# 50 HIKES
## IN THE UPPER
## HUDSON VALLEY

FIRST EDITION

Derek Dellinger

THE COUNTRYMAN PRESS

A division of W. W. Norton & Company

*Independent Publishers Since 1923*

AN INVITATION TO THE READER

Over time trails can be rerouted and signs and landmarks altered. If you find that
changes have occurred on the routes described in this book, please let us know so that
corrections may be made in future editions. The author and publisher also welcome other
comments and suggestions. Address all correspondence to:

Editor, *50 Hikes Series*
The Countryman Press
500 Fifth Avenue
New York, NY 10110

For information about permission to reproduce selections from this book, write to Permissions,
The Countryman Press, 500 Fifth Avenue, New York, NY 10110


For information about special discounts for bulk purchases, please contact
W. W. Norton Special Sales at specialsales@wwnorton.com or 800-233-4830



The Countryman Press
www.countrymanpress.com

A division of W. W. Norton & Company, Inc.
500 Fifth Avenue, New York, NY 10110
www.wwnorton.com

978-1-68268-096-4 (pbk.)

10 9 8 7 6 5 4 3 2 1

# 50 HIKES

## IN THE UPPER
## HUDSON VALLEY

## OTHER BOOKS IN THE 50 HIKES SERIES

50 Hikes in Michigan & Wisconsin's North Country Trail

50 Hikes in the North Georgia Mountains

50 Hikes in Northern New Mexico

50 Hikes in Ohio

50 Hikes in Orange County

50 Hikes in the Ozarks

50 Hikes in South Carolina

50 Hikes in the Upper Hudson Valley

50 Hikes in Wisconsin

50 Hikes in the Berkshire Hills

50 Hikes in Alaska's Kenai Peninsula

50 Hikes in Coastal and Inland Maine

50 Hikes in Kentucky

50 Hikes in the Catskills

*Dedicated to everyone*
*who works to keep our public lands*
*preserved and pristine.*

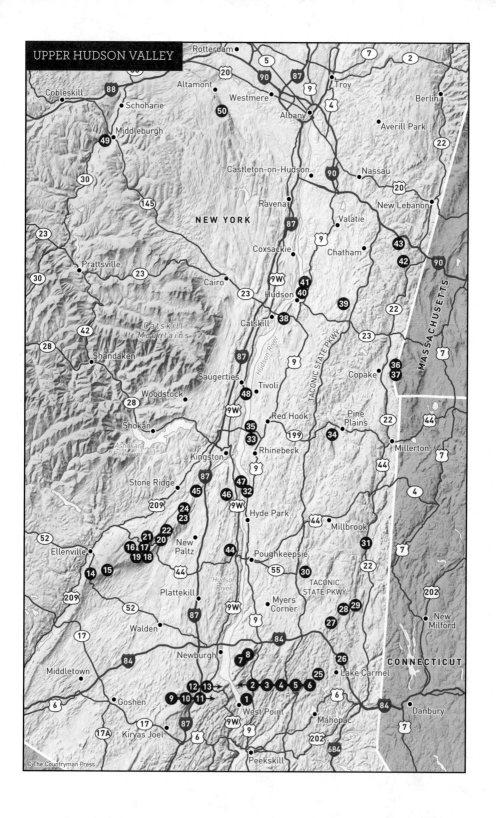

# Contents

----------------------------------------

A HIKER ENJOYS THE VIEW FROM ALANDER MOUNTAIN

# Hikes at a Glance

| Hike Name | Region | Distance (miles) | Difficulty |
|---|---|---|---|
| 1. Constitution Marsh and Indian Brook Falls | Hudson Highlands East | 1.9 | Easy |
| 2. Bull Hill (Mt. Taurus) | Hudson Highlands East | 5.2 | Strenuous |
| 3. Little Stony Point | Hudson Highlands East | 1 | Easy |
| 4. Breakneck Ridge—Arrival by Car | Hudson Highlands East | 3 | Very Difficult |
| 5. Breakneck Ridge—Arrival by Train | Hudson Highlands East | 4.2 | Very Difficult |
| 6. Sugarloaf Mountain | Hudson Highlands East | 2.5 | Moderate |
| 7. Mt. Beacon and Fire Tower | Hudson Highlands East | 4 | Strenuous |
| 8. Lambs Hill and Bald Mountain | Hudson Highlands East | 7.2 | Strenuous |
| 9. Rattlesnake Hill Loop | Hudson Highlands West | 6.7 | Moderate |
| 10. Black Rock Mountain | Hudson Highlands West | 3.8 | Strenuous |
| 11. Black Rock Forest Northern Loop | Hudson Highlands West | 6 | Moderate |
| 12. Storm King Mountain from Mountain Road | Hudson Highlands West | 4 | Moderate |
| 13. Pitching Point and North Point | Hudson Highlands West | 3.1 | Strenuous |
| 14. Bear Hill Preserve | Shawangunk Ridge | 1.3 | Easy |
| 15. Sam's Point to Verkeerderkill Falls | Shawangunk Ridge | 6.75 | Moderate |
| 16. Lake Awosting | Shawangunk Ridge | 9.8 | Moderate |
| 17. Lake Minnewaska | Shawangunk Ridge | 2.1 | Easy |
| 18. Millbrook Mountain and Gertrude's Nose | Shawangunk Ridge | 7 | Moderate |
| 19. Castle Point and Hamilton Point | Shawangunk Ridge | 8.5 | Moderate |
| 20. The Trapps Carriageway Loop | Shawangunk Ridge | 5.3 | Easy |
| 21. High Peters Kill Trail and Awosting Falls | Shawangunk Ridge | 4.7 | Moderate |
| 22. Giant's Workshop and Copes Lookout | Shawangunk Ridge | 7.5 | Difficult |
| 23. Bonticou Crag Rock Scramble | Shawangunk Ridge | 2.9 | Difficult |
| 24. Table Rocks | Shawangunk Ridge | 4.1 | Easy |
| 25. Ninham Mountain Fire Tower | Putnam and Dutchess Counties | 1.5 | Easy |
| 26. Wonder Lake | Putnam and Dutchess Counties | 3.6 | Easy |

| Good for Kids | Camping | Water-falls | Scenic Views | Notes |
|---|---|---|---|---|
| ✓ | | ✓ | ✓ | Unique boardwalk through scenic marsh |
| | | | ✓ | Abandoned quarry and dairy estate ruins |
| ✓ | | | ✓ | Easy hike to stone beach and cliff-top views |
| | | | ✓ | Popular rock scramble up a very challenging trail |
| | | | ✓ | Alternate route ideal for city-dwellers using train |
| | | | ✓ | Great Hudson River views |
| | | | ✓ | Great views, plus abandoned structures |
| | | ✓ | ✓ | Manhattan skyline visible from various viewpoints |
| | | | ✓ | Quiet forest trek around several ponds |
| | | | ✓ | Steep hike up woods road to viewpoint |
| | | | ✓ | Varied hike to views and historic buildings |
| | | | ✓ | Fantastic views of Hudson River and the Highlands |
| | | ✓ | ✓ | Little-hiked route to several great viewpoints |
| ✓ | | | ✓ | Easy hike to classic Shawangunk cliffs |
| ✓ | | ✓ | ✓ | Unique ice caves and tallest waterfall in the Gunks |
| | | ✓ | ✓ | Cliff-top views over pristine sky lake |
| ✓ | | | ✓ | Scenic loop around sky lake and cliffs |
| | | | ✓ | Fantastic views from white conglomerate cliffs |
| | | | ✓ | Fantastic views from white conglomerate cliffs |
| ✓ | | | ✓ | Easy carriage roads around popular climbing area |
| ✓ | | ✓ | ✓ | Impressive waterfall very close to trailhead |
| | | ✓ | ✓ | Quiet trail to challenging scramble and great views |
| | | | ✓ | Challenging rock scramble and great views |
| ✓ | | | ✓ | Slanted cliffs with vertigo-inducing chasms |
| ✓ | | | ✓ | Short hike to firetower |
| ✓ | | | ✓ | Loop hike around scenic pond |

| Hike Name | Region | Distance (miles) | Difficulty |
|---|---|---|---|
| 27. Mt. Egbert from Depot Hill | Putnam and Dutchess Counties | 3 | Easy |
| 28. Nuclear Lake | Putnam and Dutchess Counties | 4.3 | Easy |
| 29. Cat Rocks | Putnam and Dutchess Counties | 1.9 | Easy |
| 30. Red Wing Recreation Area | Putnam and Dutchess Counties | 2 | Easy |
| 31. Dover Stone Church | Putnam and Dutchess Counties | 2.6 | Easy |
| 32. Mills Norrie State Park | Putnam and Dutchess Counties | 4.5 | Easy |
| 33. Ferncliff Forest | Putnam and Dutchess Counties | 1.25 | Easy |
| 34. Stissing Mountain | Putnam and Dutchess Counties | 2.2 | Moderate |
| 35. Poets' Walk | Putnam and Dutchess Counties | 2.4 | Easy |
| 36. Bash Bish Falls | Northeastern Hudson Valley | 1.5 | Easy |
| 37. Alander Mountain | Northeastern Hudson Valley | 6.8 | Strenuous |
| 38. Olana | Northeastern Hudson Valley | 2.4 | Easy |
| 39. High Falls | Northeastern Hudson Valley | 1 | Easy |
| 40. Greenport Conservation Area | Northeastern Hudson Valley | 2.5 | Easy |
| 41. Harrier Hill Park | Northeastern Hudson Valley | 3.6 | Easy |
| 42. Beebe Hill Fire Tower | Northeastern Hudson Valley | 1.8 | Easy |
| 43. Schor Conservation Area | Northeastern Hudson Valley | 3.6 | Easy |
| 44. Illinois Mountain | Northwestern Hudson Valley | 4.2 | Moderate |
| 45. Joppenbergh Mountain | Northwestern Hudson Valley | 1.3 | Moderate |
| 46. Shaupeneak Ridge | Northwestern Hudson Valley | 3.5 | Easy |
| 47. Esopus Meadows Preserve | Northwestern Hudson Valley | 1.7 | Easy |
| 48. Falling Waters Preserve | Northwestern Hudson Valley | 1.7 | Easy |
| 49. Vroman's Nose | Northwestern Hudson Valley | 2.4 | Easy |
| 50. Indian Ladder Trail | Northwestern Hudson Valley | 2.4 | Easy |

## A NOTE ON DIFFICULTY RATINGS

While a hiker's perception of the difficulty of a trail will always depend, more than any other factor, on the experience level of that hiker, some trails undeniably require more effort than others. In general, "**Easy**" hikes are those which can be completed in only a few hours, with a minimum of exertion. "**Moder-ate**" hikes may be slightly longer, and will likely include several sections of steep uphill, though nothing that an inexperienced hiker could not handle. For the purposes of this guide, elevation gain and the steepness of the trail have been given the greatest consideration— a long route of 8 to 10 miles that follows a mostly level, easily-walked carriage path, therefore, will rank as "easy" to "moderate." "**Strenuous**" trails are

| Good for Kids | Camping | Waterfalls | Scenic Views | Notes |
|:---:|:---:|:---:|:---:|---|
| ✓ | ✓ |  | ✓ | Peaceful section of the Appalachian Trail |
| ✓ |  |  |  | Semi-loop on the AT around scenic pond |
| ✓ | ✓ |  | ✓ | Short hike to rock outcropping with views |
| ✓ |  |  | ✓ | Short hike to picnic area with views |
| ✓ |  | ✓ | ✓ | Unique waterfall inside cave |
| ✓ | ✓ |  | ✓ | Scenic walk along Hudson River and historic sites |
| ✓ | ✓ |  | ✓ | Short hike to firetower |
| ✓ |  |  | ✓ | Firetower and short rock scramble |
| ✓ |  |  | ✓ | Popular walk to wooden pavilion and viewpoints |
| ✓ | ✓ | ✓ |  | Short hike through ravine to impressive waterfall; camping nearby at state park |
|  | ✓ |  | ✓ | Strenuous climb to great views and summit-top cabin |
| ✓ |  |  | ✓ | Historic site with great views |
| ✓ |  | ✓ |  | Short walk to waterfall overlook |
| ✓ |  |  | ✓ | Easy walk to wooden pavilion with great views |
| ✓ |  | ✓ | ✓ | Short walk to wooden pavilion with great views |
| ✓ | ✓ |  | ✓ | Remote firetower with views to Albany |
| ✓ |  |  | ✓ | Peaceful, remote hike around scenic pond |
| ✓ |  |  |  | Hike through quiet woods around several reservoirs |
| ✓ |  |  | ✓ | Short hike to great viewpoint |
| ✓ |  |  |  | Loop hike around scenic pond |
| ✓ |  |  | ✓ | Peaceful, easy hike with Hudson River views |
| ✓ |  | ✓ | ✓ | Hudson River views and waterfall viewing area |
| ✓ |  |  | ✓ | Popular short hike with fantastic views |
| ✓ | ✓ | ✓ | ✓ | Unique trail along escarpment with camping nearby |

those which, due to their steep incline, will result in a great deal of sweating and huffing and puffing—even for experienced hikers. However, a strenuous trail may be no more than a simple woods road, easily walked and posing no technical challenges, that simply happens to be very steep. Trails rated as "Difficult" begin to demand more serious uphill climbing, may include some sections of challenging trail, and will likely be tackled over the course of a full morning or afternoon. For the final, most challenging tier of hikes, "Very Difficult" hikes are those which are both strenuous—you'll sweat a lot—and also pose a level of technical difficulty, with areas of rock scrambling and steep, narrow trail. However, no hikes in this guide require any specialized climbing equipment when hiked in good weather.

THE INITIAL ASCENT UP BREAKNECK RIDGE, GLIMPSED IN PROFILE FROM BULL HILL (MT. TAURUS)

# Introduction

reakneck Ridge is one of the most technically challenging and strenuous hikes in the northeastern United States, barely giving hikers more than a few feet of trail to acclimate to before dashing them against the hike's main scramble—an abrupt, unflinching climb over half a mile of near-vertical boulders and cliff edges. While the trail is never so difficult as to require technical climbing gear, the scramble is sure to push the limits of most hikers. Given that, it is somewhat odd that Breakneck Ridge is, in fact, the hike that introduces so many adventurers to hiking in the Hudson Valley.

On a nice weekend day, thousands will tackle the climb up Breakneck Ridge. That the unique challenges of the trail and its jaw-dropping viewpoints begat notoriety isn't surprising, but perhaps the most important factor in cementing Breakneck Ridge's popularity is the fact that this hike is easily accessible from New York City. In fact, Breakneck Ridge has its own dedicated Metro-North train stop, which deposits large hordes of hikers every weekend. Judging by the increasingly dire warnings posted around the trailhead, many of these hikers have no idea what they're getting themselves into. For the prepared adventurer, this hike can be exhilarating and memorable. Revisiting the trail never becomes repetitious: the myriad routes and challenging configurations spike your adrenaline every time. But for the unprepared—unaware just how strenuous and intimidating this

climb will be—Breakneck Ridge occasionally leads to defeat.

Perhaps there is a certain appeal to breaking yourself in with one of the most difficult hikes in the Hudson Valley. I was one of those oblivious hikers myself, years ago—like so many others, Breakneck Ridge was my (possibly ill-advised) introduction to hiking here. At the time, I was a college student in Poughkeepsie. One April weekend, a friend told me we were going on an adventure. We drove to a place far from campus that I'd never heard of before, seemingly in the middle of nowhere. All I knew was that it was about 45 minutes from Poughkeepsie. All I was told was that we would be climbing over rocks, more so than I was probably used to.

An hour later, I was clinging for dear life to the side of a steep rock face that appeared to have no handholds, no grip, and no possible safe route up. I told my friend that she would have to leave me there, to start a new life as a hermit on the side of that cliff. There was certainly no way I was making it up, and turning back was probably a suicide mission, given the severe grade of the climb we'd already undertaken.

Of course, part of the magic of hiking is how quickly our bodies adapt to the challenges of nature, relearning a sense of balance and intuition that we've mostly forgotten after years of easy domestic challenges. Humans learned many tricks of coordination and wayfinding over the thousands of years of our species; given the many physical challenges humankind has managed to overcome, the simple contortions required to summit Breakneck Ridge are nothing, really (not that this long view will give you any more energy to climb up that next steep rock face). Clinging to the side of a seemingly impassable ledge, it's all too easy to despair. Some, sadly, may be turned off from tackling any more challenging hikes by the overwhelming, humbling nature of the Breakneck Ridge Trail. Others may find their life changed, a new craving uncovered.

That first adventure in the Hudson Highlands with my friend did, in fact, put me off trying again for years. But eventually, living in Brooklyn and feeling stifled by city life, I decided I needed to give it another go. There are many reasons to hike: the views, the serenity of nature, the simple exercise (in a far more interesting setting than the treadmill at the gym), and—particularly appealing after years stuck working in a cubical—to reconnect with that lost sense of balance our species has engineered out of our daily lives. The first few attempts to tackle a trail as rough as Breakneck may be daunting, even humiliating, but that lost sense soon begins to return: the feeling that, hard as the challenge may be, it is what our bodies evolved to do. By the time I'd completed the Breakneck Ridge loop a couple of times, I found I could walk up that steep (but not nearly so steep as it had once seemed) rock face without even bending down to find a handhold. So much turns out to be a mental challenge even more than it is a physical challenge.

From Breakneck Ridge, I started pressing further. The Hudson Highlands draw hundreds of thousands of tourists each year, funneling most of them through the small towns of Cold Spring and Beacon, both with their own train stops. Cold Spring is especially popular with city hikers, as its Metro-North station is positioned in such a way that one can easily make a loop out of the Breakneck Ridge hike (or its neighboring mountain, Bull Hill), heading into town afterwards for pizza before catching the train. It's hard to imagine a more perfectly staged weekend adventure from the perspective of a city dweller—no wonder I made the trip dozens of times myself. But as I pushed further away from the crowds, my love of the Hudson Valley as a whole only grew, and soon I was aching to explore all the scenic spots that I'd barely touched back in college: the Shawangunk Ridge, a charming ecological anomaly; Storm King Mountain and the hilly Black Rock Forest at its back; and the Catskill Mountains, the rugged peaks looming over the whole of the valley.

A few years and dozens of hikes later, I packed up my stuff and moved out of the city. I settled in Beacon, with the Hudson Highlands in my backyard. The area's virtues are numerous, but for me, the beauty of the nature and the easy access to the things I appreciated most in life were the main draw. Why count the days until my next upstate excursion, spending hours on public transportation, waiting to be dropped off at a trailhead alongside the massive crowds, when I could simply live in this beautiful place? From my new apartment, I could walk to the trailhead that had first introduced me to the town of Beacon in five minutes, and enjoy views of the Manhattan skyline from the Fishkill Ridge. I could drive to Breakneck Ridge in only ten minutes. The Shawangunks, one of the most unique natural sites in the eastern United States, were half an hour away. The Catskills, an hour. Then there are those hidden gems: the trails found not in a major park system, but simply tucked away behind a small town, or along the ridge of an unassuming low hill.

New York is one of the most geographically rich states in the country—and the Hudson Valley is its heart.

Take advantage of the many excellent hiking opportunities here, and help to keep these trails protected for the enjoyment of all. Hiking is much more than just exercise, or a way to clear the mind. In the modern world, it is often our best opportunity to reorient ourselves to the true nature of the world we live in.

A HIKER RESTS AT THE CLIFFS OF CASTLE POINT

# How to Prepare for Your Hike

Preparing for a short hike ahead of time may seem like something for the paranoid, or for those prone to overcomplicating all their plans, but it should never be overlooked. Even a short, seemingly easy hike can turn on a dime with a shift of weather or some unforeseen accident or error. When hiking in the wild, it is always better to be overprepared than caught off guard, even if it means extra time spent and extra weight to carry. How well you plan could, in fact, save your life. Listed below is a set of guidelines that should aid you in your journey both on and off the trail.

Most principles of backcountry safety are based on common sense: stay on the designated trail and be extra cautious when near cliff edges or on slick rocks. Wear appropriate gear, particularly footwear, and watch the weather forecast carefully before setting out. However, there are several other steps you can take to ensure that your trip remains a safe affair.

- Leave your plans with a friend or family member. Let them know when and where you plan to hike as well as what time you expect to be finished. Establish a cutoff time a few hours after you plan to arrive home, and contact them as soon as you are able to upon returning from the trail. If your safety contact does not hear from you by the cutoff time, this will be a signal that they may need to seek help.
- Familiarize yourself with nearby towns. Look up how far your hike is from the nearest hospital and write down any necessary phone numbers beforehand. It is also a good idea to make note of nearby grocery and convenience stores, as well as gas stations on the way to your destination. Spotty cell reception in the mountains can often make looking up this information difficult once you are on the trail. However, even if you do expect cell service to be unreliable on your hike, always bring your cell phone with you anyway. Be mindful of your cell phone's battery charge before leaving for your hike. Reception may come and go, but without a charge, your phone is guaranteed to be useless in the backcountry. Simply carrying a cell phone is not a replacement for ample planning.

## WEATHER

While few summits in the Hudson Valley outside of the Catskills approach the 2,000-foot range, elevation always has a significant impact on weather conditions, temperature, and especially wind chill. Under normal circumstances, the temperature drops by roughly 3°F for every 1,000 feet of elevation gain. This can be exacerbated even further by the strong winds often encountered on open summits. For much of the year, you will need to bring extra layers to stay warm once you reach an exposed vista, especially if you intend to relax there and take in the view. Before you embark on your hike, check the weather forecast and plan to the best of your ability, but be aware that the conditions may change without warning. Extremes of weather can lead to injury or death in any season, especially on trails that feature rock ledges, cliff edges, or rock scrambles. In the event of inclement weather or an unexpected storm breaking in the middle of your hike, be prepared to turn around if necessary. Safety should always be your number one concern.

## ETIQUETTE

The subject of trail etiquette is mostly concerned with preserving the serene quality of the woods for others to enjoy, both immediately and in the future. Do your best to be courteous to those sharing the trails with you. This should be easy to do since the people you'll meet on the trail will generally be cheerful and friendly. It's not uncommon to strike up amiable conversations with fellow hikers, or to offer a neighborly greeting as you pass. Everyone hikes at a different pace, so let others pass if they wish to go faster, and yield to hikers coming downhill, especially when the trail is steep and narrow. If you are hiking in a group, try to keep your noise level low so that others may enjoy the peacefulness of the forest. Stay on the trail to minimize erosion and preserve the delicate flora that inhabits the mountains. Lastly, follow Leave No Trace principles and pack out anything you pack in. If you have the pack space, carry out any trash that may have been left behind by others. It is the responsibility of everyone to ensure that the wilderness remains pristine for future generations to enjoy.

## WHAT TO BRING ON YOUR HIKE

Ask any number of hikers what they bring on a hike, and you will likely get a variety of answers ranging from the practical to the extravagant and everywhere in between. Some people embrace the ultralight ideology, bringing only essential lightweight items that often serve dual purposes, while others prefer to carry a little bit of extra weight for the sake of comfort and security. Whatever your style may be, there are a few things that just about everyone can agree on.

## BACKPACK

A comfortable backpack is a must for any hike longer than a mile or two. Just about any pack will do as long as you find it agreeable. While not imperative, packs with hip or chest belts can increase load stability and greatly improve your balance on the trail. Other popular features include multiple compartments for frequently accessed items such as a camera or food, and hydration reservoirs. Whichever backpack you choose, make sure everything you plan on bringing will comfortably fit inside before you leave for the trailhead.

## HIKING BOOTS

The type of hiking boots you should wear is largely a matter of preference, but it is beneficial to know what options exist so you can make the choice that will suit you best. High-top hiking boots offer the most ankle support and are quite durable, but are much more expensive. Low-cut boots and trail-running shoes let feet breathe more easily, allow a greater range of motion, and are usually cheaper. A variety of different rubber soles are available, with varying levels of stickiness and durability—perhaps the most important aspect to consider, given that many of the trails are rocky and uneven. Waterproof or treated boots can help make your feet more comfortable as well. Whatever type of shoes you choose, be sure to break them in beforehand. Waiting until the day of your hike to break in your shoes will likely result in uncomfortable, hot, blistery feet.

## WATER

You will want to bring about one liter of water for every 2–3 miles you plan to hike. However, this amount is just a guideline, and you will need to carry more water during hot summer months. Never drink water directly from a stream or pond, no matter how pristine it may appear. All water must be treated before drinking to remove or kill harmful bacteria and protozoa such as *Giardia*, *E. coli*, and *Salmonella*. A number of options exist, including chemical treatments, filtration systems, or simply boiling water before you drink it. Chemical treatments such as iodine or chlorine dioxide tablets are cheap and lightweight, but they need to work for a minimum of half an hour before the water is safe to drink, and they can leave a foul taste behind. Backcountry water filters are more expensive, bulkier, and heavier, but they deliver immediate results without any impact on the flavor of the water. Many hikes may have water sources along the route, though you should not assume that you will encounter a running stream without first consulting a map—and even then, many water sources can dry up at times during the year. Nonetheless, a water filter or other treatment device can be a useful way to save on water weight for longer summer hikes. Refilling your water bottle or hydration bladder from a mountain spring or stream on a hot day is a rewarding, refreshing experience.

## FOOD

In general, you will want to bring 2–3 pounds of food per person per day of hiking. As with water, this figure should be considered a rough guideline. You may need to bring more or less food depending on how strenuous your route is, as well as your metabolism. It is a good idea to bring more than you think you'll need if you are unsure. It is better to carry extra food back to your car than it is to run out of food halfway through your hike. Energy and granola bars, dried fruit and nuts, candy bars, and jerky are excellent, highly portable choices that will provide your body with the necessary protein, carbohydrates, and electrolytes it needs to keep you energized and on the trail.

## CLOTHING

It is important to stay prepared for any sudden weather changes by bringing along extra layers of clothing. Windy, exposed summits may require you to add layers of clothing to stay warm, while the exertion of the climb up to these summits will cause you to remove layers to keep cool. The key to staying comfortable is planning for a wide variety of conditions. Choose clothing that is versatile. Wool or synthetic blends insulate well and also breathe, letting moisture evaporate quickly so that your body can regulate its temperature more naturally. Cotton clothing traps moisture and insulates poorly when wet. For this reason, you should try to avoid cotton clothing as much as possible.

It is a good idea, even in warmer weather, to always bring a long-sleeved shirt or jacket with you. A windbreaker can extend your visit to a blustery vista, and a rain jacket or poncho will further protect you from less-than-pleasant weather conditions. Bring a hat and gloves if the weather will be chilly since your hands and head radiate a significant amount of heat. Lastly, it's always a good idea to bring an extra pair of socks in case your feet become wet.

## FIRST AID KIT

Your first aid kit does not need to be extensive, but a few basic items will help alleviate any minor injuries you may sustain on your hike. You can create your own first aid kit out of things commonly found at a drugstore, such as adhesive bandages, gauze, medical tape, alcohol swabs, hand sanitizer, antibiotic ointment, tweezers, moleskin (or other blister-relief material), and over-the-counter pain medication. If you are taking any prescription medication, be sure to pack any doses you would normally take throughout the day as well. All of these items easily fit inside a plastic bag and will help ensure your safety on the trail.

## FLASHLIGHT/HEADLAMP

It is always wise to bring a headlamp or lightweight flashlight along on your hike, even if you're planning on finishing well before dusk. You never know when an innocent error reading the trail map may delay your return to your car by several hours. In spring, fall, and winter especially, nightfall can sneak up on you. If you are forced to make your return to the trailhead in the dark, don't panic. Simply pay close attention to the trail, and take extra time to orient yourself at each intersection. Most trail markers are reflective and thus easy to follow even at night, provided you have a good source of light. A decent headlamp

is a relatively inexpensive investment, and well worth keeping in your pack at all times.

## WINTER HIKING

Hiking in the winter can be an exciting undertaking. The cold air feels clean and refreshing, the lack of foliage on the trees can uncover previously hidden vistas, and the frigid landscape breathes an exciting new life into areas you may have previously visited. Additionally, outdoor winter activities are one of the best ways to combat seasonal depression and moderate the doldrums of short days. Even on gray, overcast winter days, an excursion outside can feel refreshing and enlivening. That being said, the risks associated with hiking are augmented and intensified during the winter months. For this reason, winter hiking should only be attempted by experienced hikers with the proper equipment. Weather, snow, ice, and hypothermia are very real dangers that can be fatal if you are not very well prepared, especially when combined with the magnifying effect that elevation has on these variables. The weather conditions, snow accumulation, and icy buildup are often much more drastic at elevation than at the parking area. It is imperative to plan ahead extensively if you are going to attempt hiking in the winter. No one wants to bail before they reach their desired destination, but you may need to turn around halfway through your hike even if you do come prepared. It can be difficult to make this call, but it is far better to be safe than to risk serious injury or death. Use common sense and be cautious.

Wintertime hiking often requires the use of additional equipment, both for ease of hiking and for safety on the trail. Be sure to bring hats, gloves, and extra layers of clothing. Additional items such as gaiters, hand warmers, and a thermos of hot chocolate or coffee can make your hike more comfortable and enjoyable. Snowshoes and poles should be used when snowy conditions are present, and crampons or similar traction devices are generally a must to provide steady footing.

While lower elevation hikes in the Hudson Valley may not build up snow accumulation like the mountain peaks to the north, ice formation is a very real concern for hikers and is usually exacerbated on trails. In recent years, as winters have become warmer and warmer, snow in most of the Hudson Valley tends to melt away within a few days or weeks of falling. Conditions in town, however, are often misleading, and not representative of what to expect on a hike. On trails, the frequent passage of hikers compacts the snow before it can melt, hardening it, and forming dense ice. Such compacted ice generally lingers for weeks even after the snow in surrounding areas has melted away. Additionally, ice tends to accumulate on trails more than the land surrounding them, as trails tend to form a flat surface on which runoff can accumulate as it trickles downslope. For this reason, always anticipate that you will encounter significantly more ice on the trails than is present elsewhere. Trails covered in ice can be extremely dangerous to traverse without traction devices, so hikers should always bring crampons or microspikes even if they do not expect to use them.

## BEAR SAFETY

Black bears play a vital part in New York's ecosystem, and when you are hiking and camping, it is important to remember that you are sharing their home with them—you are the visitor, not them. Most animals want a confrontation even less than you do. Always respect the creatures that call the wild their home, and protect yourself (and the bears) by taking basic precautions. Most rules of bear safety boil down to an essential principle: Do nothing that will unnecessarily attract the attention of bears in the first place. For this reason, you must always be careful when camping and hiking to not feed these intelligent and potentially dangerous animals.

Black bears are omnivorous, and in the wild, they live off of fruit, nuts, seeds, insects, grasses, and carrion. Plant foods can make up as much as 90 percent of a bear's diet. It is important to realize that bears, while powerful and imposing creatures are nonetheless scavengers much more than they are hunters. Most of their day is spent searching for sustenance. Thus, any food made available to them by lazy or unmindful humans will be happily set upon and consumed. Bears are intelligent animals that learn from past experiences. If searching a certain location or repeating a certain activity results in food, a bear will attempt to recreate this scenario again in the future. Thus, food left out around a camp, in close proximity to humans, becomes dangerous for both the bear and the humans. Likewise, if a bear encounters a human and does not acquire any food as a result of the encounter, the bear will have no reason to seek out humans again in the future.

To be clear, the chances of a deadly encounter with a black bear in the Hudson Valley are extremely low. Most of the bear population in the Hudson Valley is centered in the Catskill Mountains, though a bear can be spotted anywhere—even near heavily populated areas. In the Shawangunk Ridge, bears are sometimes spotted in mid to late summer feasting on the blueberries that grow wild throughout the ridge. While hiking the majority of the trails suggested by this book, there is very little chance that you will ever see a bear—but nevertheless, it is always good to be prepared. If you do spot a bear nearby, do not run. Back away slowly, speaking in a low, calm voice to ensure that the bear recognizes you as a human and not a prey animal. Hiking in a group is usually a deterrent on its own, but if you are alone, attempt to make yourself look as large as possible by raising your arms and taking to high ground while continuing to make noise. Make sure the bear has a clear route to flee the encounter—a bear that feels trapped is likely to behave more aggressively. Do not scream or shriek. If the bear stands up on its hind legs, it is most likely just trying to get a better sense of the situation, not issuing a threat. While black bear encounters tend not to be as deadly as encounters with brown bears or grizzlies out west, the recommended strategy in the unlikely event of an attack is much different. If a black bear does attack you, do not play dead—always fight back.

## TICKS AND LYME DISEASE

Bears may be the more dramatic threat haunting the backwoods, but a far more likely danger comes in a much smaller form. Ticks are a rapidly growing problem in the United States, with about 300,000 infections occurring each year. The northeast is, unfortunately, a hotbed for Lyme disease, with a vast majority of all cases in the United States occurring in these states.

Lyme disease is spread by an infected tick, but not every tick bite will result in Lyme disease. Of course, the tick has to bite you before it can transmit the disease, so the best way to avoid Lyme is to catch any ticks while they're still crawling on you. If you do contract Lyme, the disease may produce a rash, flu-like symptoms, and pain in joints within a few weeks. The most obvious indication that you have Lyme is the notorious "bulls-eye" rash, though not everyone develops this rash. Without the rash, the symptoms of Lyme can be difficult to distinguish from mono or simply a stubborn flu, so if you think you may have contracted Lyme, it is always best to play it safe and get tested. Untreated, it will eventually result in chronic arthritis and nervous system disorders.

Check yourself regularly while hiking, before you get in your car, and again when you return home to shower. Deer ticks are very small and can be easy to miss. Tuck your pants into your socks and boots, and apply insect repellent containing DEET. Wearing light-colored clothing will make it somewhat easier to see any unwanted passengers crawling on you. Finally, showering and changing clothes immediately following your hike is the best way to prevent the parasites from digging in.

# Subregions
# of the Upper Hudson Valley

---

## HUDSON HIGHLANDS

The Hudson Highlands are an area of fjords and mountains on both the west and east banks of the Hudson River, between Newburgh Bay and Haverstraw Bay. The range forms the northern section of the New York–New Jersey Highlands, but the prominent peaks of the Hudson Highlands overlooking the Hudson River make for a particularly memorable landscape. While this guide covers only the section of the Hudson Highlands from Cold Spring, NY, and north, there are countless classic hikes throughout the range. Some, like Breakneck Ridge, are easily accessible by train, and are estimated to be among the most popular hikes in the entire country.

The northern Hudson Highlands serve as both a natural border between the upper and lower portions of the Hudson Valley, and also a cultural center for the region as well. Towns like Beacon, Newburgh, and Cold Spring have seen an influx of tourism from New York City in recent years, and a corresponding boom in local culture and business development. Beacon and Cold Spring are ideal for a post-hike visit, as a number of key trailheads are located on the outskirts of both towns, and there are many diverse offerings for food and drink to be found. Both Beacon and Cold Spring offer an easily walked Main Street. Beacon, the larger of the two towns, is home to an excellent brewery (Hudson Valley Brewery) and several coffee shops with outdoor seating. Just across the river, Newburgh's shopping district is found primarily around the intersection of Washington and Liberty Street. Another great brewery, Newburgh Brewery, is located in a grand converted warehouse down the hill, near to a variety of cafés, restaurants, and bars.

## SHAWANGUNK RIDGE

Whether you're hiking in the Hudson Highlands, cresting a hill on a backroad in Poughkeepsie, or driving along NY-87, two natural landmarks are so prominent and distinct, they can be seen from all over the Hudson Valley. The Catskills, as the highest mountains in New York outside of the Adirondacks, dominate the skyline for miles in every direction. The Shawangunk Ridge, though rising to only about half the height of most peaks in the Catskills, nonetheless cuts a memorable sight across the central Hudson Valley. Heading toward the town of New Paltz, one of the most distinct sections of the ridge rises dramatically over the town, crowned by the Sky Top observation tower. In the "Gunks" themselves, you will find a landscape so gorgeous and distinct, it may feel as if you've stumbled through a portal into some fantasy land. Here, a unique ecosystem supports an unusual diversity of vegetation, including distinct dwarf pitch pine forests, and jagged cliffs of white rock rise to mesmerizing prominence over pristine sky lakes.

The Shawangunks are known especially for these picturesque white cliffs, which have long been a popular destination for climbers, hikers, and wealthy tourists vacationing at the Shawangunks' mountain resorts (only one of which remains today: the Mohonk Mountain House). Today, the Gunks are considered one of the premiere climbing destinations in America, bringing so many climbers and tourists from all across the East Coast, the main parking areas often run out of space on weekends. While most tourism congregates around the northeastern end of the Gunks—which contain the most distinct areas of cliffs and ridges—the Shawangunk Ridge actually extends for many more miles to the southwest, into New Jersey, where it is known as the Kittatinny Mountains, and the Blue Mountains where it overlaps into Pennsylvania.

The ridge's eye-catching cliffs are formed of Shawangunk conglomerate, a hard, silica-cemented sedimentary rock composed of white quartz pebbles and sandstone. Beneath the conglomerate is shale, deposited when the area was covered by a deep ocean some 400 million years ago. The Shawangunk conglomerate is very hard and thus resists erosion, while the shale is far less resistant to weathering. Erosion of the edges of the ridge over time has thus sculpted the quartz conglomerate into cliffs and talus slopes, leaving the distinct formations found today. The harsh soil conditions have led to the proliferation of dwarf pitch pine on the ridge. Blueberry pickers in the 1800s were known to set fires to handicap the growth of competing vegetation, the practice of which helped the pitch pine to flourish even further. This ridgetop environment is considered to be extremely unique, with perhaps only one other area like it in all the world. Exploring the carriage roads that navigate the woods and cliffs, you will quickly come to appreciate the unique qualities of this place.

New Paltz—a busy college town even when it's not crowded with adventure enthusiasts and leaf peepers—is relatively small, but home to dozens of dining, drinking, and shopping options, from quick and cheap burrito joints to upscale fine dining. Nearby Rosendale, situated just beyond the northeast tip of the Shawangunk Ridge, is much smaller, but features a scenic, easily walked downtown area with cafés, restaurants, and a coffee shop/bookstore. Both towns are excellent destinations to pair with a hike.

## PUTNAM AND DUTCHESS COUNTIES

The rolling hills and fields of Dutchess County contain a diverse mix of culture and geography: bustling riverside towns with busy highways and train stations whisking commuters and tourists alike down to the city, and only miles away, vast expanses of quiet, scenic farmland. The most famous trail in America runs through Dutchess County, spanning both the suburbs and the farmland alike. The Appalachian Trail crosses over the Hudson River on the Bear Mountain Bridge, at the border of Westchester and Putnam counties, and works its way through the Fahnestock State Park in Putnam County, before crossing over into Dutchess County just south of NY-84. Before reaching Connecticut, the AT offers several sections that can be carved up into ideal day hikes. Nuclear Lake, Depot Hill, and Cat Rocks are all excellent excursions accessible to any level of hiker.

At the southwestern corner of

Dutchess County, the riverfront town of Beacon has become one of the most popular destinations in the region, and is covered previously under the Hudson Highlands section. To the north, the town of Poughkeepsie is larger and more sprawling, but has several notable destinations for food and drinks near its long Main Street. Rabbit and Turtle Pub and Schatzi's Pub are both excellent choices for a sit-down meal and beers, while locally focused Plan Bee Farm Brewery offers a rustic taproom on a quiet farm setting that is a perfect pairing with a nearby hike.

## CATSKILLS

It's virtually impossible to ignore the Catskill Mountains when hiking in the Upper Hudson Valley: the distant outline of these peaks can be glimpsed at some point during the majority of hikes in this guide. The Catskill's park covers 700,000 acres and contains hundreds of mountains, and thus there are a large number of potential hikes within this beautiful and historic subregion of the Hudson Valley. As such, 50 of these hikes are covered in a separate guidebook, *50 Hikes in the Catskills*, also available from Countryman Press.

## NORTHERN HUDSON VALLEY

The northeastern Hudson Valley is comparatively flat next to the hills and rugged mountains that comprise much of the rest of the region, though the trails in this area have a special charm to them. In Columbia County, parks like Poets' Walk, the Greenport Conservation Area, and Harrier Hill Park are home to pleasant footpaths over small but scenic hills and fields, with idyllic, romantic viewpoints looking out over the Hudson River with the Catskill Mountains just beyond. At these viewpoints, you will find benches and gazebos fashioned in a particular woven-wood style shared by parks throughout Columbia County.

The town of Hudson, NY is undoubtedly the cultural and culinary capital of this region, with numerous shopping and dining opportunities, several coffee shops, and art galleries. Nearby, those searching for a post-hike beer should visit Suarez Family Brewery, where the large sunny taproom looks out to views of the countryside almost as nice as those found on your hike.

Even further north, on the west side of the river, several unique geological formations rise to prominence just as the hills north of the Catskill Mountains trail off. Near the town of Middleburgh, the wedge-like Vroman's Nose is the result of ancient glacial movements, and a popular destination for families due to the easy trails and exceptional views. Closer to Albany, the Helderberg Escarpment forms a dramatic series of cliffs rising over the Hudson Valley. Waterfalls cascading over the cliff tops create numerous unique photo opportunities.

# I.

# HUDSON HIGHLANDS EAST

# Constitution Marsh and Indian Brook Falls

**TOTAL DISTANCE**: 1.9 miles

**TYPE**: Out and Back

**HIKING TIME**: 1–2 hours

**TOTAL ELEVATION GAIN**: 300 feet

**MAXIMUM ELEVATION**: 335 feet

**DIFFICULTY**: Easy

This well-hidden gem just outside the town of Cold Spring is certainly one of the most unique hikes in the Hudson Valley, with its boardwalk tour over a quiet, sprawling marsh. Still, this strikingly beautiful riverside spot doesn't get nearly the attention that the more strenuous ridgetop hikes just north of town receive. That's probably for the best: this is not a robust trail system designed for hundreds of hikers, and accordingly, the parking area is only built to hold a couple of vehicles. From the lot, you will have access to two technically separate hikes, combined into one here since both are quite short and accessed from the same parking area. The Indian Brook Falls segment of this hike is a short walk to a small, but beautiful waterfall, while the walk from the Constitution Marsh Audubon Center offers a chance to explore quintessential Hudson Valley scenery in a unique setting. The boardwalk loop at the end of the hike explores an area of beautiful wetlands, while looking out to some of the most notable Hudson Highland summits: Storm King Mountain, Bull Mountain, and Breakneck Ridge.

## GETTING THERE

From the village of Cold Spring, drive south on NY-9D. About a mile out of town, after passing the Boscobel historic estate, turn right onto Indian Brook Road. The parking area is just ahead, with room for about eight cars. Do not drive past the parking area in either direction where the road splits. Parking is strictly limited to the designated parking area. Parking anywhere else along the road is not allowed, and will likely result in your car being ticketed or towed.

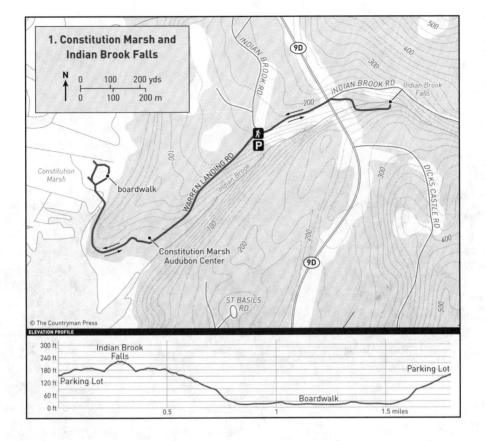

## 1. Constitution Marsh and Indian Brook Falls

ELEVATION PROFILE

## GPS SHORTCUT

Type "Marsh Audubon Center and Sanctuary Parking" into Google Maps and your GPS will navigate you to the appropriate trailhead.

## THE TRAIL

With the parking area squarely in the middle, this is essentially two separate, short out-and-back hikes connected by a joint parking area. From the parking lot, continue up Indian Brook Road, heading back in the direction of NY-9D (you'll hear the traffic) and away from the Hudson River. Following the street, you will soon see the large red bridge where 9D

spans the creek bed far below. After a short distance, the street splits in a V, with the road continuing to the left and the trail angling down toward the creek, to the right. A metal gate separates the trail from the road.

Continue downhill on the trail, across a small stone bridge, until the trail again splits, with another path doubling back along the edge of the creek chasm, toward the large metal 9D bridge. Take the smaller foot trail that cuts to the left, marked by occasional green blazes. You will now be walking along the creek bed itself. The trail seems to disappear entirely at points, forcing you to hop across rocks where trees block the way.

THE BOARDWALK AT CONSTITUTION MARSH

Only 0.3 mile from the parking area, you will come to Indian Brook Falls, a compact two-section waterfall that is quite scenic, despite its small size.

Please note that swimming is illegal here, and given the small number of cars that can fit in the parking area, might prevent other hikers from being able to enjoy this unique area. Please respect the rules and your fellow adventurers, and do not linger here for too long.

When you are ready to continue on to the second leg of the hike, return along the same route back to the parking area.

From here, continue straight past your car, down the gravel road that leads in the direction of the river. Warren Landing Road, with several private homes just off to the right, may seem to be a driveway, but it also serves as the access road to the Constitution Marsh Audubon Center, and is marked by several trail posts along the way. As a reminder, you may not drive down this road, and must leave your car in the same parking area and continue on foot.

Warren Landing Road will begin to slope downhill after a short distance.

The trail climbs briefly as you crest the ridge. A short distance up, a wooden bench looks out to a gorgeous view of the marshlands and river, with views of West Point on the far side of the Hudson. From here, follow the blazes as the trail makes its way back down the ridge, toward the marsh.

A large sign marks the entrance to the boardwalk section of the hike, where wooden platforms weave like a maze through the reeds. This is a truly special place, one that you may feel shocked to find nestled in the busy center of the Hudson Valley, so off the radar despite its easy accessibility. The wooden pathways through the marsh are a treat to navigate themselves, with various placards explaining the flora and fauna of the area, and benches at intervals where you can sit and take in the quiet. While there are various extensions branching off, the boardwalk ultimately makes a rough circle leading back to the ridge trail. The views are equally spectacular from all points of the boardwalk, whether looking north toward Storm King Mountain and Breakneck Ridge, or southwest, toward West Point.

On your way back, just before reaching the open area and the Audubon Center, you will see a yellow trail branching off to the left, seeming to continue toward the other end of the ridge. This short, optional trail can be taken around to the other side of the Audubon Center, though it does not lead to any views.

When you are done exploring, walk back up Warren Landing Road to your car.

About 0.3 mile from the parking area (after crossing over from the first leg of the hike), you will come to the Audubon Center building, a small dock, and an open area with two blazed trailheads. Look for the blue blazes, to the right of the dock behind the Audubon Center building, which will take you on a trail heading north up the rocks along the water.

# Bull Hill (Mt. Taurus)

**TOTAL DISTANCE**: 5.2 miles

**TYPE**: Loop

**HIKING TIME**: 3–4 hours

**TOTAL ELEVATION GAIN**: 1,400 feet

**MAXIMUM ELEVATION**: 1,420 feet

**DIFFICULTY**: Strenuous

A hike up Bull Hill (also sometimes referred to as Mt. Taurus) offers a little bit of everything—it's a moderately challenging, incredibly pretty, historically rich snapshot of the Hudson Highlands, and also happens to be easily accessible by train. A hike up Bull Hill offers a chance to scale an imposing peak, presents iconic viewpoints, dramatic rock ledges, and just-challenging-enough rock scrambles. There's history, both in the form of the old ruins that haunt the woods toward the end of the hike and in the dramatic abandoned quarry that dominates the hillside just after the trail begins. There are river views, city views, gurgling streams, and secluded backwoods foot trails. The ascent here is more exciting than that up nearby Mt. Beacon, and less intimidating for inexperienced hikers than the scramble up neighboring Breakneck Ridge.

The most prominent feature of Bull Hill is undoubtedly the abandoned quarry found only a quarter of a mile into the hike. The area that is now the Hudson Highlands State Park was logged, mined, and quarried throughout the nineteenth century. In 1931, the Hudson River Stone Corporation opened the quarry that you see today on Bull Hill, despite protests from locals seeking to reclaim the mountains here for recreational purposes. The quarry operated until 1967, and soon after became part of the Hudson Highlands State Park in 1970.

Later on in the hike, you will encounter the ruins of the Cornish estate. In 1917, Edward Joel Cornish and his wife Selina decided to move upstate and create a home in the woods, acquiring 650 acres in the area. The massive estate, which included a dairy operation, was known as "Northgate." The couple died

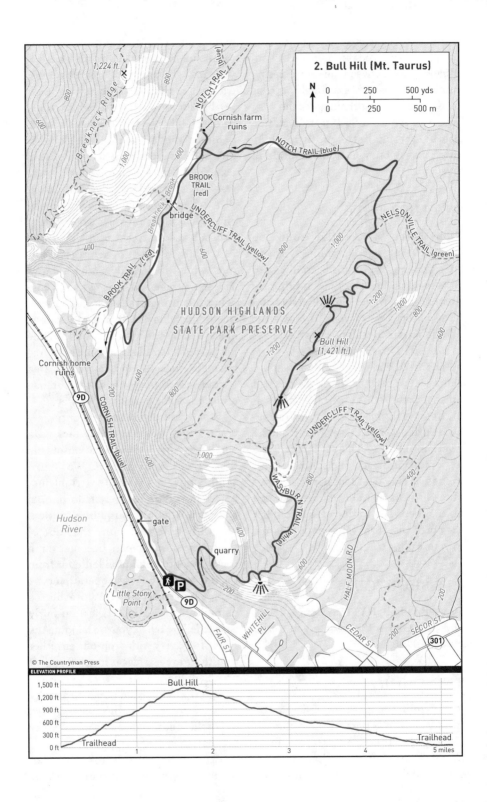

1,224 ft.

*Breakneck Ridge*

800

600

1,000

400

NOTCH TRAIL (blue)

Cornish farm ruins

NOTCH TRAIL (blue)

NELSONVILLE TRAIL (green)

BROOK TRAIL (red)

*Breakneck Brook*

bridge

UNDERCLIFF TRAIL (yellow)

BROOK TRAIL (red)

600

800

1,000

1,200

HUDSON HIGHLANDS
STATE PARK PRESERVE

1,200

×  Bull Hill
(1,421 ft.)

1,000

600

800

Cornish home ruins

CORNISH TRAIL (blue)

UNDERCLIFF TRAIL (yellow)

9D

Hudson
River

200

400

600

800

400

1,000

gate

WASHBURN TRAIL (white)

quarry

Little Stony
Point

P

9D

200

400

600

HALF MOON RD.

FAIR ST.

WHITEHILL PL.

CEDAR ST.

SECOR ST.

301

200

© The Countryman Press

**ELEVATION PROFILE**

| | Bull Hill | | | | |
| 1,500 ft | | | | | |
| 1,200 ft | | | | | |
| 900 ft | | | | | |
| 600 ft | | | | | |
| 300 ft | Trailhead | | | | Trailhead |
| 0 ft | 1 | 2 | 3 | 4 | 5 miles |

within two weeks of each other in 1938, and a fire destroyed the mansion several decades later. Between these fascinating ruins and the several extremely popular hikes surrounding them, plus the easy access to the Cold Spring train station nearby, the final stretch of this hike can get very busy on summer and fall weekends.

## GETTING THERE

From Beacon, NY, drive south on Route 9D. After about 5 miles, you will pass under a tunnel at the trailhead to Breakneck Ridge. Continue driving for another mile, when you will arrive at a large parking area, to your left, as well as additional parking along the street next to signs for Little Stony Point.

The trailhead for this hike is just a short walk north of the town of Cold Spring, making this hike easily accessible from NYC, via Metro-North. Walk up Cold Spring's Main Street away from the river, until you reach Fair Street. Turn left onto Fair Street, and follow it until it ends at NY-9D. From here, turn left onto NY-9D and walk a short distance up the road. The trailhead is located at the north end of the large parking area, to your right.

## GPS SHORTCUT

Type "Bull Hill, NY" into Google Maps and your GPS will navigate you to the main parking area.

## THE TRAIL

Walk from the parking area to the trailhead, at the north end of the lot. Here, paper trail maps are available by the signs that mark the trailhead. Immediately after starting out on the white-blazed Washburn Trail, you will see a blue-blazed trail directly ahead of you. You will eventually return on this trail, which runs north–south parallel to 9D, but for now, follow the white blazes as the trail hooks to the right. The path begins a moderate climb upslope, at one point traversing a section of trail collapsed from erosion, where a huge trench has formed to the left of the path.

After you make it up this first steady climb, you will begin to see what appears to be a huge clearing through the trees. At 0.3 mile, you will reach this "clearing," which is actually an old quarry. The short trees and dense grasses covering this unnaturally flat area give it the unique vibe of a displaced savanna, shadowed by sheer cliffs of rock. While not part of the trail, you should of course take a few minutes to explore this area to your satisfaction—it has a very unique atmosphere for the Hudson Valley.

When you are ready to continue—don't forget, you have only tackled a small fraction of the elevation of this hike so far!—return to the Washburn Trail, which makes a hard right just before the quarry, loosely following its southern rim as it gains in elevation. You will climb up around the edge of the quarry, and the path becomes quite rocky. A long metal pipe left over from the days of the quarry's operation runs along your path here. White blazes painted onto rocks make the route fairly easy to follow, but as you are hugging the edge of a quarry with drop-offs on either side, there are few places to go off-trail at first. Eventually, however, you will leave the quarry behind and climb up a rocky hillside, where the path weaves in and out of the trees, and can be a bit harder to follow in spots.

At 0.5 mile, you will reach a rocky overlook with views downriver. This

THE QUARRY BELOW BULL HILL, SEEN FROM ACROSS THE HUDSON RIVER

vista is directly above the village of Cold Spring—close enough that you could watch townspeople mowing their yard. It is an impressive view for the little distance you've come. Return to the trail and continue uphill. The grade becomes slightly easier, though you have some distance of moderately strenuous ascent still to go before you reach the summit. Around the 1-mile mark, you will come to a second viewpoint. Here, you will have views to the south and west, but even more (and better) are yet to come.

A short distance after, you will reach an intersection with the yellow-blazed Undercliff Trail. This trail also makes a loop around Bull Hill / Mt. Taurus, but skirting the slope of the mountain about halfway to the summit. An excellent vista can be found on this trail around the central point of the mountain's western slope, only about 0.4 mile from this intersection—a good option for a side excursion, if you wish to add on to your hike. To continue along the main route, head straight from your original path, following the white blazes uphill. The ascent becomes a bit more strenuous for a time, and at 1.35 miles, watch for an area of boulders to the side of the trail. Here—easily missed, as it is not obvious from the trail itself—is an excellent viewpoint from atop a rocky area. From this spot, you will enjoy a straight-on view of the Hudson River as it curves and slices south. This is perhaps the best view of the entire hike, so be sure to watch out for it, as it's very easy to walk right past.

At 1.6 miles, the trail begins to level. The summit of Bull Hill is just ahead. The views from the summit are not quite as dramatic as those you have already experienced, but you will catch a nice profile view of Breakneck Ridge to your north, as it runs into the Scofield Ridge and Fishkill Ridge.

Continuing on from the summit, still following the white blazes, the path will begin to switchback downhill. The descent is fairly moderate and follows a broad, clear trail. At 2.3 miles the Washburn Trail ends at an intersection with the blue-blazed Notch Trail, which heads north, and the green-blazed Nelsonville Trail, which heads east. Take the blue-blazed trail to your left.

The descent here is gentle, and soon you will cross a stream, hiking by a gully with stone walls on either side. The trail makes a sharp left, now heading west, down into a valley. At 2.85 miles, you will reach a spot where a large tree has fallen across the path. Either bored hikers or frivolous forest gnomes have taken the time to construct small stone cairns all across this downed tree, making for a very curious landmark.

Continue, as the trail follows two parallel stream beds for some time. At 3.4 miles, you will reach an intersection: the red-blazed Brook Trail, which heads south toward the river and 9D. The blue trail cuts right, toward the ridges, and is a common route taken by hikers returning to the Cold Spring train station after hiking Breakneck Ridge (Hike #5). Just up the blue trail, you will notice ruins in the woods. This is the old Cornish farm estate and is a fascinating place to explore. Take a few minutes to observe these ruins—being extremely careful, as old ruins in the woods are not always the safest and most stable environments—then return to the intersection. You will be hiking out on the red trail.

Follow the red blazes for about a quarter of a mile, walking along the stream. Soon, you will see a wooden bridge crossing the water to your right and a yellow trail that heads over the bridge to the ridgeline. This is the Undercliff Trail, the same yellow trail from near

RUINS OF THE OLD CORNISH ESTATE CAN BE GLIMPSED JUST OFF THE TRAIL

the beginning of your hike, which cuts across the slope of Bull Mountain. Here, it provides yet another route down from Breakneck. Continue on red, and a short distance beyond, you will pass a green trail, to your right. Stay straight.

At 3.75 miles, at another fork, the red trail heads to the right. A sign indicates that the red-blazed trail makes its way back toward the tunnel which passes beneath Breakneck Ridge. You will want to stay left, on the blue-blazed Cornish Trail, which will bring you back to 9D and the parking area. The trail makes a gradual descent here, morphing into an easily traversed woods road. You will soon pass a service road branching off to your right. At 4.3 miles, the path becomes asphalt. Just after this are more ruins, including the main home of the Cornish estate. The ruins of this huge, impressive building are available from a short side path. Walk to the left of the house, where the building's porch once was, and try to imagine how incredible of a view the residents of this home once enjoyed, with the trees cleared to the river in front of them.

Continuing down the path, you will hike for another half a mile on a very easy, gradually sloping asphalt woods road. At 5 miles, you will approach a gate leading back to 9D, though you are still about a quarter mile north of your car and the main parking area. To the left of the gate, you will notice a blue foot trail leading back into the woods. Take this path, which runs along the road, with the sound of traffic not far away. This trail can be very muddy throughout the year but is much safer than walking along the shoulder of 9D. At 5.2 miles, you will return to the trailhead and the main parking area.

# Little Stony Point

**TOTAL DISTANCE**: 1 mile

**TYPE**: Loop

**HIKING TIME**: 1 hour

**TOTAL ELEVATION GAIN**: 120 feet

**MAXIMUM ELEVATION**: 140 feet

**DIFFICULTY**: Easy

Tucked behind a bridge over the train tracks off of NY-9D, across the street from the busy Bull Hill (Mt. Taurus) parking lot, Little Stony Point can be easy to overlook. It is dwarfed by its neighboring hiking destinations, but for as short as its trails, it offers surprisingly fantastic views. With a rocky cliff rising just a little more than a hundred feet above the Hudson River, and yet offering dramatic open views up and down the river, Little Stony Point almost seems designed to show off the Hudson Highlands in miniature form. You won't have to work too hard to reach the top of the cliffs, but the jump of rocks dropping away in front of you is no less impressive despite the low elevation. Around the rest of this peninsula, various rocky beaches grant their own unique river views. Signs posted around these beaches expressly forbid swimming, though they seem to be widely ignored in summer. Regardless, stay out of the water and enjoy this beautiful, easy loop in combination with a longer hike, or for a leisurely outing somewhere between a hike and a walk. With the trailhead so close by, Little Stony Point is especially appealing at sunset and sunrise.

## GETTING THERE

From Beacon, NY, drive south on Route 9D. After about 5 miles, you will pass under a tunnel at the trailhead to Breakneck Ridge. Continue driving for another mile, when you will see parking along the right side of the street next to signs for Little Stony Point. Additional parking can be found in a large parking area, to your left.

Little Stony Point, as well as the trailhead for Bull Hill (Mt. Taurus), are just a short walk north of the town of Cold

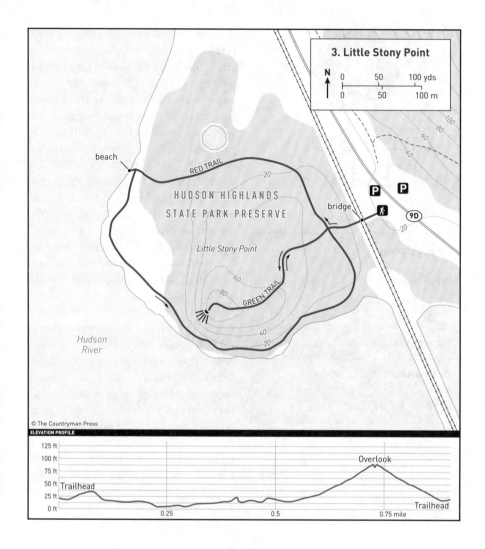

**ELEVATION PROFILE**

Spring, making this hike easily accessible from NYC, via Metro-North. Walk up Cold Spring's Main Street away from the river, until you reach Fair Street. Turn left onto Fair Street, and follow it until it ends at NY-9D. From here, turn left onto NY-9D and walk a short distance up the road. The trailhead is located at the bridge crossing the train tracks, to your left.

## GPS SHORTCUT

Type "Little Stony Point" into Google Maps and your GPS will navigate you to the trailhead.

## THE TRAIL

There are two lots near the trailhead, with the trail actually beginning in the smaller lot on the west side of the road. If you park in the larger lot, carefully cross the road, to the smaller (and quickly

SUNSET FROM THE CLIFFS AT LITTLE STONY POINT

filled) lot. The trail begins beyond this parking area, at the large bridge crossing over the train tracks.

Cross the bridge, following the red blazes. Past the bridge, you will come to a tree with both green and red blazes. A green trail heads straight, deeper into the woods, toward the overlook on the cliffs. You will take this trail after you complete your loop around Little Stony Point, but for now, turn right to begin the loop portion of the hike.

Follow the red blazes, and soon you will reach a fork. Stay to the left, still following the blazes. After a short distance, you will reach a side trail that heads down to the water. Several signs warn against swimming here, but this rule does not seem to be commonly followed. In the summer, many families can be found gathered on the beaches around Little Stony Point, though swimming in the waters of the Hudson River is not recommended.

Continuing around the loop, various side trails veer closer to the rocky cliffs, or toward the water's edge. After enjoying views of Storm King, Cold Spring, and West Point, you will pass a cave at the base of the cliffs at 0.4 mile.

At 0.6 mile you will complete the loop portion of the hike. Turn left, now taking the green-blazed trail. This path makes its way through the woods, before ascending briefly to reach the cliffs. At 0.75 mile, you will reach the top of the cliffs, which come to a jagged peak before slouching away north, decreasing in height. The views of the river here are excellent, and there are many places to perch and take in the scenery.

When you are ready to return, retrace your steps back down the green-blazed trail. Cross the bridge over the train tracks and head to your car.

# Breakneck Ridge— Arrival by Car

**TOTAL DISTANCE**: 3 miles

**TYPE**: Loop

**HIKING TIME**: 3–5 hours

**TOTAL ELEVATION GAIN**: 1,440 feet

**MAXIMUM ELEVATION**: 1,200 feet

**DIFFICULTY**: Very Difficult

Some estimates have claimed that Breakneck Ridge is the most popular hike in the United States, and if you show up around 10 am on a Saturday in early fall with pristine weather, it's easy to believe it. But don't let the massive crowds scare you off—there is a reason the Breakneck Ridge rock scramble is so popular. The unique views and the challenge of the hike make it easy to see why: it is the longest, highest, and most varied rock scramble in the region, and certainly one of the most exhilarating trails in all of the East Coast. Signs have been erected at the trailhead in recent years to warn hikers how challenging this hike is, and in this case, they aren't exaggerating. If you haven't hiked much before—and especially if you haven't attempted any rock scrambles, or hiked up larger, rockier mountains elsewhere in the country—this is probably not the trail you should start with.

The scramble that comprises the first half of the hike is a physical challenge on its own, requiring dexterity, strength, and confidence, even if it never approaches the level of a technical climb. (In other words, there's no need for ropes or harnesses to climb the ridge.) At several points, the trail demands clever scrambling up some rocky crevasse or chimney, and when there's a steep cliff only a few feet away, plummeting hundreds of feet to the ground, a less experienced hiker can easily become intimidated and freeze up. Rescue teams are regularly called upon to evacuate hikers who find themselves unable to continue, to the point where a renovation of the parking area will create a zone specifically for rescue vehicles to park closer to the trailhead. Once again, as fun as this trail can be, you should not attempt to climb Breakneck

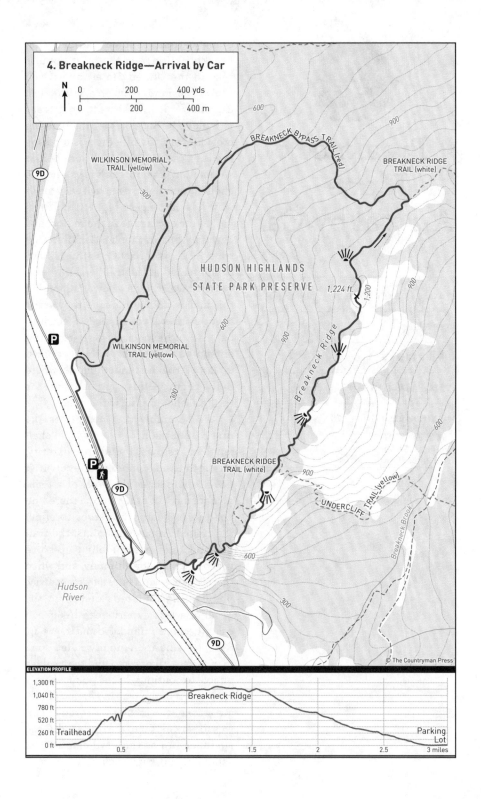

## 4. Breakneck Ridge—Arrival by Car

N

| 0 | 200 | 400 yds |
| 0 | 200 | 400 m |

9D

BREAKNECK BYPASS TRAIL (red)

WILKINSON MEMORIAL
TRAIL (yellow)

BREAKNECK RIDGE
TRAIL (white)

600

900

HUDSON HIGHLANDS
STATE PARK PRESERVE

1,224 ft.

1,200

900

300

600

900

Breakneck Ridge

WILKINSON MEMORIAL
TRAIL (yellow)

P

300

600

BREAKNECK RIDGE
TRAIL (white)

P

9D

900

UNDERCLIFF TRAIL (yellow)

Breakneck Brook

600

Hudson
River

600

300

9D

© The Countryman Press

**ELEVATION PROFILE**

| 1,300 ft | | Breakneck Ridge | | | | |
| 1,040 ft | | | | | | |
| 780 ft | | | | | | |
| 520 ft | | | | | | Parking |
| 260 ft | Trailhead | | | | | Lot |
| 0 ft | | 0.5 | 1 | 1.5 | 2 | 2.5 | 3 miles |

Ridge unless you feel confident in your ability to complete the hike. The Hudson Valley offers several other shorter rock scrambles, and while they are all challenging in their own unique ways, attempting a similar but easier hike is a good idea if you are unsure whether you can handle Breakneck Ridge. Bonticou Crag (Hike #23), located in the northeastern Shawangunks, offers a shorter, somewhat less strenuous rock scramble to test yourself on.

## GETTING THERE

The parking area for Breakneck Ridge is located on NY-9D roughly 5 miles south of Beacon, NY, and 2.3 miles north of Cold Spring, NY. Parking can be found on both sides of the road, and while there is ample parking available, spots fill up very quickly on weekends.

## GPS SHORTCUT

Type "Breakneck Ridge" into Google Maps and your GPS will navigate you to the main parking area.

## THE TRAIL

From the parking area, walk on the footpath to the right of the guard railing alongside 9D. Right before the tunnel, you will come to a small shed where volunteers are stationed with information on busy days. The trail begins, heading uphill, alongside a large stone structure next to the train tracks. Below this structure is a pumping station for the system that transports water from the Catskills to New York City. The trail climbs above the tunnel and the pumping station, and a short distance up, there is a rocky area with a lookout to the river.

The trail bends left, over the tunnel for 9D, and begins up the ridge. The next several legs of this hike are very deceptive when measured in miles—you're climbing vertically much more than you're hiking horizontally, and so a mere quarter mile of distance traversed may take you 45 minutes, and feel as if you've hiked five times farther than you actually have. From the trailhead to the first viewpoint of Breakneck Ridge is only 0.25 mile, but includes the steepest, most intense section of climbing. As this area of rock is broad and extremely varied, there are many possible routes. White paint blazes indicate the suggested, and easiest route, though if you diverge from the "trail," it is usually very simple to hop a few rocks and return. While this area may be the most grueling, it is not particularly challenging in a technical sense.

Approaching the first viewpoint, you will spot an American flag on the edge where the cliff looms toward the Hudson. This spot is extremely popular for photos, and tends to be very crowded on most weekends. Nonetheless, the remarkable views here shouldn't be missed. To the south is Bull Mountain / Mt. Taurus and the southern section of the park, which offers several excellent hikes of its own. Straight ahead, directly opposite you on the other side of the Hudson, is Storm King Mountain, another very popular hiking destination. To the northwest, on a clear day, you may spot the Shawangunk Ridge near New Paltz, and the Catskill Mountains in the distance beyond.

When you are ready, follow the trail markers up the rocks and along the ridgeline. At this point, the trail begins to follow a much narrower portion of the ridge. While the first section was a broad scramble up a steep hill, here, you will feel as if you are navigating a narrow cliff. At 0.35 mile, you will tackle one of the more challenging "scramble" portions of the hike. As with all semi-technical spots on Breakneck, take your time, and be careful with your hand and foot placements. Almost all climbs here are very simple once you figure out where to wedge your foot for balance and find the right handholds for leverage. There is no single point on this hike in which you will be dangling off a rock without a proper handhold or foothold available. Carefully observe your surroundings, all possible points of purchase, and plan your route in your head before making the attempt.

At 0.4 (though once again it will feel as if you have gone much further), you will reach the second vista. The views are just as impressive as the first, though you will find the crowds tend to thin out the further along you go. There are four main viewpoints on this hike, and many more minor vistas.

Continuing on, at 0.5 mile, you will see a white trail to your left offering an easier ascent. Take this if you wish, or continue on the main trail. Cross a ledge on the south side of the ridge, which is narrow but easily traversed. The views here are as impressive as at the vistas. The trail moves back up the ridge to your left, climbing a section of broad, flat rock face that can seem particularly imposing from below. Depending on your angle, it may appear as if there are no obvious routes up the rock face, and that any attempt will result in you sliding back down, dangerously close to a cliff edge. However, to the right of this rock face is a narrow crevasse, which has foot and handholds. And once attempted, you will find that the rock face is not nearly as steep as it seems from the bottom, and can be walked up without assistance, if your shoes have good grip and you keep your center of gravity low.

Just after this, you will reach the third viewing area. Continue on the trail, and soon after, at 0.65 mile, you will pass the Undercliff Trail to your right. This yellow-blazed trail cuts down into the clove on a rocky, challenging footpath, and will bring you back to the road south of the original trailhead, closer to the town of Cold Spring. While this route can also be taken to complete a loop hike, another trail, further along, makes for an easier hike. And of course, there's the fact that you haven't even reached the true summit yet!

The yellow trail departs from a low point between the ridge's peaks, and immediately after, the trail makes another ascent. Tackle another rock scramble, shorter and less challenging than those previous, with views near the top. Afterwards, the trail levels, as you are nearing the high point of the ridgeline. At 0.8 mile, you will reach another viewpoint, again looking toward Storm King. Shortly after is yet another vista, this time looking out to the northwest, with the Shawangunk Ridge visible in the distance.

Follow the trail, which now resembles a more typical hiking path—horizontal, rather than vertical. At 1.15 miles, you will reach the high point of the ridgeline. Just beyond, at 1.25 miles, you will arrive at a rocky outcrop with excellent views to the north. Sugarloaf Mountain is directly below you, rising to nearly 900 feet, much less than the height of Breakneck Ridge.

BREAKNECK RIDGE FEATURES SEVERAL STAGES OF ROCK SCRAMBLES, EACH WITH INCREDIBLE VIEWS

At 1.5 miles, look for red paint markers on the rocks to your left, indicating the return trail to the parking area. Climb up these rocks before the trail finally begins to descend. From here, the path weaves through the woods, making a moderate and steady downhill. The trail is never strenuous or challenging, but may be muddy and slick with runoff after rain or snowmelt. Occasionally, you may spot Sugarloaf through the trees, growing larger as you descend.

At 2 miles, you will pass a large teepee made from branches.

At 2.25 miles, you will reach an intersection with a yellow-blazed trail. This trail, if taken to the right, heads up Sugarloaf Mountain (Hike #6), an excellent hike on its own. Turn left to descend and return to the parking area. At 2.8 miles, you will return to the road, to the north of the main parking area. Walk down the side of 9D, being very mindful of traffic. Cross the road and return to your car.

# Breakneck Ridge—Arrival by Train

| | |
|---|---|
| **TOTAL DISTANCE**: 4.2 miles | |
| **TYPE**: Loop | |
| **HIKING TIME**: 3–5 hours | |
| **TOTAL ELEVATION GAIN**: 1,480 feet | |
| **MAXIMUM ELEVATION**: 1,200 feet | |
| **DIFFICULTY**: Very Difficult | |

There's no doubt that Breakneck Ridge is one of the most exciting, challenging hikes in the northeast, but part of its popularity certainly stems from the fact that this hike is easily accessible by Metro-North on weekends. Trains northbound from Manhattan deposit thousands of hikers every Saturday and Sunday. This route follows a slightly different course than Hike #4, as most hikers returning to the city in the evening will wish to arrive at the Breakneck Ridge station (merely a small platform next to the tracks) in the morning and depart from the Cold Spring train station after completing their hike. In Cold Spring, hikers will find a variety of food and refreshment options with which to reward themselves following their adventure, as well as easy access to trains returning to Manhattan, about once an hour throughout the day and evening.

## GETTING THERE

Metro-North trains on the Poughkeepsie line stop at Breakneck Ridge on weekends. Trains depart Grand Central about once an hour. A return train can also be taken from the same Breakneck Ridge train platform, however—as the station is merely a small platform alongside the tracks—it is generally more convenient and enjoyable to return from the Cold Spring train station. This guide is routed to end on the outskirts of Cold Spring. The Cold Spring train station is located on Market St., about 0.3 mile south from Main Street.

## THE TRAIL

From the train platform, walk toward NY-9D, away from the river, following the rough path. The trailhead begins about half a mile from where the train dropped you off. Walk south, toward the ridge and the tunnel passing through it, until you pass the large parking area for cars. Past the parking area, walk on the footpath to the right of the guard railing alongside NY-9D. Right before the tunnel, you will come to a small shed where volunteers are stationed with information on busy days. The trail begins, heading uphill, alongside a large stone structure next to the train tracks. Below this structure is a pumping station for the system that transports water from the Catskills to New York City. The trail climbs above the tunnel and the pumping station, and a short distance up, there is a rocky area with a lookout to the river.

The trail bends left, over the tunnel for NY-9D, and begins up the ridge. The next several sections of this hike are very deceptive when measured in miles—you're climbing vertically much more than you're hiking horizontally, and so a mere quarter mile of distance traversed may take you 45 minutes, and feel as if you've hiked five times farther than you actually have. From the trailhead to the first viewpoint of Breakneck Ridge is only 0.25 mile, but includes the steepest, most intense section of climbing. As this area of rock is broad and extremely varied, there are many possible routes. White paint blazes indicate the suggested, and easiest route, though if you diverge from the "trail," it is usually very simple to hop a few rocks and return. While this area may be the most grueling, it is not particularly challenging in a technical sense.

Approaching the first viewpoint, you will spot an American flag on the edge where the cliff overlooks the Hudson. This spot is extremely popular for photos and tends to be very crowded on most weekends. Nonetheless, the remarkable views here shouldn't be missed. To the south is Bull Mountain / Mt. Taurus and the southern reaches of the Hudson Highlands. Straight ahead, directly opposite you on the other side of the river, is Storm King Mountain (Hike #12), another very popular hiking destination. To the northwest, on a clear day, you may spot the Shawangunk Ridge near New Paltz, and the Catskill Mountains in the distance beyond.

When you are ready, follow the trail markers up the rocks and along the ridgeline. At this point, the trail begins to follow a much more narrow portion of the ridge. While the first section was a broad scramble up a steep hill, here, you will feel as if you are navigating a narrow cliff. At 0.35 mile, you will tackle one of the more challenging "scramble" portions of the hike. As with all semi-technical spots on Breakneck, take your time, and be careful with your hand and foot placements. Almost all climbs here are very simple once you figure out where to wedge your foot for balance and find the right handholds for leverage. There is no single point on this hike in which you will be dangling off a rock without a proper handhold or foothold available. Carefully observe your surroundings, all possible points of purchase, and plan your route in your head before making the attempt. However, if you realize you are not up for this particular climb, there is also an alternate route marked with wide blazes that will bypass this section, a short distance before the difficult section begins.

Past this climb, there is a small side trail to your right leading to a flat rock ledge that is easily missed. This ledge offers an excellent view down toward the first overlook (where the flags are posi-

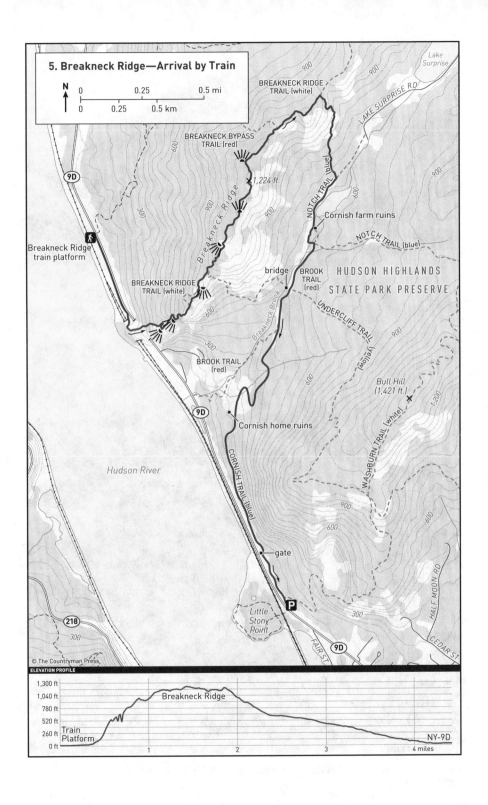

5. Breakneck Ridge—Arrival by Train

N

0        0.25              0.5 mi

0    0.25        0.5 km

BREAKNECK RIDGE
TRAIL (white)

Lake
Surprise

900

900

LAKE SURPRISE RD

9D

600

BREAKNECK BYPASS
TRAIL (red)

600

300

900

1,224 ft.

NOTCH TRAIL (blue)

900

600

Cornish farm ruins

Breakneck Ridge
train platform

Breakneck Ridge

900

NOTCH TRAIL (blue)

HUDSON HIGHLANDS
STATE PARK PRESERVE

BREAKNECK RIDGE
TRAIL (white)

bridge    BROOK
TRAIL
(red)

600

UNDERCLIFF TRAIL (yellow)

900

300

Breakneck Brook

600

Bull Hill
(1,421 ft.)

1,200

BROOK TRAIL
(red)

600

WASHBURN TRAIL (white)

9D

Cornish home ruins

Hudson River

CORNISH TRAIL (blue)

900

600

gate

300

HALF MOON RD

218

300

P

Little
Stony
Point

300

FAIR ST

9D

CEDAR ST

© The Countryman Press

ELEVATION PROFILE

1,300 ft

1,040 ft                    Breakneck Ridge

780 ft

520 ft

260 ft    Train
Platform                                                    NY-9D

0 ft           1              2              3        4 miles

THE FIRST VIEWPOINT ON THE BREAKNECK RIDGE SCRAMBLE, REACHED AFTER ONLY HALF A MILE OF STEEP UPHILL CLIMBING

tioned) and across the river to Storm King.

Continuing on, at 0.4 mile, you will see another white trail to your left offering an easier ascent. Take this if you wish, or continue on the main trail. Cross a ledge on the south side of the ridge, which is narrow but easily traversed. The views here are as impressive as at the main vistas. The trail moves back up the ridge to your left, climbing a section of broad, flat rock face that can seem particularly imposing from below. Depending on your angle, it may appear as if there are no obvious routes up the rock face, and that any attempt will result in you sliding back down, dangerously close to a cliff edge. However, to the right of this rock face is a narrow crevasse, which has foot and handholds. Once attempted, you will find that the rock face is not nearly as steep as it seems from the bottom, and can be walked up without assistance, if your shoes have good grip and you keep your center of gravity low.

Just after this, you will reach the third viewing area. Continue on the trail, and soon after, at 0.65 mile, you will pass the Undercliff Trail to your right. This yellow-blazed trail cuts down into the valley below you on a rocky, challenging footpath, and will bring you back to the road south of the original trailhead, closer to the town of Cold Spring. While this route can also be taken to complete a loop hike, another trail, further along, makes for an easier and more interesting hike. And of course, there's the fact that you haven't even reached the true summit yet!

Immediately after, the trail begins to ascend once again. Tackle yet another rock scramble, shorter and less challenging than those previous, with views near the top. Afterwards, the trail levels, as you are nearing the high point of the ridgeline. At 0.8 mile, you will reach another viewpoint, though this vista is mostly obscured by foliage in the summer.

Follow the trail, which now resembles a more typical hiking path—horizontal, rather than vertical. At 1.15 miles, you will reach the high point of the ridgeline. There are no views from the high point, but just beyond, at 1.2 miles, you will pass a short side trail leading to a large rocky area with excellent views to the north. Sugarloaf Mountain (Hike #6) rises directly below you, while Storm King, Schunemunk Mountain, Bannerman's Island, Denning's Point, the city of Beacon, the Shawangunks, and the Catskills are all visible.

Shortly after, the trail begins to head downhill. At 1.5 miles, you will pass a red-blazed trail on your left. This is the Breakneck Bypass Trail, which offers an ideal return trail to complete a loop back toward the parking area for those who arrived by car (Hike #4). Continue on the white-blazed trail, and soon you will come to another bald, rocky area with limited views. From here, the trail begins to descend once again.

At 1.75 miles, the white trail continues straight, heading north toward Mt. Beacon, while the blue-blazed Notch Trail intersects to your right. Take the blue trail, heading steeply downhill. After descending for about half a mile, you will come to a T-intersection, with a woods road heading left and right. To the left, the road heads toward private property, and is thus off limits to hikers. Turn right, and soon you will find yourself walking next to a large marshy area. The remains of a dam at the far end hint that this used to be a reservoir.

Just past the marsh, around mile mark 2.5, you will see the first of several large ruins in the woods. These struc-

RUINS FROM THE OLD CORNISH ESTATE ARE SCATTERED THROUGHOUT THE WOODS ALONG MORE THAN A MILE OF TRAIL

tures are the remains of the old Cornish dairy estate. Multiple structures can be found all throughout this valley between Breakneck and Bull Mountain.

You will pass a blue trail to your left, but continue straight, hiking along a small creek. Soon, you will see two arrows, red and blue, pointing you to make a left turn, where an old trail has been rerouted. This route will bring you across the creek, after which the blue-blazed trail heads straight, climbing toward Bull Hill. Turn right onto the red trail, and follow as it meanders through the woods, roughly parallel to the creek.

Soon, you will see a wooden bridge crossing the water to your right, and a yellow trail that heads over the bridge to the ridgeline. This is the Undercliff Trail, which you passed earlier in the

hike, as it made an early descent from the ridge before reaching the true summit. Continue on red, and a short distance beyond, you will pass a green trail. Stay left.

At the next fork, the red trail heads to the right. A sign indicates that the red-blazed trail heads toward the tunnel that passes beneath Breakneck Ridge. You will want to stay left, on the blue-blazed Cornish Trail, which will bring you back to NY-9D, the road leading into the town of Cold Spring. The trail makes a gradual descent here, morphing into an easily traversed woods road. You will soon pass a service road branching off to your right. At 3.3 miles, the path becomes asphalt. Just after this are more ruins, including the main home of the Cornish estate. The ruins of this huge, impressive building are available from a short side path. Walk to the left of the house, where the building's porch once was, and try to imagine the incredible view the residents of this home once enjoyed, with the trees cleared to the river in front of them.

Continuing down the path, you will hike for another half a mile on a very easy, gradually sloping asphalt woods road. Eventually, you will approach a gate leading back to NY-9D, though you are still about a quarter mile north of the "exit" trailhead that you will wish to emerge from. To the left of the gate, you will notice a blue foot trail leading back into the woods. Take this path, which runs along the road, with the sound of traffic only a few feet away. This trail can be very muddy throughout the year but is much safer than walking along the shoulder of busy NY-9D. At 5.2 miles, you will emerge at a trailhead by a large parking area.

From here, walk south on NY-9D, with the Hudson River to your right. Be very watchful for traffic; this is a busy road. After less than a quarter mile, however, turn onto Fair St., which veers right. Walk along this quieter town road for about 0.6 mile, at which point you will hit Main St. in Cold Spring. Here, you can shop, explore, and enjoy dinner before returning to the train.

To find the Cold Spring train station, walk along Main St. toward the Hudson River, and cross under the train tracks via the underground pedestrian tunnel. On the other side, turn left onto Market St. Walk south for about 0.3 mile, and soon you will see the train station on your left.

# 6

# Sugarloaf Mountain

**TOTAL DISTANCE**: 2.5 miles

**TYPE**: Out and Back

**HIKING TIME**: 2 hours

**TOTAL ELEVATION GAIN**: 870 feet

**MAXIMUM ELEVATION**: 900 feet

**DIFFICULTY**: Moderate

Sugarloaf Mountain may be home to the most famous tree in the Hudson Valley—or at least the most commonly photographed. The exposed rock ledges at the pinnacle of this hike are home to a perfectly perched dead tree with two gnarled, twisting branches, overlooking a million-dollar view of Bannerman's Island below. It's nearly impossible to pass by this memorable spot without snapping a photo, but even still, in terms of popularity, Sugarloaf Mountain is overshadowed by neighboring Breakneck Ridge—literally. The rock scramble looming over your shoulder shares a common parking area and a short stretch of trail on its return loop. While there's enough elevation gain heading up Sugarloaf to give you a proper workout, the 2.5 miles round trip means this hike doesn't have to be a long excursion for an in-shape hiker. Given the exceptional views, memorable summit, and modest time commitment, Sugarloaf Mountain is an ideal sunset hike.

## GETTING THERE

Sugarloaf Mountain shares a main parking area with Breakneck Ridge, though several other smaller parking areas are available, a few hundred feet north up the road. The main parking area is located on NY-9D roughly 5 miles south of Beacon, NY, and 2.3 miles north of Cold Spring, NY. Parking can be found on both sides of the road, but these lots fill up very quickly on weekends.

## GPS SHORTCUT

Type "Breakneck Ridge" into Google Maps and your GPS will navigate you to the main parking area. Additional

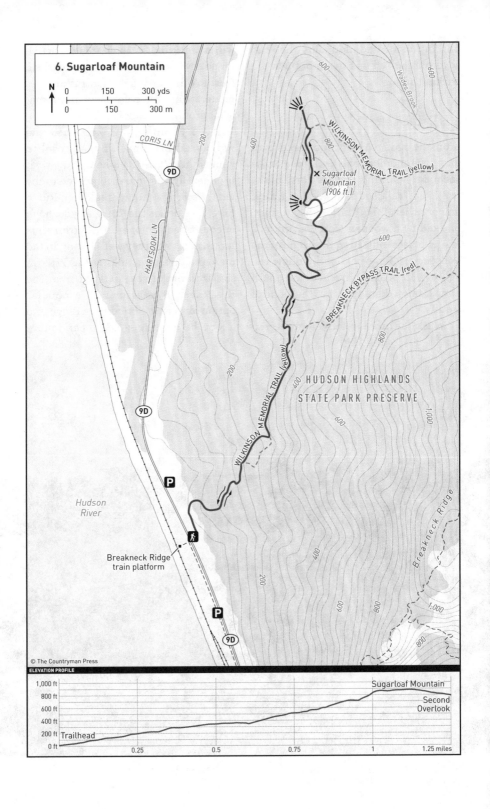

# 6. Sugarloaf Mountain

N

| 0 | 150 | 300 yds |
| 0 | 150 | 300 m |

CORIS LN

9D

HARTSOOK LN

WILKINSON MEMORIAL TRAIL (yellow)

✕ Sugarloaf
Mountain
(906 ft.)

BREAKNECK BYPASS TRAIL (red)

Wades Brook

600

800

400

200

600

800

HUDSON HIGHLANDS
STATE PARK PRESERVE

1,000

WILKINSON MEMORIAL TRAIL (yellow)

400

600

200

Breakneck Ridge

9D

P

Hudson
River

Breakneck Ridge
train platform

P

9D

400

200

600

800

1,000

© The Countryman Press

**ELEVATION PROFILE**

| | | | | | |
| 1,000 ft | | | | | Sugarloaf Mountain |
| 800 ft | | | | | |
| 600 ft | | | | | Second |
| 400 ft | | | | | Overlook |
| 200 ft | Trailhead | | | | |
| 0 ft | | 0.25 | 0.5 | 0.75 | 1 | 1.25 miles |

parking is located alongside the road several hundred feet north of the main parking area.

## THE TRAIL

From the main parking area, walk north along the shoulder of NY-9D (one of the secondary parking areas is north of the trailhead; walk south to find the trail if you park here). The trail is easy to spot, marked by a wooden sign bearing yellow tri-blazes indicating the origin of the Wilkinson Memorial Trail. Follow the yellow blazes as the trail begins uphill almost immediately, first in the slope of a gully.

While the hike is relatively short, you will be tackling some degree of incline for nearly the entire ascent up Sugarloaf. During this starting section, the grade is moderate at first, before leveling somewhat around 0.2 mile in.

At 0.56 mile, you will pass the red-blazed Breakneck Bypass trail to your right. While the hike up Sugarloaf is generally very quiet compared to the vastly more popular Breakneck Ridge hike just down the road, if you have encountered anyone on the trail thus far, chances are they were hiking in the opposite direction, taking the Wilkinson Trail back to the parking area. The Breakneck Bypass trail is a popular option for turning Breakneck Ridge into a loop hike (Hike #5). You can ignore

THE GNARLED, DEAD TREE ON TOP OF SUGARLOAF MOUNTAIN IS A POPULAR SUBJECT FOR AREA PHOTOGRAPHERS, AND ADDS TO THE EXCELLENT VIEWS FOUND HERE

BANNERMAN'S ISLAND, SEEN FROM SUGARLOAF

this trail for the purpose of this hike, continuing straight, still following the yellow blazes.

Shortly after, you will cross a stream. Just after this, the incline will increase once again as Sugarloaf looms overhead. The trail switchbacks and climbs up a series of stone steps before veering around the south side of the mountain slope, and beginning an even steeper ascent.

After a short, easy scramble up the final stretch of rocky trail, you will reach the summit area. Here the trail cuts back southwest, toward a viewpoint. At 1.1 miles, you will reach the famous tree of Sugarloaf and an incredible vista overlooking the Hudson, with a variety of purchases to be found around the open rocky summit.

Continue past "the tree," and in a short distance, you will reach a second vista, on the north side of the mountain's round summit. From here, simply turn around and retrace your steps to return to NY-9D and the parking area.

# Mt. Beacon and Fire Tower

| | |
|---|---|
| **TOTAL DISTANCE**: 4 miles | |
| **TYPE**: Out and Back | |
| **HIKING TIME**: 3–4 hours | |
| **TOTAL ELEVATION GAIN**: 1,100 feet | |
| **MAXIMUM ELEVATION**: 1,520 feet | |
| **DIFFICULTY**: Strenuous | |

Another classic, popular hike of the eastern Hudson Highlands, Mt. Beacon towers over its bustling namesake town. The weekend crowds that wander Beacon's main street for its many dining and shopping destinations translate to crowds on the nearby trails as well. This hike holds plenty of appeal besides its convenience for city dwellers, though. While the steep, short hike up the slope's switchbacks will leave even experienced hikers winded, the rewards at the summit are many. From the first main vista, by the ruins of an old hotel and incline railway, Mt. Beacon offers dramatic views over town, and beyond, to Newburgh, the Shawangunk Ridge, and the Catskill Mountains. And that's before you even get to the fire tower!

Multiple excellent vistas and a fire tower would be draw enough, but then there's the unique history of these mountains. Visible from all across town, the remains of an old incline railway leave a scar from top to bottom on the mountainside: a hint that, for many decades, one didn't have to sweat quite so much to reach the top. The Beacon Incline Railway was opened in 1902, and proved quite popular, with tens of thousands of riders taking the trip to the top each year. Once there, visitors to Mt. Beacon could enjoy the Beacon-crest Hotel and Casino, a resort that brought a bit of the famous Catskill mountain-house charm to the Hudson Highlands. Today, only the foundations of these buildings remain, along with the massive gears that once operated the railway. While the hotel and casino eventually went the way of their doomed Catskill brethren, the railway lasted until 1978, when it too ceased operations due to financial problems. The railway was added to the National Register of Historic Places in 1982, but only the

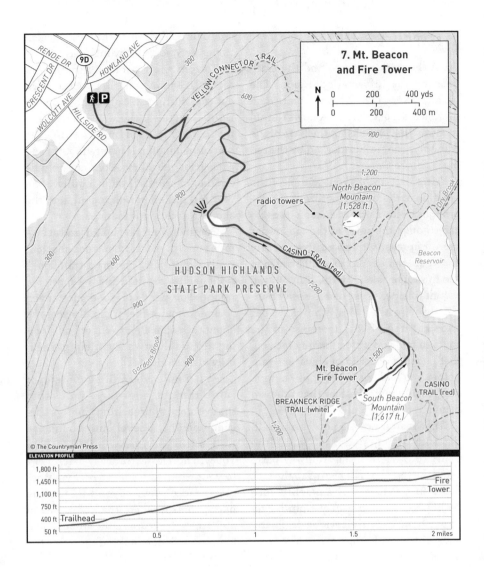

## 7. Mt. Beacon and Fire Tower

RENDE DR
CRESCENT DR
WOLCOTT AVE
HILLSIDE RD
HOWLAND AVE
9D
YELLOW CONNECTOR TRAIL
HUDSON HIGHLANDS
STATE PARK PRESERVE
Gordons Brook
radio towers
North Beacon Mountain (1,528 ft.)
CASINO TRAIL (red)
Beacon Reservoir
Mt. Beacon Fire Tower
South Beacon Mountain (1,617 ft.)
BREAKNECK RIDGE TRAIL (white)
CASINO TRAIL (red)
© The Countryman Press

**ELEVATION PROFILE**

Trailhead — Fire Tower

next year, a suspicious fire destroyed most of the buildings. Now, the Mount Beacon Incline Railway Restoration Society is working to rebuild the railroad and restore service, though there is no estimate yet for when this ambitious project might be completed.

## GETTING THERE

The parking area is located just off of NY-9D, heading south out of town from Beacon. From I-84, simply drive south on NY-9D for 2.5 miles, and the parking area will be on your left, at the base of the mountain. The lot is large, but is very busy on weekends, and may fill up during peak periods.

## GPS SHORTCUT

Type "Mt. Beacon Trailhead" into Google Maps and your GPS will navigate you to the parking area.

## THE TRAIL

From the parking area, find the trailhead by the informational sign. The path is a very broad, level woods road for this first section, as it follows the old roadway that once led to the base of the tramway. The trail is marked by the red blazes of the Casino Trail.

After 0.2 mile, you will see the remains of the infrastructure that once brought visitors up Mt. Beacon by cable car—though the ruins at the top are far more impressive. Viewed from nearly anywhere in Beacon, you will be able to see the route taken by the tram up the mountainside, here visible as a channel through the trees. The cable car once boasted of the steepness of the route taken, and unfortunately for you, that means a good bit of elevation gain before you will reach the top! There is no glossing over the fact that this is a grueling march uphill.

That march begins not with a trail, but with a long staircase. Tackle the stairs to the left of the tramway path. From the top, the trail begins to the left, ascending over a rocky patch before beginning a steep ascent uphill. The grade here is fairly serious from the start, as you trudge up a series of switchbacks. At the curve in the first switchback, you will see a yellow-blazed trail heading straight. This is a connector trail heading northeast toward the other main route and trailhead in this area: the Fishkill Ridge Trail, which begins at Pocket Road. Continue on the main path, taking the Casino Trail as it cuts to the right.

At the next switchback, an unmarked trail once again continues straight, this time to an overlook by the tramway, with a small viewing platform. From here,

continue up the trail to the left, as it continues its steep, steady incline.

Toward the top of this section, at around 0.6 mile, you will notice a shortcut trail cutting sharply uphill, to your right. Several of these shortcut trails tackle the hill head-on to shorten the distance, but offer less sure footing and a much tougher climb. Continue on, past another shortcut through a gully. Soon the trail switches right again, and the shortcuts rejoin the main path.

Continue your slog uphill, and at 0.75 mile you will see another steep shortcut trail to your right. The main trail hooks right itself soon after, and the shortcuts rejoin. The path here becomes much rockier, though the grade of ascent is about the same. Be careful of your footing around these rocky areas, particularly after a rain.

At 0.9 mile, you will begin to spot ruins through the trees, indicating that you are approaching the top. The grade begins to level out, though the trail is still very rocky in this section. You will notice old tramway machinery to your right, and a large rocky pinnacle ahead of you. Beyond that is the flat open area where the hotel, casino and other structures once stood, and a man-made ledge looking out over the town of Beacon.

Once you are done exploring this area, find the trail again around the backside of the casino area. The trail over this next section is a woods road commonly used by ATVs and Jeeps to access Mt. Beacon. This road is often in rough condition due to the aggressive traffic, but it is flat and easy to travel on foot.

At 1.3 miles, you will reach a three-way intersection, with another woods road heading left toward the

THE TOWN OF BEACON, SPRAWLED OUT BELOW MT. BEACON

RUINS OF THE WHEELHOUSE AT THE TOP OF MOUNTAIN SHOW THE PATH OF THE OLD INCLINE RAILWAY

Beacon reservoir. Take the path to the right, still following the red blazes of the Casino Trail. Soon the trail will become a typical footpath once again, climbing over several more rocky areas. At 1.5 miles, you will pass a flat area where someone has constructed dozens of small rock cairns alongside the trail.

At 1.75 miles, the red trail veers left, and a white-blazed trail begins, heading to your right. This intersection is actually the northern terminus of the Breakneck Ridge Trail, which begins at the popular rock scramble by the Hudson River. Take this trail, following the white blazes uphill.

Soon, you will begin to hike up a ridgeline with views to the east. At spots, you will see the fire tower looming above you. One final climb up a rocky area stands between you and fire tower now, which you will reach at the 2 mile mark.

From the tower, retrace your steps to return to the parking area.

# Lambs Hill and Bald Mountain

**TOTAL DISTANCE**: 7.2 miles

**TYPE**: Partial Loop

**HIKING TIME**: 4–5 hours

**TOTAL ELEVATION GAIN**: 1,720 feet

**MAXIMUM ELEVATION**: 1,470 feet

**DIFFICULTY**: Strenuous

There are many qualities with which to recommend this hike as one of the Hudson Valley's finest: the more predictable, like a gorgeous waterfall, a lush gorge, and views of the Hudson River. There are more esoteric draws here, too: an abandoned bulldozer hidden deep in the woods, slowly being reclaimed by the forest. And even the viewpoints leading up to and from Lambs Hill, this hike's first summit, would be enough to recommend this adventure all on their own. But the hike only gets better from there, as one heads further along the quiet trails of the northern Fishkill Ridge.

Bald Mountain is a special place, and while the views are some of the best around, perhaps one of its most compelling qualities is its solitude. The crowds that flock to nearby Mt. Beacon and its fire tower very rarely make their way to the northeastern end of the ridgeline, where you'll discover a remarkable vantage over the surrounding region—nearly 360 degree views of the Hudson Valley can be enjoyed here. From the Bald Mountain summit and the many ledges on the trail leading to it, the Manhattan skyline can even be glimpsed on a clear day. Enjoying a quiet moment at this incredible spot, you may be glad that the crowds stick to the area's better-known tourist traps.

## GETTING THERE

From Main Street in Beacon, turn right onto East Main Street at the "dummy light," crossing Fishkill Creek. Continue following East Main Street for just under 1 mile. At this point, the road forks. Take Pocket Road, to the right. Pocket Road continues for only a short distance before reaching a dead end. A small parking area is at the end of the road.

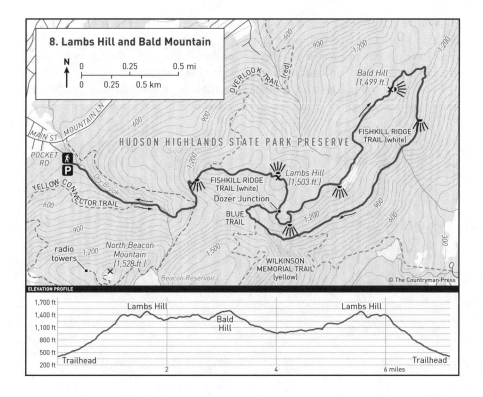

8. Lambs Hill and Bald Mountain

ELEVATION PROFILE

There are only spaces for a few cars here, and signs warning you not to block the gate at the end of the road. This road is surrounded by private property; be careful not to block the driveway of a private residence.

## GPS SHORTCUT

Type "Pocket Road" into Google Maps and your GPS will navigate you to the short road leading to the parking area.

## THE TRAIL

Walk up the road toward the gate, then cross around to continue on the gravel road up the hill. A large, squat water "tower" will be to your left. Up the hill,

you will walk past the Beacon water reservoir and pumping station, a small city of sorts. The trail climbs a small bank here before heading into the woods.

Continue up the trail, following the white blazes of the Fishkill Ridge Trail. The ascent is easy at first, making a slow climb up the side of a col along a creek. About half a mile from the parking area, you will pass a yellow-blazed trail heading upslope to your right. Continue on the white-blazed trail. The path is fairly rocky for most of this run, requiring you to pay extra attention to your footing despite the moderate grade. Be careful during periods of high runoff or after a rain, however, as there are steep drop-offs down to the creek below you for much of the way.

At 0.65 mile, after a somewhat

steeper ascent up a hill bank, you will descend briefly toward the water and cross over the stream. Watch your footing and climb up the bank on the northern side of the water. The trail ascends more aggressively uphill here, following a narrow trail, before tackling a compact switchback and heading toward a footbridge. Cross the footbridge to the other side of the stream once more, and hike up the bank as the trail cuts into the hillside. You will tackle a short burst of ele-

THE MANHATTAN SKYLINE IS VISIBLE FROM VARIOUS VIEWPOINTS AROUND BALD MOUNTAIN

vation here before the trail levels, then climbs again. Soon you will approach an access road, at 0.9 mile. To your right is a small clearing with a primitive campsite. The road running perpendicular to your path is an access road leading to the Beacon Reservoir, which lies up the hill about half a mile. This road, and several other routes around the surrounding hills, are very popular for ATVs and Jeeps.

Turn left onto the woods road, walking downhill, until you see the white blazes of the Fishkill Ridge Trail leading back into the woods to your right. Climb over a bank, then begin a steady ascent uphill. The trail will ascend at a moderate grade over the next leg of the hike: this is the most significant elevation change of the hike, and while the climb is not particularly strenuous compared to some other hikes, the prolonged uphill for the first stretch of this route can certainly be tiring. Soon, however, you will be rewarded for your efforts with excellent views, starting at around 1 mile. The open rocks and dwarf pines here make for impressive mountaintop vistas, looking south toward Mt. Beacon and the South Mt. Beacon Fire Tower, and west toward the Hudson River, with the Shawangunk Ridge visible in the distance. The viewpoints here continue one after the other, and each is equally grand. If one spot has already been occupied, continue uphill and you will likely find a perch at the next open rock.

At 1.25 miles, you will reach the high point and an intersection with a red-blazed trail. This trail, splitting off to your left, heads north toward an alternate trailhead. Keep right, following the white blazes. At 1.6 miles, you will reach Lambs Hill, the major summit of the northern Fishkill Ridge. The summit features views to the west and north. After this, you will descend briefly, before reaching Dozer Junction at 1.9 miles. The reason for the name of this intersection is quite obvious, and

DOZER JUNCTION

the abandoned bulldozer along the trail here provides a unique backwoods sight.

Dozer Junction falls in a deep gully, with a woods road following the gully perpendicular to your path. Continue across to the other side of the gully, where the white blazes ascend and continue east. The trail continues to the south, but will soon hook back around and head northeast. At around 2.05 miles, you will encounter the first of several viewpoints from which you might catch a glimpse of the Manhattan skyline. This remarkable view is very distant and easy to miss if you are not paying attention, shaded by the 60 miles or so of rolling hills that separate you from North America's largest city. This first viewpoint to the far-away metropolis is only a taste, and there will be many more spots offering similar or better views. Several of the best views lay near the northern terminus of your route, a good distance further still.

At 2.5 miles, the trail makes a moderate but short climb uphill. Here, at a rocky outcropping, you will find an excellent view south to the Hudson River, and once again, Manhattan. At 2.6 miles, you will arrive at Bald Mountain, an incredible open vista that seems to rise out of the surrounding countryside like a mountaintop island above the forest.

From the summit of Bald Mountain, the trail descends once more for a short distance, then tackles an uphill on the ridgeline again at 2.8 miles. Climb for roughly a quarter mile, before the way becomes level again, as you approach the northern terminus of the ridgeline. From here, the trail will descend before hooking back around to complete its loop. At 3.1 miles, you will reach a vista with a straight-on view south toward Manhattan—one of the best of the hike. At 3.25 miles, begin your descent at the far end of the ridge. Soon, the trail doubles back, heading south, and levels.

At 3.4 miles, the trail will make its way downhill next to a streambed, then level again at 3.5 miles. Following the underside of the ridge, the trail continues relatively uneventfully for the next mile. At 4.7 miles, you will intersect with a yellow-blazed trail. Continue straight, now on yellow.

At the 5 mile mark, you will arrive at a blue-blazed trail, to your right. This short bypass trail will bring you back to Dozer Junction. Follow this trail for a short distance before it cuts sharply to the right—watch carefully to be sure you do not miss this turn and lose track of the blazes. Soon the trail will make its way up a rocky gully. The gully will narrow as you approach Dozer Junction, until the familiar sight of the abandoned bulldozer is once again before you.

At Dozer Junction, turn left onto the white-blazed Fishkill Ridge Trail. You will now re-cross Lambs Hill, following your original route. From here, simply retrace your steps from the first 2 miles of this hike to return to the parking area.

# II.

# HUDSON
# HIGHLANDS
# WEST

# Rattlesnake Hill Loop

**TOTAL DISTANCE**: 6.7 miles

**TYPE**: Loop

**HIKING TIME**: 4–5 Hours

**TOTAL ELEVATION GAIN**: 1,100 feet

**MAXIMUM ELEVATION**: 1,240 feet

**DIFFICULTY**: Moderate

While this loop through the eastern section of the Black Rock Forest may not be able to compete with neighboring Storm King Mountain for stunning views, the quiet wood roads and meandering footpaths of this hilly preserve offer an enchanting sense of solitude. 1,100 feet of elevation gain is spread out over several short climbs, meaning this hike won't beat you up too bad, but can still be counted on to provide a solid workout. With excellent views from Rattlesnake Hill and several scenic bodies of water along the way, you won't be starved for scenery—and you'll likely get to enjoy them on your own. This section of the Black Rock Forest is accessed from a large parking area, off of which a number of trails begin. Nonetheless, the crowds rarely venture too far into the preserve, and you may go several miles without seeing another hiker on a quiet day.

From this parking area, the road continues up the mountain to the facilities of the Black Rock Forest Consortium's Science Center. The Black Rock Forest Consortium is a not-for-profit organization that manages the park, with the goal of advancing scientific understanding of the natural world.

## GETTING THERE

From the city of Newburgh, drive south on US-9W S for just over 8 miles. As the road begins to climb into the Hudson Highlands, about 3 miles past the town of Cornwall, prepare to turn right onto Reservoir Road. Follow this road a short distance, until you reach a T-intersection. Turn right, and the parking area is a short distance up the road.

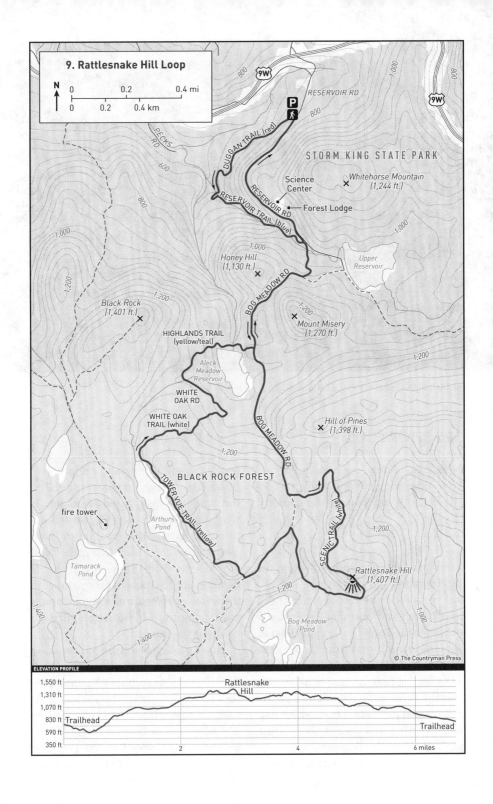

## 9. Rattlesnake Hill Loop

N

| 0 | 0.2 | 0.4 mi |
| 0 | 0.2 | 0.4 km |

9W

RESERVOIR RD

9W

PECKS RD

DUGGAN TRAIL (red)

RESERVOIR RD

RESERVOIR TRAIL (blue)

Science Center

Forest Lodge

STORM KING STATE PARK

Whitehorse Mountain (1,244 ft.)

Upper Reservoir

Honey Hill (1,130 ft.)

BOG MEADOW RD

Black Rock (1,401 ft.)

Mount Misery (1,270 ft.)

HIGHLANDS TRAIL (yellow/teal)

Aleck Meadow Reservoir

WHITE OAK RD

WHITE OAK TRAIL (white)

Hill of Pines (1,398 ft.)

BOG MEADOW RD

BLACK ROCK FOREST

fire tower

TOWER VUE TRAIL (yellow)

Arthurs Pond

Tamarack Pond

SCENIC TRAIL (white)

Rattlesnake Hill (1,407 ft.)

Bog Meadow Pond

© The Countryman Press

**ELEVATION PROFILE**

| 1,550 ft | | | Rattlesnake |
| 1,310 ft | | | Hill |
| 1,070 ft | | | |
| 830 ft | Trailhead | | Trailhead |
| 590 ft | | | |
| 350 ft | | 2 | 4 | 6 miles |

THE TRAIL ALONG THE ALECK MEADOW RESERVOIR

## GPS SHORTCUT

Type "Black Rock Forest Main Parking Area" into Google Maps and your GPS will navigate you to the parking area.

## THE TRAIL

Several trails branch off right from the parking area. Just above the lot, you will see a road that continues to head uphill from the entrance, eventually leading to the Forest Lodge and Science Center. Heading east from there is the yellow-blazed Stillman Trail and Highlands Trail. From the far end of the lot, past the information kiosk, is a newly constructed paved foot trail, which parallels the road, and the red-blazed Duggan Trail. Take the Duggan Trail.

The Duggan Trail begins to head downhill, staying relatively straight for most of the next half mile. At 0.45 mile, you will descend to an intersection with a gravel carriage road. The red trail ends here, but ahead of you is the blue-blazed Reservoir Trail. Take this trail, continuing straight to cross over the stream. Just after, the trail curves away from the creek and begins heading uphill. You will hike parallel to the water as you gain elevation. Soon, a small waterfall will be visible through the trees to your left.

At 0.85 mile, as you are still working your way uphill, you will see the Black Rock Forest Consortium's Science Center across the ravine, to your left. At 0.9 mile the trail will level off, and you will arrive at an intersection with the white-blazed Honey Hill Trail to your right, and an access trail to left heading toward the Science Center, across Mailey's Mill Bridge on your left. The blue trail you have been following continues straight, heading toward the creek now.

Upon reaching the creek, the trail will bend right. Just after a mile, you will spot blazes for a yellow trail cutting across the creek to the road on the other side. Another yellow trail continues straight. Stay straight, hiking uphill past a boulder marked with a yellow blaze.

At 1.2 miles you will reach an intersection with a woods road. Turn right and follow the woods road for some distance. At 1.6 miles, you will see a trail to your right marked with yellow and teal blazes—the Highlands Trail—and a gate across an access road to your right. Shortly after you will cross a small stream, and in another quarter mile, the woods road will split. Turn left, taking the path that heads uphill. The woods begin to make a relatively steady ascent.

At 2.2 miles, you will reach another split in the woods road. Continuing straight would bring you to an intersection you will arrive at later on in the hike, cutting out your ascent of Rattlesnake Hill. While this would save you over a mile of hiking, Rattlesnake Hill offers the best views of this hike, and the climb to the top is moderate. Turning left onto this woods road, continue until you see a white-blazed trail to your right at 2.4 miles. Take this footpath, which now begins to climb up toward the crest of Rattlesnake Hill. The climb is short, and the trail will begin to level around 2.5 miles, before dipping briefly and then climbing briefly again.

Soon you will begin to catch partially obscured views to the southwest from rocky outcroppings alongside the trail, though the best will be yet to come. A short distance beyond, at 2.8 miles, you will arrive at a large, open, rocky area with the best views so far. Continuing on, the bald summit of Rattlesnake Hill, at 2.9 miles, offers one of the best vistas of the hike. As you are now close to the southern border of the Black Rock Forest, from here you'll be looking out to the sprawling hills of Harriman State Park, with Bog Meadow Pond visible just below you.

From this spot, the trail makes a steady downhill, before looping back around the base of the hill, heading north. Pass a stream at 3.2 miles, and soon after you will intersect with a woods road—the same that branched off from the intersection before you ascended Rattlesnake Hill. Follow the woods road left. At 3.75 miles, look for a rock cairn to the right of the road, marking the start of a yellow trail which makes its way sharply uphill.

Take this yellow-blazed path up a winding, mossy trail, until you reach the crest of the ridge. At 4 miles, you will see Arthur's Pond through the trees below the ridge. While this viewpoint is fairly overgrown, you should also be able to spot the abandoned fire tower across the pond. At 4.4 miles, descend from the ridge to a dam at the tip of Arthur's Pond. Walk into the woods, then stay straight on the white-blazed White Oak Trail, which also heads left toward the other side of the pond.

Just under 5 miles, you will reach another woods road. Turn left, as the path makes a moderate uphill climb. Soon after you will see boulders off to the right of the trail, marking a very short spur trail that climbs up a slope to join another. Turn right to now follow the yellow and teal blazes of the Highlands Trail. You will soon come to another intersection, at 5.2 miles, with a white-blazed trail. Stay right, following the yellow and teal blazes.

Approaching another body of water, the trail turns left to follow the underside of a second dam. This is the Aleck Meadow Reservoir. After crossing to the other side of the dam, follow the road as it loops up the other side of the reservoir. Look for the yellow blazes of a foot trail entering the woods, while the woods road continues straight, around the side of the reservoir. Turn left onto this woods road, intersecting with the Oak Road woods road very soon, at 5.5 miles. You have now rejoined your route from earlier in the hike. Turn left onto the woods road, following it until you reach an intersection with the yellow-blazed trail to your left. Turn left and follow this yellow trail, retracing your steps from earlier in the hike.

Soon you will reach the intersection by the creek near the Science Center. Here, you can take the blue trail downhill to retrace your original route back to your car, or, to differentiate the final leg of your hike, cross the stream and return to the parking area along the road, which offers new views and a gentler grade.

If you wish to return via the road, look for the yellow blazes marking the stream crossing. The crossing can be difficult if there has been heavy run-off or a lot of rain recently; exercise extra caution crossing the water here in spring. On the other side of the creek, take the broad road to the left. The road will soon pass the Science Center and Mailey's Mill Bridge to your left, winding around the slope of a mountain before reaching an expansive viewpoint of the ravine below you and the northwestern expanse of Black Rock Forest. While a gravel road may not be the most idyllic setting, the view here is surprisingly stunning.

Continue following the road as it meanders downhill, returning to the parking area on the slope above the lot, at 6.7 miles. Descend to the lot and your car.

# 10

# Black Rock Mountain

| | |
|---|---|
| **TOTAL DISTANCE**: 3.8 miles | |
| **TYPE**: Out and Back | |
| **HIKING TIME**: 2–3 hours | |
| **TOTAL ELEVATION GAIN**: 1,050 feet | |
| **MAXIMUM ELEVATION**: 1,260 feet | |
| **DIFFICULTY**: Strenuous | |

The many woods roads of the Black Rock Forest create a paradox for hikers: these dirt and gravel roads are not the most exciting trails to hike on, but they make it easy to get where you're going, with little risk of getting lost in the woods due to missing a trail marker. The approach to the park's namesake summit, Black Rock Mountain, follows such a woods road for almost the entirety of the hike, meaning there's little chance for confusion or ambiguity here. This road nonetheless makes for a strenuous hike, making a steady, unrelenting uphill climb from the parking area for about a mile, before relaxing considerably just below the summit of the mountain. So while this hike is never very challenging on a technical level, you can certainly expect to sweat. The vista from the top is worth it, though, looking north up the Hudson River, and offering a unique perspective of the Moodna Viaduct at Schunemunk Mountain, to the west.

## GETTING THERE

From the city of Newburgh, drive south on US-9W S for about 8 miles. Just as the road begins to climb into the Hudson Highlands, a little less than 2 miles past the town of Cornwall, prepare to turn right onto Pecks Road. This small road is gated off, but there is a small parking area for hikers before the gate.

## GPS SHORTCUT

Type "Pecks Rd, Cornwall, NY" into Google Maps and your GPS will navigate you to the appropriate parking area.

## THE TRAIL

From the parking area, walk up the gravel road around the gate. Look for a

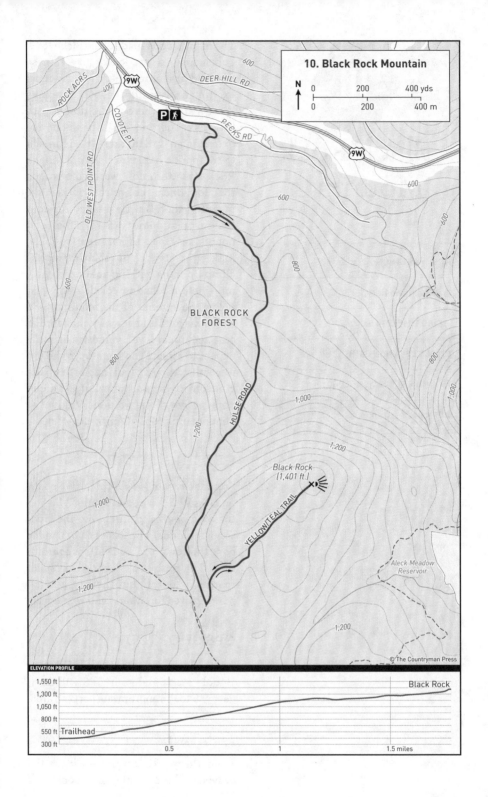

**10. Black Rock Mountain**

N

| 0 | 200 | 400 yds |
|---|-----|---------|
| 0 | 200 | 400 m |

ROCK ACRS

DEER HILL RD

9W

COYOTE PT

PECKS RD

9W

OLD WEST POINT RD

600

600

600

600

600

600

800

800

800

1,000

1,000

1,000

1,000

1,200

1,200

1,200

1,200

1,200

**BLACK ROCK FOREST**

HULSE ROAD

YELLOW/TEAL TRAIL

Black Rock
(1,401 ft.)

Aleck Meadow Reservoir

© The Countryman Press

**ELEVATION PROFILE**

| | | | | |
|---|---|---|---|---|
| 1,550 ft | | | | Black Rock |
| 1,300 ft | | | | |
| 1,050 ft | | | | |
| 800 ft | | | | |
| 550 ft Trailhead | | | | |
| 300 ft | | | | |
| | 0.5 | 1 | 1.5 miles | |

white blaze painted on a rock to indicate the start of the trail. The trail follows an access road into the woods for several hundred feet, passing a triangular information kiosk. Just past the kiosk, turn right onto the woods road heading uphill.

The path will follow this road for the next mile and a half, snaking through the woods as it makes a steady ascent. The grade will not become any easier until you are a mile into the hike, so brace for a strenuous, uphill slog. While this portion of the hike may be fairly exhausting, the broad, obvious woods road presents no technical challenges— all you need here is endurance, and most likely, frequent rest stops.

Just after the 1-mile mark, the grade will finally begin to level out, and at 1.3 miles the trail briefly dips downhill. At 1.5 miles the woods road continues straight, and a footpath makes a hard left turn, cutting back into the forest toward the Black Rock summit. Take this trail, marked by yellow and teal blazes.

There's good news from here: very little elevation gain separates you and the rounded, rocky summit of Black Rock Mountain. The trail here is surprisingly level, winding through the woods for another quarter mile. Soon you will see the dome of the mountain rising through the forest before you. The trail makes one final, short ascent: a moderate rock scramble before the summit of Black Rock opens up before you.

Here, views reach from the north to the west. The Catskills can be glimpsed in the distance, beyond the river, while to the west you will see Schunemunk Mountain and the Moodna Viaduct connected to it.

A loop hike can be attempted by following the yellow / teal blazes down the other side of Black Rock Mountain, but this section of trail is not commonly hiked, and can be extremely difficult to follow in places. It is recommended to simply retrace your original route back to your car.

THE VIEW FROM BLACK ROCK, LOOKING NORTH UP THE HUDSON

# Black Rock Forest Northern Loop

| | |
|---|---|
| **TOTAL DISTANCE**: 6 miles | |

**TYPE**: Loop

**HIKING TIME**: 4–5 hours

**TOTAL ELEVATION GAIN**: 625 feet

**MAXIMUM ELEVATION**: 1,430 feet

**DIFFICULTY**: Moderate

It's hard to say a hike or even a park system is "underrated," but hiking the quiet trails of the Black Rock Forest, there's certainly a sense that this wonderful hike is underappreciated compared to others in the area. Not that there's anything wrong with the solitude—it's perhaps for the best that this loop hike remains a relaxed backwoods ramble, where you might spot only a few other hikers even on a nice day. But don't mistake quiet for boring: this loop hike has a bit of everything. Quirky clocks mounted by the parking area, cliffside climbs, cliff-top boulder vistas, valley views, ponds, fire towers, pine forests, waterside pavilions, historic houses, notable trees, and everyone's favorite, a labyrinth of yellow trails. (You'll see what I mean with that last one). While this loop might be lacking a true mountain summit, it really does have just about everything else—it's hard to imagine a better encapsulation of backwoods trails in one setting. There's very little elevation change over the course of the hike, making it an excellent choice for hikers of all skill levels, but at 6 miles, more advanced hikers won't feel cheated either. Whatever you're looking for, you'll enjoy a workout and a fascinating array of scenery here too.

## GETTING THERE

From the city of Newburgh, drive south on NY-9W S for about 3.5 miles. Take the Angola Road exit, just past the town of Cornwall, then turn left onto Angola Road. Drive for 1.2 miles, then turn left onto Mine Hill Road. Drive for a mile on Mine Hill Road, then the parking area will be up the hill, just after the sharp bend, on your right. The parking area is small, with room for only a few vehicles.

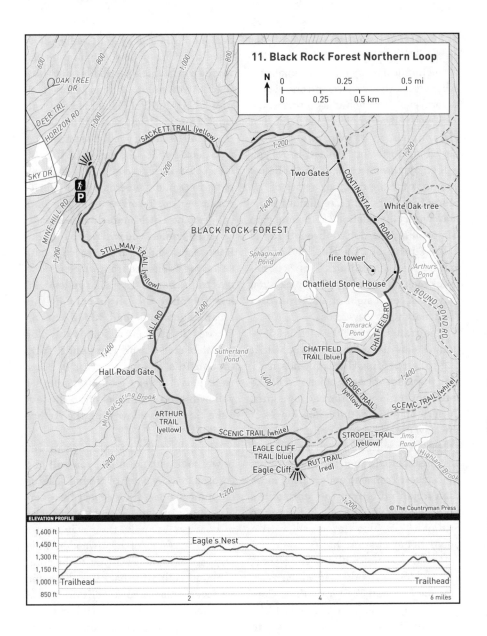

## 11. Black Rock Forest Northern Loop

N

| 0 | 0.25 | 0.5 mi |
| 0 | 0.25 | 0.5 km |

**ELEVATION PROFILE**

Eagle's Nest

Trailhead                                        Trailhead

1,600 ft
1,450 ft
1,300 ft
1,150 ft
1,000 ft
850 ft

2                    4                    6 miles

## GPS SHORTCUT

Type "Black Rock Forest—Northern Loop Trailhead" into Google Maps and your GPS will navigate you to the appropriate parking area.

## THE TRAIL

From the parking area, cross the road and turn to your right, walking a short distance uphill to the trailhead. The trail's entry into the woods is marked by a sign with the tri-blaze trail terminus indicator. Begin following the yellow blazes of the Mine Hill Trail, the first of many yellow-blazed paths you will encounter on this hike. The trail tackles a moderate incline up a rocky incline, though this ascent is relatively short, and one of only several significant climbs on this whole loop. You will very quickly reach the first vista, which, on its own, offers a wonderful payoff for little effort. Here, you will enjoy views west and north. Below you, look for the open air estate of the Storm King Art Center. A number of the massive art installations at the museum can be glimpsed, dotted throughout the fields. Further out, the Moodna Viaduct can be seen stretching off of Schunemunk Mountain, and if you are lucky, you may even catch sight of a Metro-North train making its way across.

The trail switchbacks at this viewpoint. Follow the yellow blazes uphill. At 0.25 mile, the Mine Hill Trail ends at a T with the yellow-blazed Sackett Trail. The intersection is well-marked by signs. Turn right to follow the yellow blazes of this new trail. This path continues more or less level, with slight ups and downs, as it meanders through the woods. Soon, the Sackett Trail also ends, a little more than a half mile from the start of the hike, and you will make a left onto the Stillman Trail, also blazed yellow. (Are you noticing a pattern here?)

At 0.8 mile, you will descend a short hill, and join a woods road which overlaps the Stillman Trail for a time. Continue straight, still following yellow. The path will now be broad and very easy to follow, with tire grooves on either side of the road. (A number of woods roads run throughout the park, and given that they can be hiked much more quickly than many of the foot trails, can also serve as "shortcuts" between sections of the park, or to shorten a loop hike).

At 1 mile, yet another yellow trail branches left. (Seemingly, whoever designed this trail system really, really liked the color yellow.) Remain on the woods road, which is still blazed yellow itself. At 1.2 miles, another yellow trail (the "Short Cut Trail") intersects to your right. This trail leads back up to the Stillman Trail (which, if you'll remember, was also blazed yellow) toward a further-off viewpoint. If this system of "every trail is blazed yellow" seems unnecessarily confusing, don't worry—the color palate will become a little more diverse shortly.

At 1.35 miles, you will reach the Hall Road Gate, which isn't so much a gate as a large open area from which several new trails branch. There is a yellow trail heading off to the left (of course); this an another woods road, which you can ignore. Go straight to follow the blue / teal blazes of the Highlands Trail, though this change in color is but a "red" herring. Very soon after, another yellow-blazed trail forks off to the left. Take this new yellow trail, the Arthur Trail.

Here, the trail passes through an area of wetlands. At 1.6 miles, you will hop across a marshy patch of ground on large stepping stones, then repeat the exercise over a stream. Soon after, a series of boardwalks make their way across the swamp. Many of these wooden walkways are extremely warped, to the point of almost collapsing back into the water. At several places, makeshift bridges of new boards have been placed on top of the sinking boards, to create a walkway over the walkway.

At the next intersection, shortly after leaving the wetlands, make a left onto the white-blazed Scenic Trail. In about a quarter mile, you will pass a blue-blazed trail intersecting to the left. Continue straight, following the white blazes, for another quarter mile. Soon, the trail will make a slight ascent once

THE TRAILS OF THE BLACK ROCK FOREST CROSS A DIVERSE RANGE OF LANDSCAPES AND ECOSYSTEMS

more, though this section is not particularly strenuous. At 2.3 miles, you will arrive at a second blue trail, this time on your right. This, the Eagle Cliff Trail, makes a detour to the best viewpoint of the hike. Follow the blue blazes for a short distance, before reaching a series of massive rock boulders at the edge of a cliff. Here, you may scramble up the rocks to a stunning vista. Just the rock formations of Eagle Cliff would be fun on their own, but standing atop them, you'll see the layers of hills stretching south, from the forestlands of West Point Academy, to Harriman State Park beyond. To your left, Jim's Pond stretches long and narrow at the underside of the cliff. And straight on before you, Wilkins Pond and Round Pond glimmer beneath the forest canopy. Eagle Cliff makes for an excellent spot to catch the fall foliage, as the layers of hills create dramatic waves of color, and as these trails are not particularly busy, there's a good chance you'll have this vista all to yourself, especially on weekdays.

From Eagle Cliff, take the red trail, which runs parallel to the cliff itself. Of course, by now it's been some time since you've seen a yellow-blazed trail, and the Black Rock Forest would like to fix that oversight. Take a left onto the yellow-blazed Stropel Trail (which, if taken to the right, would bring you down to Jim's Pond at the underside of the cliff). This yellow trail will return you to the white-blazed Scenic Trail shortly after. Turn right. Soon after, just under the 3 mile mark, you will spot the Ledge Trail to your left, working its way uphill. It is clearly marked with a sign, and you might be able to guess what color the blazes are. Follow the yellow for about 0.2 mile, until the Ledge Trail ends at an intersection with the blue-blazed Chat-field Trail. Turn right onto blue, and follow this path a short distance until you come out onto a woods road.

Here, at 3.25 miles, the blue trail ends, and the woods road heads to your left and right. Directly in front of you, visible through the trees, is Tamarack Pond. In spots, you might catch a glimpse of a fire tower on a hill looming over the pond; sadly, this tower is closed off to the public. Head to the right, as the woods road makes it way around the southern end of the pond before veering northward. At 3.5 miles, you will see a rocky area to your left looking out over the pond. Continue, and soon the road enters a pleasantly shady conifer grove, where many of the trees were recently planted.

A short distance ahead, you will spot a pavilion through the trees. This is the Moretti Outpost—not a lean-to, but a large, open-sided pavilion that makes for a charming rest spot, with the pond visible through the trees from the seats of the outpost. The pine forest here is particularly idyllic, as if transplanted from some pine-scented valley in the west. Just past the Outpost, the woods road curves to the right, and you will spot another curious backwoods structure. This is the Chatfield Stone House, a large stone farmhouse built in 1834, and still in good condition today. There is a campground next to the house, and several other outbuildings nearby. Today, the Stone House serves as a site for visiting classes.

Continue on the woods road. Soon, you will cross the white-blazed White Oak Trail, which first intersects on your right, then shortly after, on your left. Keep on the woods road, and soon you will see the white oak tree for which the trail is named, framed by an intersection of woods roads. Continue straight.

THE CHATFIELD STONE HOUSE, BUILT IN 1834

At 4.5 miles, you will reach the Two Gates intersection, where a number of trails diverge. Continue straight through the intersection, past one yellow trail, before coming to a second yellow trail. Take this left onto the Sackett Trail—one of the original trails from the beginning of your hike, meaning you're on the last leg.

At the 5 mile mark, a fork will intersect with the Sackett Trail from behind you. Here, a woods road heads north, toward the northeastern end of the park. Continue straight ahead on the yellow trail, and a short distance after, you will spot blue blazes heading to your left. Stay on yellow, to your right. Soon you will arrive at a huge stone cairn on a rocky outcropping. Beyond the cairn, cross a stream, and at 5.25 miles, navigate a second stream crossing.

At 5.5 miles, a large wooden sign indicates another trail split. Here, the trail to your right heads toward Kenridge Farm and the Museum of the Hudson Highlands. Remain on the yellow trail, which heads left, to the west. Around 5.75 miles, you will reach the ridgeline where you first ascended, with familiar views out to the northwest and the Storm King Art Center. Shortly after, the yellow-blazed Mine Hill Trail intersects to your right. Follow this hike downhill, retracing your steps to the parking area and your car.

# Storm King Mountain from Mountain Road

**TOTAL DISTANCE**: 4 miles

**TYPE**: Loop

**HIKING TIME**: 2–3 hours

**TOTAL ELEVATION GAIN**: 1,050 feet

**MAXIMUM ELEVATION**: 1,295 feet

**DIFFICULTY**: Moderate

With a name as dramatic as "Storm King," this mountain dominating the west side of the Hudson River has a lot to live up to—fortunately, the views from the summit really will blow you away, regardless of the weather. Storm King directly faces Breakneck Ridge (guides #4 and #5) and the picturesque Fishkill Ridge on the east bank of the Hudson, but the best views from the top are actually to the north. From the exposed rocky peak, one can enjoy a straight-shot view directly up the Hudson River, providing a unique perspective of several river towns, the Newburgh-Beacon bridge, and landmarks as far north as the Catskills. It is a view so dramatic, it helped to inspire an entire school of painting. The artists of the Hudson River School took inspiration from Storm King Mountain, transforming the landscapes of the Hudson Valley into a romantic ideal, full of drama and intrigue.

While Storm King now boasts openly of its dramatic nature, history almost failed to give the mountain its proper due. Early Dutch colonists decided an appropriate name for this imposing landmark was "Boterberg," thinking that the mountain resembled a lump of butter. The name didn't stick, but was later applied to one of the summits flanking Storm King. Fortunately, one of the Hudson Valley's most impressive views thus earned a name befitting its rugged drama.

## GETTING THERE

From the city of Newburgh, drive south on NY-9W S for about 8 miles. As the road begins to climb into the Hudson Highlands, look for Mountain Rd. on your left. Turn left onto Mountain Rd., then continue for about 0.75 mile before reaching the parking area, on the right.

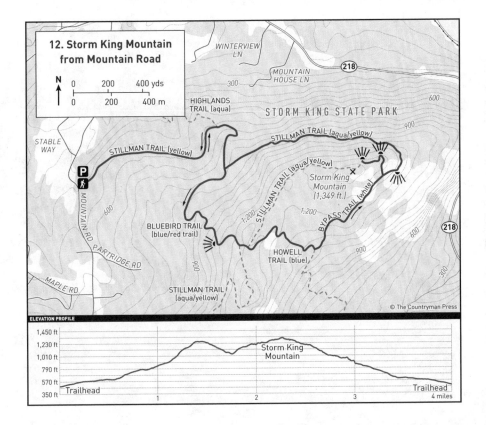

**12. Storm King Mountain from Mountain Road**

N

| 0 | 200 | 400 yds |
| 0 | 200 | 400 m |

WINTERVIEW LN

MOUNTAIN HOUSE LN

218

HIGHLANDS TRAIL (aqua)

STORM KING STATE PARK

STILLMAN TRAIL (aqua/yellow)

STILLMAN TRAIL (yellow)

STABLE WAY

STILLMAN TRAIL (aqua/yellow)

Storm King Mountain (1,349 ft.)

BYPASS TRAIL (white)

BLUEBIRD TRAIL (blue/red trail)

HOWELL TRAIL (blue)

MOUNTAIN RD

PARTRIDGE RD

MAPLE RD

STILLMAN TRAIL (aqua/yellow)

218

© The Countryman Press

**ELEVATION PROFILE**

| | |
|---|---|
| 1,450 ft | |
| 1,230 ft | |
| 1,010 ft | Storm King Mountain |
| 790 ft | |
| 570 ft | |
| 350 ft | Trailhead ... Trailhead |

1    2    3    4 miles

The parking area is small, with room for about a half dozen cars.

## GPS SHORTCUT

Type "Storm King Mountain Trailhead" into Google Maps and your GPS will navigate you to the appropriate parking area.

## THE TRAIL

From the parking area on Mountain Road, cross through the gate to the trail. The Stillman Trail, marked by yellow blazes, is a broad and easily followed path, making a gentle ascent for the first half mile. The path traces the route of an old woods road for the first section of the hike. Just under 0.5 mile into the hike,

you will cross the first of several stone bridges, just one of several hints that a stately, sprawling mountain property once covered these grounds.

At 0.6 mile, the trail turns right. To the left is a narrower aqua and yellow-blazed footpath which you will later return on. For now, continue uphill on the broad woods road. At about the 1-mile mark, the trail levels briefly. You will spot a large clearing to your right, and just ahead through the woods, the stone foundation of an old house after a fork. Going to the right will keep you on the main route. If you wish to explore the ruins, go to the left. From the stone steps at the far end of the ruins, a small side trail cuts through the woods back to the main trail. Otherwise, retrace your steps back to where the trail split.

THE VIEW FROM STORM KING, LOOKING NORTH UP THE HUDSON RIVER

Turn right onto the blue-red trail, heading uphill. You will now follow the blue-red blazes, switchbacking steeply up the mountain, tackling the bulk of the elevation change in this short stretch. In places, stone stairs are set into the ground to make the ascent somewhat easier. Soon, you will have partial views through the trees (particularly when the leaves are down) to the west, with the Schunemunk Ridge and the Moodna Viaduct visible in the distance. Around the 1.4 mile mark, the trail will begin to level and you will reach an open viewpoint with clear views of the countryside.

After the viewpoint, the trail switchbacks once more to the left, making a less severe ascent. In a tenth of a mile, you will reach an intersection marked by a large stone cairn. Here, the aqua blazes of the Highlands Trail combine with yellow blazes, while the blue-red trail ends. Continue on this trail for a short distance, until you reach a second intersection where a dark blue trail heads south. Here, an optional route can be taken by making a left onto the aqua-yellow trail. This trail will bring you to the summit of Storm King in about 0.75 mile. A longer route, circling the southern edge of the summit, offers distinct views toward Cold Spring and Pitching Point (Hike #13). This guide follows the longer route, marked by blue blazes. In a short distance, you will crest the western ridge of the mountain before descending to its southern slope. Just under the 2 mile mark, after a short downhill, you will reach an intersection with a white-blazed trail. Here, the blue trail continues south toward the southern section of the Storm King State Park. Turn left and follow the white blazes of the Bypass Trail.

Soon you will begin to hit vistas looking south over the Hudson River and the Highlands, as well as the clove between the two sections of the Storm King State Park. Soon after, you will tackle a short rock scramble, bringing you uphill once again. Views continue to open up through the trees to your right, until you once more reach an intersection with the aqua-yellow trail. (This is the end point of the shorter trail that you might optionally take to the Storm King summit, which you diverged from earlier). While you will be returning to your car by taking the right fork at this intersection, for now, to reach the main viewpoints of Storm King Mountain, take a left. Ascend uphill following the aqua-yellow blazes. You will only have to climb here for a short distance before you reach the high point of the hike, and the most dramatic viewpoint of the western Hudson Highlands.

At 2.4 miles, you will arrive at the Storm King Mountain summit. Enjoy incredible views looking north up the Hudson River and east toward Breakneck Ridge. Several rock outcroppings around the summit offer slightly different versions of this north-to-east view, making this one of the best vistas in the Hudson Valley. There is plenty of space here at the summit to enjoy a snack and a break, even on busy days.

When you are ready to continue, retrace your steps back to the last trail intersection, just downhill from Storm King Summit. Turn left to continue on the aqua-blue blazes of the Stillman Trail, which you will now follow all the way back to your car. Immediately after this intersection is another vista on the right side of the trail, looking south.

Before meeting up with your original route, however, you will hike for nearly a mile along the steep northeastern slope of Storm King, quickly descending a few hundred feet beneath the summit. Given its sheer nature and a lack of sunlight striking this region of the mountain, this section of trail has a distinct feel from the rest of the hike, and can be quite beautiful. It is also very narrow and can be precarious in places—be extra cautious with your footing and look for handholds at sections with particularly steep drop-offs. Due to the lack of sunlight this trail receives in winter, on top of water runoff from the mountain and the steady passage of hikers compacting the snow, it is not recommended to attempt this section of trail in winter without good traction devices. Entire portions of the trail may be entirely iced over even early in the season, and under certain conditions, may range from unsafe to nearly unpassable, even with crampons. If attempting this hike in the winter months, turn back at the first sign that this section of trail is iced over and simply retrace your original route back from the summit of Storm King. However, under normal conditions, this narrow trail is well-marked and easy to follow.

After the initial descent, the trail eases downhill gradually over the next mile. Continue following the aqua-yellow blazes until you rejoin the main woods road that you began your hike on. From here, follow the woods road down to the parking area and your car.

# Pitching Point and North Point

**TOTAL DISTANCE**: 3.1 miles

**TYPE**: Loop

**HIKING TIME**: 2.5 hours

**TOTAL ELEVATION GAIN**: 1,130 feet

**MAXIMUM ELEVATION**: 1,050 feet

**DIFFICULTY**: Difficult

On a beautiful morning from spring to autumn, when the parking areas of some of the Hudson Highlands' most popular destinations will be packed with cars, you can expect to encounter only a handful of other hikers on the trails of the Pitching Point loop. Why this route remains an obscure, hidden gem is a mystery—it's a nearly perfect tour of the Hudson Highlands, with top-notch vistas and varied terrain, all over a mere 3.1 miles. This hike circles the southern portion of Storm King State Park, and boasts Hudson River views every bit as good as those found on its more popular neighbors. Indeed, from the many vistas you'll find along the way here, the mighty Storm King itself enters the picture, perfectly framed against the backdrop of the Hudson River and the distant Catskills. Treasure the relative quiet of this hike while you can—it's too good to stay obscure for long.

The hike itself is typical of the Hudson Highlands, with sections of steep ascent that'll leave even experienced hikers winded, followed by a more gentle, gradual descent. Still, while strenuous, the trail here is not particularly technically challenging, making it accessible to hikers of all skill levels.

## GETTING THERE

From the city of Newburgh, drive south on NY-9W S for 3 miles, then exit to the right toward Cornwall. Continue on Academy Ave. for 0.7 mile, until it becomes Hudson St. Continue through the town of Cornwall. In another 0.7 mile, Hudson St. turns slightly right and becomes NY-218 S / Bayview Ave. Drive for about 2 miles. Soon, you will see the parking area to the left of the road, across the street from several large boulders and a waterfall.

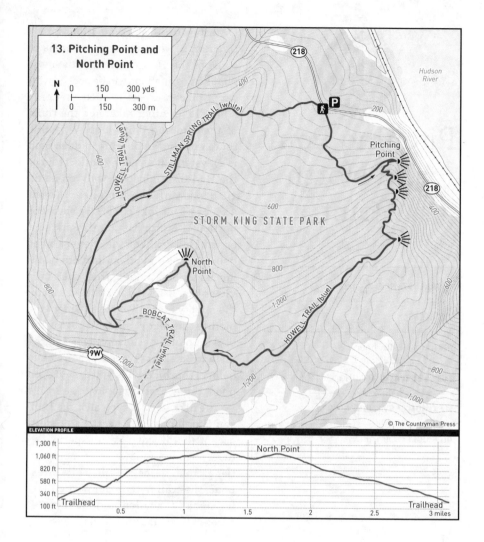

13. Pitching Point and North Point

N
0    150    300 yds
0    150    300 m

STILLMAN SPRING TRAIL (white)

HOWELL TRAIL (blue)

218

Hudson
River

P

Pitching
Point

218

STORM KING STATE PARK

600

800

1,000

North
Point

BOBCAT TRAIL (white)

HOWELL TRAIL (blue)

9W

1,000

1,200

800

1,000

© The Countryman Press

ELEVATION PROFILE

1,300 ft
1,060 ft
820 ft
580 ft
340 ft
100 ft

North Point

Trailhead

Trailhead

0.5        1        1.5        2        2.5    3 miles

## GPS SHORTCUT

The closest searchable, tagged area on Google Maps is "Target Point, West Point, NY," which is about 0.8 mile south of the trailhead along NY-218 S.

## THE TRAIL

From the parking area, cross the street, watching carefully for cars—the road bends and it is sometimes difficult to see distant traffic. Look for the blue blazes marking the start of the trail to the left of the large boulders and the small waterfall running down off of the mountain.

Climb up a series of stones to begin on the trail. The path makes its way uphill, away from the stream, and the ascent is immediately a fairly steady, strenuous climb. Around 0.4 mile, the trail levels briefly, then dips slightly downhill for a short distance. At the half-mile mark, you will make a sharp right uphill, climbing up a series of stone steps.

PITCHING POINT OFFERS EXCEPTIONAL VIEWS ACROSS THE HUDSON TO BREAKNECK RIDGE AND BULL HILL

At 0.6 mile, you will make another sharp right at a rocky overlook, with a second overlook following very soon after—but the best views are yet to come. At 0.7 mile, you will arrive at the first major viewpoint, an open, rocky area with clear views across the river to Breakneck Ridge and Bull Mountain / Mt. Taurus. At the next viewpoint, a tenth of a mile further up, you will be able to see Butter Hill lurking behind Storm King's distinct mass. Finally, at 0.85 mile, you will reach the upper portion of the rocky ridge that gave you your first vista, further down the slope. Each of these viewpoints is excellent, and all would make a great spot for an extended relaxation break or picnic.

At the 1-mile mark, you will begin hiking through an open rocky area with more views. Continue, and at 1.4 miles return to the woods. A short distance beyond will descend briefly, and will likely start to hear the sounds of traffic from nearby NY-9W. The trail begins to head north, roughly parallel to the road.

At 1.85 miles, you will reach the open summit of North Point, which was cleared of most trees in a fire. This rocky hilltop offers more fantastic views up the river, particularly of the dramatic, severe eastern face of Storm

King Mountain. A large boulder sits just off the summit at the high point of your hike.

The trail descends slightly from here, and at 2.2 miles, you will arrive at an intersection with the white-blazed Bobcat Trail. Turn right, staying on the blue trail, and hike parallel to the stream. At 2.6 miles the trail splits, with the blue trail now heading left, deeper into the col between Pitching Point and Storm King. A white trail turns right, descending the slope, back toward Storm King Highway and the parking area from which you set out. Take the white trail.

Hike downhill following the white blazes for another half mile. The trail crosses a stream just before the road, and follows the water out to the road. Carefully cross the road and return to the parking area.

PITCHING POINT AND NORTH POINT OFFER UNIQUE PERSPECTIVES OVER NEIGHBORING STORM KING MOUNTAIN AND THE HUDSON RIVER

# III.

# SHAWANGUNK RIDGE

# 14

# Bear Hill Preserve

**TOTAL DISTANCE**: 1.3 miles

**TYPE**: Out and Back

**HIKING TIME**: 1 hour

**TOTAL ELEVATION GAIN**: 180 feet

**MAXIMUM ELEVATION**: 1,930 feet

**DIFFICULTY**: Easy

Tucked away in the western section of the Shawangunk Ridge, miles from the immensely popular Minnewaska and Mohonk areas, Bear Hill Preserve is one of the ridge's hidden, little-known treasures. The Shawangunk Ridge continues west from here to New Jersey, eventually becoming part of the Kittatinny Mountain area. The ridge rises to a high point of almost 2,000 feet in this area, before losing elevation as it continues west. Bear Hill Preserve, therefore, can be viewed as the western end of the ridge's most dramatic section, even if it is not a true geographical boundary. The hike to the top is short but sweet, with an ascent of less than 200 feet. Nonetheless, the views are fantastic, and as with many hikes in the Shawangunks, the rock formations throughout the hike would be interesting enough to warrant a visit even if there weren't any views to be earned.

## GETTING THERE

From the town of Pine Bush, NY, drive west on NY-52 W for 7.5 miles. Make a sharp right onto Cragsmoor Road, then continue for 1.5 miles. Turn left onto Dellenbaugh Road, then immediately after turn left again to stay on Dellenbaugh Road. After 0.3 mile, the parking area will be on the left.

## GPS SHORTCUT

Type "Bear Hill Preserve Parking" into Google Maps and your GPS will navigate you to the appropriate parking area. Getting directions to just "Bear Hill Preserve" will not navigate you to the correct parking area.

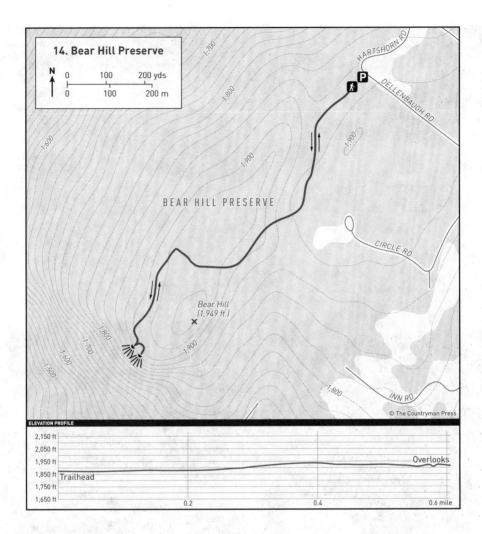

## THE TRAIL

From the parking area—after paying at the kiosk—walk past the kiosk to the trail. Several boulders cross the trail to block off the path from vehicles. The trail continues mostly straight, and is very easy to follow. A few hundred feet down the path you will spot a house through the woods to your left. Soon, at 0.3 mile, you will pass a trail on the left leading to private property, well-marked by signs to discourage you from accidentally following this path.

The trail will begin to make a slight uphill from here, and soon after you will come to a T-intersection where there is a sign warning you against littering (generally, please don't litter whether or not there is a sign to suggest that you not!) After turning left at this intersection, the trail swings uphill, and soon, at 0.55 mile, reaches a rocky area. You will encounter huge open views to your right.

From here, several narrower foot trails thread into the woods to further explore the Bear Hill area. The path

THE VIEW FROM BEAR HILL

heading to your right crosses a crevasse to a large rocky outcropping, with plenty of boulders, ledges, and open vistas to explore. Doubling back, take the center path to reach another section of the cliffs, separated from the first vista area by a crevasse. Thread through the dwarf pitch pines to enjoy more shielded views to the east and south.

Several footpaths will return you to the original main path, at the first open rocky vista. From here, turn right onto the wide gravel path and retrace your steps to return to the parking area.

# 15

# Sam's Point to Verkeerderkill Falls

**TOTAL DISTANCE**: 6.75 miles

**TYPE**: Out and Back

**HIKING TIME**: 4–5 hours

**TOTAL ELEVATION GAIN**: 610 feet

**MAXIMUM ELEVATION**: 2,235 feet

**DIFFICULTY**: Moderate

Sam's Point—the arrow-shaped tip of one of the several distinct plateaus formed by the northwestern Shawangunk Ridge—contains the highest point of the ridge in New York, at 2,289 feet. Lake Maratanza, the highest lake on the ridge, is also located within the Sam's Point area, but the park is best known for the Ellenville Fault Ice Caves, a series of dramatic fissures that maintain cold temperatures even through the heat of summer. With more dramatic conglomerate cliffs like those found elsewhere in the Shawangunks, a visit to Sam's Point offers a tour through almost all of the Ridge's unique environmental highlights.

The Sam's Point area is sometimes referred to as the Dwarf Pine Ridge Preserve, due to prevalence of dwarf pitch pines here. The Sam's Point name was coined, as the story goes, after a man named Sam who jumped off a cliff while being pursued by Indians, surviving against all odds thanks to a conveniently located tree breaking his fall. Nonetheless, as many of the vistas here are found at dramatic cliffs with steep drop-offs, you should exercise extra caution around the edges—you aren't likely to enjoy the same luck as Sam.

## GETTING THERE

From the town of Pine Bush, NY, drive west on NY-52 W for 7.5 miles. Make a sharp right onto Cragsmoor Road, then continue for another 1.5 miles. Turn right onto Sam's Point Road, and drive for 1.3 miles to reach the parking area. The parking area is a large, though very busy on weekends. Sam's Point is managed by the Minnewaska State Park Preserve, and there is a fee ($10 per vehicle, as of 2017). However, the Empire Pass is accepted here.

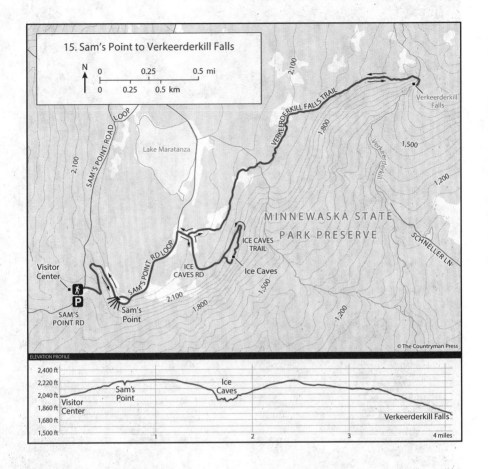

## 15. Sam's Point to Verkeerderkill Falls

Lake Maratanza

VERKEERDERKILL FALLS TRAIL

Verkeerderkill
Falls

MINNEWASKA STATE
PARK PRESERVE

ICE CAVES
TRAIL

ICE
CAVES RD

Ice Caves

SCHNELLER LN

SAM'S POINT RD LOOP

SAM'S POINT ROAD LOOP

Visitor
Center

SAM'S
POINT RD

Sam's
Point

© The Countryman Press

**ELEVATION PROFILE**

Visitor
Center

Sam's
Point

Ice
Caves

Verkeerderkill Falls

## GPS SHORTCUT

Type "Sam's Point Dwarf Pine Ridge" into Google Maps and your GPS will navigate you to the appropriate parking area.

## THE TRAIL

From the parking area, walk around the gate and take the right fork of the Loop Road (a gravel road, closed to private vehicles). Follow the road uphill, following the switchbacks. In about half a mile, you'll start to pass under large, looming cliffs on your left. Soon, views will begin to open up from rock outcrops on the right. Just beyond, you'll see a dirt road veering away to the left, back toward the top of the cliffs. Turn left to follow this road, and soon you will arrive at the top of Sam's Point. From these white conglomerate cliffs, you will enjoy incredible views to the south and east. As this vista arrives only a short distance into the hike, it is very popular, and can become crowded on weekends.

When you are ready to continue, return to the main trail and turn left. The road levels off, and the vegetation changes dramatically: you will now be hiking through a ridgetop dwarf pitch pine forest. Blueberries and huckleberries, having long made this area a popular summer destination for both humans and bears, also grow here.

INSIDE THE CAVES

Continue along the road for another half a mile. You will arrive at an intersection where a gravel road descends to the right. A sign indicates that you are turning onto Ice Caves Road. Turn right, and in a short distance, you'll see another sign marking the start of the Verkeerderkill Falls Trail to the left. You will take this trail later, but for now, stay straight on the Ice Caves Road. The path begins to hook to the east, giving you a glimpse of the northern section of the Shawangunk Ridge.

At the end of the road, you'll arrive at a large open area. This was once a parking area, when the road to the Ice Caves was open to vehicular traffic. Ahead, a sign indicates the start of the Ice Caves Loop Trail. Take this trail, and begin to descend into the Ice Caves. You will follow a winding footpath through the caves, with wooden guardrails erected in places to aid you. You will quickly notice that the difference in temperature implied by the name is quite pronounced.

Follow the white blazes, which cross several wooden bridges and eventually begin to lead along the base of cliffs, on the left.

Soon, the trail turns left and makes its way through a deep rock crevice. Here, the caves are not only cool but also very dark, and you will notice that motion-sensitive lighting has been installed to illuminate the way.

Eventually, the trail bears left once more and heads on a raised boardwalk into a narrow crevice. At this spot, ice and snow can often be found even in summer.

After this crevice, you will climb a wooden ladder to an outcrop, where you'll find the solar panel that provides power to the lights in the caves. After this, the white-blazed trail turns right and returns to the beginning of the loop.

Follow the trail back to the open area where you started your descent into the Ice Caves. From the open area, return to the intersection with the Verkeerderkill Falls Trail, just up the path. Turn right to take this aqua-blazed trail (shared by the Long Path), heading east.

About 0.65 mile from the beginning of the Verkeerderkill Falls Trail, you will cross the outlet stream of Lake Maratanza. About 1.75 miles from the start of the Verkeerderkill Falls Trail, you will arrive at the Verkeerderkill. Cross the stream, using the stepping stones—the crossing is generally not too difficult, except in spring. The open rock slabs found alongside the stream offer a tempting place for a picnic, though there are better spots to break not far ahead.

Continue along the path, and soon you will arrive at a rock ledge overlooking the 180-foot-high Verkeerderkill Falls, the highest waterfall in the Shawangunks. Be very careful here, as the drop down to the base of the falls is very sheer, and losing your footing could easily prove deadly.

When you are ready to return, retrace your steps back to the intersection of the Verkeerderkill Falls Trail and the Ice Caves Road. Turn right into the Ice Caves Road, and in a short distance, at the T-intersection, turn left onto the trail leading back to Sam's Point. From here, retrace your steps from the first leg of the hike back to the parking area.

# 16

# Lake Awosting

| | |
|---|---|
| **TOTAL DISTANCE**: 9.8 miles | |
| **TYPE**: Loop | |
| **HIKING TIME**: 6 hours | |
| **TOTAL ELEVATION GAIN**: 675 feet | |
| **MAXIMUM ELEVATION**: 1,975 feet | |
| **DIFFICULTY**: Moderate | |

There's no denying that 9.8 miles is a long hike, but this loop around the scenic and remote Lake Awosting is well worth the mileage. It's also not nearly as challenging as the distance might imply: for most of this trek, you'll be following easy carriage roads, with only moderate, short sections of elevation gain. The first 3 miles are the easiest and will pass quickly, but once you arrive at the lake itself, you'll find countless spots that would be ideal for a rest stop or snack. The trail around the lake stays close to the water's edge, turning nearly every foot of the trail into a viewpoint. And before veering back into the woods, you'll hike to a large stone beach, which becomes a popular destination on its own in the summer months. But the best is yet to come: from a series of cliffs overlooking the lake's northeastern end, you'll encounter some of the best views in the Shawangunks.

Over a mile in length, Awosting is the largest of the five sky lakes in the Shawangunks, and the second highest in elevation. With its dramatic cliffs and far-reaching views, miles from the crowds that flock to Minnewaska, it may be one of the area's finest destinations.

## GETTING THERE

From the town of New Paltz, NY, drive west on NY-299 W for about 6 miles. You will reach a T-intersection, with the Mountain Brauhaus restaurant to your left. Turn right onto US-44 E. Follow this road as it climbs the ridge, taking care on the extremely sharp switchback. Drive for 4.5 miles, until you reach the Minnewaska State Park Preserve, on your left. Pay the entrance fee at the booth, then continue to park in the Lower Awosting Lot.

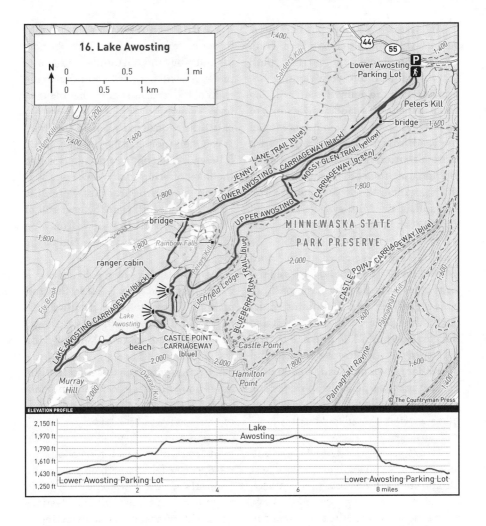

**16. Lake Awosting**

*Elevation profile shows: 2,150 ft / 1,970 ft / 1,790 ft / 1,610 ft / 1,430 ft / 1,250 ft, marked at Lower Awosting Parking Lot, rising to Lake Awosting, and returning to Lower Awosting Parking Lot, over 8 miles.*

## GPS SHORTCUT

Type "Minnewaska State Park Preserve" into Google Maps and your GPS will navigate you to the main Minnewaska Preserve parking entrance. Park in the Lower Awosting Lot.

## THE TRAIL

From the large lower parking area, look for the information sign at the far end of the lot, opposite of the road. The sign here marks the start of the Lower Awosting Carriageway Trail and gives information about the first segment of this hike. The path for the first section of the trail—nearly 3 miles—is a wide, easy carriage road, typical of those found throughout the Shawangunk parklands.

Only a short distance after the trailhead, you will see a trail intersecting from the woods to your left. This is the Mossy Glen Trail, blazed yellow, which you will be taking on your return route. Stay straight on the carriage road. The path makes a very gradual slope uphill, though the grade is not challenging.

At 1.4 miles, you will pass an intersection with the Blueberry Run Trail, which crosses over the carriage path and runs downhill to your right, where it meets with the Jenny Lane Trail. The Jenny Lane trail is a foot trail leading to an alternate parking area further down the road from where you began, with more elevation gain and a more challenging trail. In another half a mile, you will pass under the power lines that run throughout the Minnewaska area, and can be seen at different points on various trails covered in this guide.

At 2.3 miles, you will arrive at an intersection with the Long Path and the light-blue blazed Jenny Lane path, to your right. This is the beginning of the Jenny Lane path, which runs parallel to the carriage path. The gravel carriage path turns left—follow it downhill and over a large wooden bridge. After the bridge the trail will begin uphill for one of the more challenging sections of this hike—a steady, though not terribly long, slog upslope.

At 2.7 miles, the trail levels out, and soon after you will catch your first glimpse of Lake Awosting. While each of the Shawangunk sky lakes have their unique charms, the sheer size and remoteness of Awosting makes this an impressive, serene place. There is plenty to explore around just this northeastern side of the lake, so those wishing for a shorter hike may choose to simply turn around from here, taking the carriage road back to the parking area for an abridged hike of about 5.6 miles. However, exploring the loop around the entire lake is well worth the extra mileage, as the views are exceptional and the trail around the far end of the lake is usually not too busy, giving hikers the chance to relax and appreciate the majesty of nature in solitude.

Continue on the path to your right to begin your loop of the lake. A short distance beyond, just under the 3 mile mark, you will pass a ranger cabin to the right of the trail. Just after that the trail forks—stay to the left, on the path that skirts the edge of the lake. The trail here is rougher, though still wide and easily followed. The path remains close to the lake, offering many views out over Awosting. Note the beautiful white cliffs rising to your left, near the east end of the lake—you will enjoy views from atop these cliffs later, toward the end of the loop.

At 4.1 miles you will reach the far end of the lake, and shortly after, the trail makes a U-bend to begin heading back northeast. Then you will pass a trail on your right heading toward Murray Hill, with an informational sign at the trailhead giving details on this route. At 4.65 miles you will reach a small peninsula on your left with a short side trail leading out to views of the lake.

Continuing on, just before the 5 mile mark, you will pass an intersection with the Spruce Glen footpath on your right. Soon after, you will come to a large stone beach area, the primary destination for many visiting Lake Awosting in the summertime. In the colder months, when this beach is generally deserted, the unique rock structures and lonely dwarf pine trees make this yet another fascinating landmark of the Shawangunk region.

Past the beach, you will enter a thick, shady forest of tall conifer trees. The trail will begin winding slightly uphill through the woods, gaining elevation as you approach the cliffs glimpsed earlier in the loop. The first overlook will arrive around the 5.6 mile mark, though the best views are still to come. At 5.85 miles, you will intersect with

THE STONE BEACH AT LAKE AWOSTING

THE CLIFFS OVER LAKE AWOSTING, LARGEST OF THE SHAWANGUNK SKY LAKES, OFFER SPECTACULAR VIEWS

the blue-blazed Castle Point carriage way, which can be taken to access the main vista at Castle Point (Hike #19). To continue on this loop, turn left. The trail heads uphill once again. At 6 miles, views will open up over the lake, with a long cliff-line beyond offering numerous opportunities for looking out over the lake, and to the Catskills in the north. The views here are among the best in the whole region, combining nearly every sort of attraction found in the Shawangunks all in one location.

From the cliffs, return to the carriage road to continue on. At 6.3 miles, the trail intersects with the Upper Awosting Carriageway, which leads back to Lake Minnewaska's upper parking area. Take this trail to the right. The trail weaves back and forth below various rock overhangs, before passing below the Litchfield Ledges around the 7-mile mark. These ledges are quite dramatic in winter, when water runoff freezes into icicles up and down the various rock layers, creating the impression of something like a dripping, frozen, tiered wedding cake. The trail itself can become very icy in winter, so one should be prepared with traction devices if attempting to do this portion of the hike in colder months.

Just past the ledges, you will pass a trail to the left that leads down to Rainbow Falls, through a ravine. Shortly after, you will come to a small overlook ledge with a view out to the waterfall itself.

Continuing on, at 7.85 miles you will once again intersect with the Blueberry Run Trail, on your left. Take this trail, leaving the wide carriage path for the narrow, rocky footpath. This blue-blazed trail makes a steady but relatively easy descent, and at 8.1 miles, you will reach an open, rocky clearing. Here, you will see a small waterfall just ahead, and the yellow-blazed Mossy Glen Trail on your right. Take this trail into the woods. Soon you will be hiking alongside the Peters Kill stream. The trail frequently crosses rocky areas just along the water's edge, making this an especially scenic trail with a unique feel. However, in winter, the heavy runoff over the rocks to the creek means persistent ice formation, and one should again be especially careful, only attempting this path with appropriate traction devices.

At 8.65 miles, cross a boardwalk, then a wooden bridge at the 9-mile mark. Several more boardwalks and bridge crossings soon follow. At 9.2 miles, you will cross a bridge over the Peters Kill itself, and begin heading into the woods away from the water, back toward the carriage way. At 9.35 miles, the footpath will come close enough to the Lower Awosting Carriageway that you hiked in on that you will be able to see it through the trees. Continue hiking parallel to the Carriageway until 9.75 miles, when the two trails again reunite at an intersection just before the main trailhead. From here, you will be able to see the parking area beyond. Continue on to your car.

# 17

# Lake Minnewaska

**TOTAL DISTANCE**: 2.1 miles

**TYPE**: Loop

**HIKING TIME**: 1 hour

**TOTAL ELEVATION GAIN**: 175 feet

**MAXIMUM ELEVATION**: 1,795 feet

**DIFFICULTY**: Easy

Lake Minnewaska, one of the five sky lakes in the Shawangunks, is the site of much history, and home to some of the most striking examples of the conglomerate cliffs for which the ridge is famous. The pairing of these unique white rocks rising starkly above the calm lake waters, with the Catskill Mountains coming up above the trees in the background, makes for an unforgettable scene. On a flat section of ground above the highest cliffs, an open picnic area marks the spot of the defunct Minnewaska Mountain House. This mountain house, opened in 1879, was built by the Smiley family, who also constructed the nearby Mohonk Mountain House, which remains in operation today. Soon after, the Smileys built the Wildmere hotel nearby. The "Cliff House" at Minnewaska was able to accommodate more than 200 guests, who enjoyed views every bit as fine as those from the famous and popular Catskill mountain houses. These Minnewaska resorts continued operating for much longer than the Catskill mountain houses as well: Minnewaska State Park was not born until the early 1970s, when the Cliff House finally ceased operations; the Wildmere continued operating until 1979.

Today, a great number of trails branch off from Lake Minnewaska, which has two large parking areas, an upper and lower. Longer hikes to Lake Awosting, Castle Point and Hamilton Point, and Gertrude's Nose and Millbrook Mountain, all begin here. But Lake Minnewaska is one of the most gorgeous sites in the Shawangunks on its own, and this short loop of the lake is ideal for an easy, quick hike. Expect the trails to be busy throughout the year. In winter, the old carriage roads are groomed for cross-country skiing, and are closed to

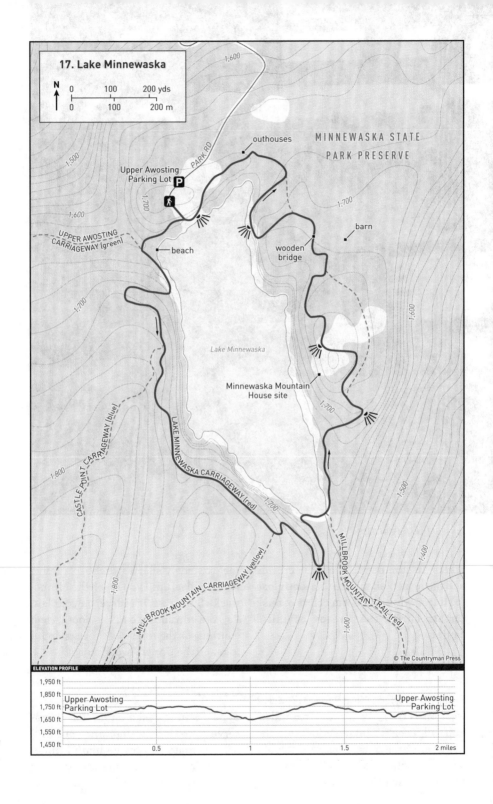

17. Lake Minnewaska

N

| 0 | 100 | 200 yds |
| 0 | 100 | 200 m |

1,600

MINNEWASKA STATE
PARK PRESERVE

outhouses

PARK RD

1,500

Upper Awosting
Parking Lot

1,700

1,600

barn

1,700

UPPER AWOSTING
CARRIAGEWAY (green)

beach

wooden
bridge

1,700

1,600

Lake Minnewaska

Minnewaska Mountain
House site

1,700

CASTLE POINT CARRIAGEWAY (blue)

LAKE MINNEWASKA CARRIAGEWAY (red)

1,800

1,700

1,500

1,800

MILLBROOK MOUNTAIN CARRIAGEWAY (yellow)

MILLBROOK MOUNTAIN TRAIL (red)

1,400

1,600

© The Countryman Press

**ELEVATION PROFILE**

| 1,950 ft |
| 1,850 ft |
| 1,750 ft | Upper Awosting Parking Lot | Upper Awosting Parking Lot |
| 1,650 ft |
| 1,550 ft |
| 1,450 ft |

0.5          1          1.5          2 miles

SUNSET AT LAKE MINNEWASKA

hikers. In summer, to avoid the crowds and the heat, plan to hike this loop close to sunset, when the warm colors of dusk further enrich the already beautiful setting.

## GETTING THERE

From the town of New Paltz, NY, drive west on NY-299 W for about 6 miles. You will reach a T-intersection, with the Mountain Brauhaus restaurant to your left. Turn right onto US-44 E. Follow this road as it climbs the ridge, taking care on the extremely sharp switchback. Drive for 4.5 miles, until you reach the Minnewaska State Park Preserve, on your left. Pay the entrance fee at the booth, then continue as the road switchbacks uphill to reach the Upper Awosting Lot.

## GPS SHORTCUT

Type "Minnewaska State Park Preserve" into Google Maps and your GPS will navigate you to the main Minnewaska Preserve parking entrance. Pay the entrance fee at the booth, then con-

THE WHITE CONGLOMERATE CLIFFS OF THE SHAWANGUNKS CREATE SOME OF THE MOST MEMORABLE SETTINGS IN THE REGION

tinue as the road switchbacks uphill to reach the Upper Awosting Lot.

## THE TRAIL

From the large upper parking area, walk toward the house at the end of the lot. Take the gravel driveway to your left. The road Ts; you will see a fenced area overlooking the lake to your left, but for now, head to the right. Immediately after will be another fork. Follow the red blazes to the left. At most major intersections on this route, the trail is marked not only by blazes but also by large signs with maps and comprehensive information on the nearby routes.

At the bottom of the hill, you will see a dock area with views out over the water, including the dramatic ridges of the eastern side of the lake. At the next split in the road, continue straight, uphill. The path winds dramatically through the woods, uphill and around switchbacks, never straying far from the water. Along the way, you will pass a number of beautiful views looking to various parts of the lake, but most are partially obscured by tree cover to some extent. At 0.8 mile, you will reach an intersection with the yellow-blazed Millbrook Mountain Carriageway path (which also heads toward Hamilton Point before the trails split). Stay straight. Immediately after, the trail switchbacks downhill. At 0.9 mile, you will arrive at a viewpoint looking out over the Hudson Valley to the south.

At 1 mile, you will reach the southern tip of Lake Minnewaska. Here you will pass a trail junction with the Millbrook Mountain Trail, which heads off to your right. Continue straight. The trail begins uphill once more after veering away from the tip of the lake, sticking close to the lake's edge as it navigates the eastern bank. You will pick up elevation as the cliffs rise around you, and at 1.25 miles, you will reach a series of rock ledges with more extensive views out to the Hudson Valley. The trail splits to the right, but go straight, continuing uphill.

At 1.4 miles, you will reach a large open area, at the top of the ledges you spotted earlier in the hike. This area is the site of the former Minnewaska Mountain House, though few signs of the resort remain today. In modern times, this area offers a wonderful spot for a picnic, and the views aren't too shabby either. Peer out over the cliffs and ogle this incredible scenery—Lake Minnewaska and its surroundings may truly be one of the most beautiful places in all of the northeastern United States.

When you are ready to continue back to your car, walk to the north end of the clearing and pick up the trail once more, here an easily followed roadway. Walk left down the road, and at 1.6 miles, you will spot an old barn off a side path to your right. Stay left, and soon after cross under an arched wooden bridge. Immediately after crossing under the bridge, turn left as a narrow foot trail cuts sharply back toward the lake, uphill. The area around the cliffside house here is private property; watch out for signs and be mindful of where you can and can't go. Stay to the right at the intersection and continue, before the trail hooks back toward the lake on the northern side of the house. You will spot wooden stairs going down toward a rocky overlook— another wonderful spot for viewing the lake or taking photographs.

Head downhill. At 1.9 miles, you will continue onto a broad road toward outhouses. If you need to use the bathroom, here's your chance: other bathroom facilities around the lake are often closed depending on the season or the day. Past the toilets, go left and follow the red blazes back toward the northern end of the lake. Soon you will see the wooden fence running along the path, with views out to the lake. From here, the parking area is to your right. Walk up the hill to return to the parking area and your car.

# 18

# Millbrook Mountain and Gertrude's Nose

**TOTAL DISTANCE**: 7 miles

**TYPE**: Loop

**HIKING TIME**: 4 hours

**TOTAL ELEVATION GAIN**: 920 feet

**MAXIMUM ELEVATION**: 1,680 feet

**DIFFICULTY**: Moderate

The Shawangunks offer a number of exciting loop hikes with world-class views, but most are reached by meandering over miles of broad, mostly flat carriage paths. While carriageways may be a blessing for covering extra miles with little extra effort, there's something to be said for the oft-changing terrain and scenic twists and turns you'll cover on your way to Millbrook Mountain and Gertrude's Nose. Only two of the seven hiking miles here are on carriage roads, and the trails you'll take are often as interesting as the scenery itself—or at least they would be if the scenery wasn't so jaw-droppingly impressive. The cliffs at Gertrude's Nose set a high bar for viewpoints in the area, with some of the most impressive rock formations in the whole region. With steep drop-offs into a ravine below, and paths over rocks fractured by fissures, this may not be the best hike for someone with a serious fear of heights, or for those with young children.

## GETTING THERE

From the town of New Paltz, NY, drive west on NY-299 W for about 6 miles. You will reach a T-intersection, with the Mountain Brauhaus restaurant to your left. Turn right onto US-44 E. Follow this road as it climbs the ridge, taking care on the extremely sharp switchback. Drive for 4.5 miles, until you reach the Minnewaska State Park Preserve, on your left. Pay the entrance fee at the booth, then continue as the road switchbacks uphill to reach the Upper Awosting Lot.

## GPS SHORTCUT

Type "Minnewaska State Park Preserve" into Google Maps and your GPS will

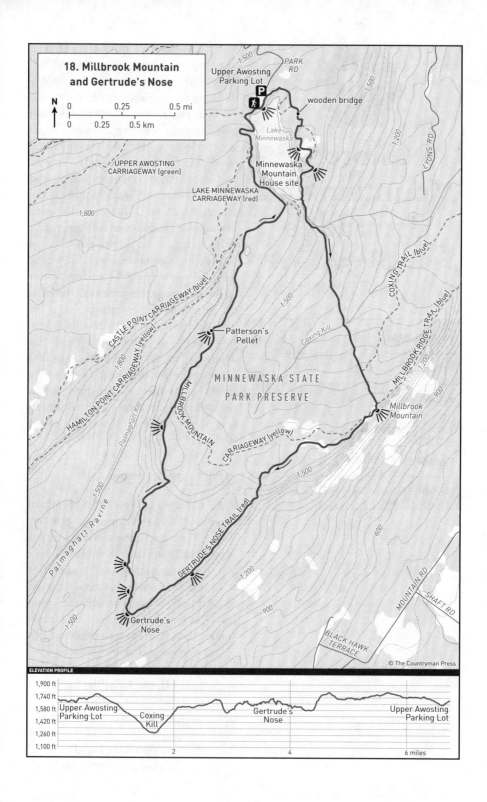

## 18. Millbrook Mountain and Gertrude's Nose

N

| 0 | 0.25 | 0.5 mi |
| 0 | 0.25 | 0.5 km |

Upper Awosting Parking Lot

PARK RD

wooden bridge

1,500

1,500

1,200

LYONS RD

Lake Minnewaska

UPPER AWOSTING CARRIAGEWAY (green)

Minnewaska Mountain House site

LAKE MINNEWASKA CARRIAGEWAY (red)

1,800

COXING TRAIL (blue)

CASTLE POINT CARRIAGEWAY (blue)

HAMILTON POINT CARRIAGEWAY (yellow)

1,800

Patterson's Pellet

MILLBROOK RIDGE TRAIL (blue)

1,500

Coxing Kill

MINNEWASKA STATE PARK PRESERVE

1,200

Palmaghatt Kill

MILLBROOK MOUNTAIN

Millbrook Mountain

CARRIAGEWAY (yellow)

1,500

900

Palmaghatt Ravine

1,500

GERTRUDE'S NOSE TRAIL (red)

600

MOUNTAIN RD

SHAFT RD

1,200

900

1,500

Gertrude's Nose

BLACK HAWK TERRACE

© The Countryman Press

**ELEVATION PROFILE**

| 1,900 ft | | | |
| 1,740 ft | | | |
| 1,580 ft | Upper Awosting Parking Lot | | Upper Awosting Parking Lot |
| 1,420 ft | | Gertrude's | |
| 1,260 ft | Coxing | Nose | |
| 1,100 ft | Kill | | |

2          4          6 miles

navigate you to the main Minnewaska Preserve parking entrance. Pay the entrance fee at the booth, then continue as the road switchbacks uphill to reach the Upper Awosting Lot.

## THE TRAIL

From the large upper parking area, walk toward the house at the end of the lot. Take the gravel driveway to your left. The road Ts; you will see a fenced area overlooking the lake to your left; go left. Enjoy incredible views out to the lake from behind the fence, then follow the red-blazed carriage trail until you pass an area with outhouses. Continue around the eastern side of the lake, following the carriage trail as it winds uphill.

Soon you will round a bend, climbing uphill, and spot a small gazebo on a rock perch over the lake. Continue on the path, and soon you will pass under an arched wooden bridge. Not far down the trail, you will spot an old barn down a side path to your left. You are now close to the main cliffs overlooking the lake. At the next split in the carriage trail, stay to the left, heading in the direction of the lake until you reach a large, open, rocky clearing. This area is the site of the former Minnewaska Mountain House, though few signs of the resort remain today. In modern times, this area offers a wonderful spot for a picnic, with incredible views. The distinct white conglomerate rock of the Shawangunks, looming jaggedly over the pristine water of this sky lake, makes this a truly special place.

When you are ready to continue, find the carriage path and take it downhill, keeping right at the next intersection. Stay on this trail as it heads toward the southern tip of the lake. At just under one mile from the start of the hike, you will reach the southern end of the lake. There, you will see a footpath heading into the woods, marked by red blazes. Leave the easy carriage path behind and take this trail, the Millbrook Mountain Trail. You will cross a stream, and the rocks and this area are often wet. The trail heads downhill, crossing a few narrow rocky ridges where you should be especially careful, especially if there is water on the path.

Soon, through the trees, enjoy views to the east of Skytop Tower. The steep descent will end when you will cross the Coxing Kill and begin hiking back uphill. The trail heading up out of the valley is often very wet, particularly in spring. Soon the trail will become drier as you approach the crest of the ridge, and a little more than a quarter mile from the stream crossing, you will pass an intersection with the blue-blazed Coxing Trail on your left. Continue uphill on the Millbrook Mountain Trail for another quarter mile, before turning right into the Millbrook Ridge Trail, and continuing a short distance until you see signs indicating that you've arrived at Millbrook Mountain, at around 2 miles. Just below the rock ledges of Millbrook is a turn-around for the Millbrook Mountain Carriageway, which heads southwest from here before looping back toward Lake Minnewaska. You will rejoin with the Carriageway later on in the hike, but it does not head all the way to Gertrude's Nose.

On the rock ledges of Millbrook Mountain, you'll enjoy excellent views out over the Hudson Valley, and up the ridge to Skytop and the Mohonk Preserve. When you are ready to continue, take the red-blazed Gertrude's Nose Trail, which will follow the ridgeline to the southwest for most of this segment

A HIKER LOOKS OUT FROM A LEDGE AT GERTRUDE'S NOSE

HIKERS ON THE CLIFFS NEAR GERTRUDE'S NOSE

of the hike. The carriage path, to your right, will run parallel to the footpath for a short distance before veering off into the woods.

The trail meanders along the ridge, occasionally opening up to viewpoints and rock ledges looking south. In half a mile, you will come to an open plateau marked by a rock cairn. At various points, you will be able to see the Hudson Highlands to the southeast, and from this angle, you will be able to see just how much this landscape resembles a classic fjord: the twin profiles of Breakneck Ridge and Storm King Mountain rise to dramatically frame the Hudson River. At other points, you will be able to see the rocks of Gertrude's Nose looming out over the valley ahead of you.

About three-quarters of a mile from

Millbrook Mountain, you will cross under the power lines that traverse Minnewaska State Park. Soon after, you will descend a short rock scramble. About a mile and a half from Millbrook Mountain, it will become apparent that you are approaching Gertrude's Nose. The cliffs open up to views to the south and east, looking out over the Wallkill Valley (the subregion of the Hudson Valley below the Shawangunk Ridgeline). The most dramatic of the rock formations can be mostly found further on, around the west side of the cliffs, but you will come to the "tip" of the nose 3.75 miles into the hike.

The cliffs here provide incredible views, and this is a good spot to take a break—but almost anywhere over the next mile will also be a great spot to take a break, and as mentioned, the most unique sections of the cliff are yet to come. When you are ready, continue on the red-blazed Gertrude's Nose Trail as it curves around the "Nose" and heads northeast. For the next half mile, you will navigate a rocky expanse of cliffs, crevasses, pitch pines bursting from improbable perches, and sheer drops of several hundred feet into the Palmaghatt Ravine. Given the inherent danger around these cliffs, it should go without saying that you will want to be extra careful here with every step.

The trail roughly follows the cliff line, but weaves in and out of the woods here and there. The exact trail may be hard to follow at some of the more open areas, but watch for painted blazes on the rocks. The trail begins to leave the cliff line and head back into the forest about half a mile from the Nose, and soon you will descend a rocky area and cross under the power lines a second time. Continue through a mossy conifer grove, just beyond.

Around 4.6 miles, tackle a short rock scramble uphill. After another quarter mile, you will come to another series of ledges, with excellent views of the ravine below, and glimpses of the cliff line all the way out to Gertrude's Nose. A short distance past the ledges, you will come to an intersection with the Millbrook Mountain Carriageway, the same path first encountered early in your hike at its origin on Millbrook Mountain. Turn left to continue hiking back in the direction of Lake Minnewaska.

Continue now on the Carriageway path. The remainder of the hike will follow this broad, easy trail, making for a refreshingly simple walk to the finish line—2 miles remain between you and your car. After a half mile, you will arrive at Patterson's Pellet (the most famous pellet in the Hudson Valley). Deposited during the last ice age, this glacial erratic is another show of nature's power and occasionally odd whims: stacked on the edge of this cliff, the Pellet makes for a memorable landmark, and can also be glimpsed from the far side of the ravine.

In another half mile, now at the 6 mile mark, you will reach an intersection with the yellow-blazed Hamilton Point Carriageway, which cuts back to your left, following the far side of the ravine opposite of your route. Continue straight. In another quarter mile you will reach another intersection. You have arrived back at Lake Minnewaska. Turn left onto the red-blazed Lake Minnewaska Carriageway, and follow this as it loops back around the west side of the lake. Several other carriage paths will branch off at points, but you can ignore them and continue following the main route marked by red blazes.

At 7 miles, the Carriageway climbs uphill from the lake, returning you to the parking area.

# 19

# Castle Point and Hamilton Point

| | |
|---|---|
| **TOTAL DISTANCE**: 8.5 miles | |
| **TYPE**: Loop | |
| **HIKING TIME**: 4.5 hours | |
| **TOTAL ELEVATION GAIN**: 855 feet | |
| **MAXIMUM ELEVATION**: 2,155 feet | |
| **DIFFICULTY**: Moderate | |

Sometimes, to truly appreciate a landmark, you have to view it from a distance. A loop hike around Castle Point and Hamilton Point—two sections of prominent conglomerate cliffs with excellent views to the south and west—allow hikers to appreciate the scale and majesty of other classic Shawangunk features. This route follows broad, easy carriage roads for most of its length, making it a much easier hike than its relatively long mileage would imply. And while tackling the long road back from Hamilton Point, you'll witness the enormity of distant Gertrude's Nose, which appears as a large wedge of earth jutting out from the main ridge. As you return to Lake Minnewaska, however, the two "wedges" will reconnect as the Palmaghatt Ravine grows narrower, until you pass this rift's origin at a humble creek. That the Shawangunk Ridge offers so many distinct loops to world-class cliff-top views only serves to demonstrate that it truly is one of the world's great places.

## GETTING THERE

From the town of New Paltz, NY, drive west on NY-299 W for about 6 miles. You will reach a T-intersection, with the Mountain Brauhaus restaurant to your left. Turn right onto US-44 E. Follow this road as it climbs the ridge, taking care on the extremely sharp switchback. Drive for 4.5 miles, until you reach the Minnewaska State Park Preserve, on your left. Pay the entrance fee at the booth, then continue as the road switchbacks uphill to reach the Upper Awosting Lot.

## GPS SHORTCUT

Type "Minnewaska State Park Preserve" into Google Maps and your GPS will

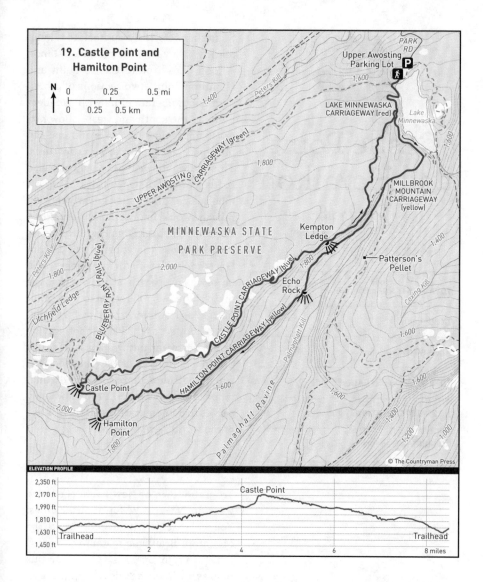

© The Countryman Press

**ELEVATION PROFILE**

navigate you to the main Minnewaska Preserve parking entrance. Pay the entrance fee at the booth, then continue as the road switchbacks uphill to reach the Upper Awosting Lot.

## THE TRAIL

From the large upper parking area, walk toward the house at the end of the lot. Take the gravel driveway to your left.

The road Ts; you will see a fenced area overlooking the lake to your left, but for now, head to the right. Immediately after will be another fork. Follow the red blazes to the left. At most major intersections on this route, the trail is marked not only by the blazes, but also by large signs with maps and comprehensive information on the nearby routes.

At the bottom of the hill, you will see a dock area with views out over the

HIKERS ENJOYING THE VIEW FROM HAMILTON POINT

water, including the dramatic ridges of the eastern side of the lake. At the next split in the road, continue straight, uphill. The path winds dramatically through the woods, uphill and around switchbacks, never straying far from the water. Along the way, you will pass a number of beautiful views looking to various parts of the lake, but most are obscured by tree cover to some extent. At 0.8 mile, you will reach an intersection with the yellow-blazed Millbrook Mountain Carriageway path, to the right, which also heads toward Hamilton Point before the trails split. Take

this trail, following the yellow blazes. At 0.95 mile, the Carriageway paths split; take the right fork to stay on the Hamilton Point path. At 1 mile the trail forks yet again, this time with a branch trail veering right to connect with the Castle Point Carriageway path. Stay left, following the yellow blazes of the Hamilton Point Trail.

Soon after you will see the beginning of the Palmaghatt Ravine open up to your left, with the deceptively humble Palmaghatt Kill flowing down into the valley. While this rift starts small, it will very quickly open up into the massive ravine that serves as the backdrop for most of this hike. The ravine widens very quickly, and at 1.8 miles, you will reach an overlook called Echo Rock, with a dramatic slab of stone jutting out into the empty space of the chasm. Here, you can glimpse just how vast the ravine stretching out along the trail has already become, and how much broader it will become still. Soon, the far edge of the ravine extending out to Gertrude's Nose will seem to be merely a distant geological feature, a ridge of rocks that just happens to run parallel to your own path in the distance.

The path continues undramatically through the woods for some time after this—the trail is mostly level, and easily followed. At 2.75 miles, at an overlook, turn back and look to your left to spot Skytop Tower in the distance behind you. At 3.5 miles, you will arrive at Hamilton Point, a series of rocky outcroppings rising above the valley. While the views here are impressive—especially if you are daring enough to step near the edge and look down, to witness the massive rock slabs that lay dashed across the forest—you will shortly be looking down on this spot from Castle Point, which is visible now to your right. Exercise caution around the steep cliffs, where a fall would certainly prove deadly.

When you are ready to continue, follow the yellow blazes once more as the trail veers to the north. Just under the 4-mile mark, you will arrive at an intersection. Here, the yellow trail continues to the left, toward Lake Awosting. Veer right onto the blue-blazed connector trail toward Castle Point. The path will begin a slight uphill, heading toward a series of dramatic rocky ledges, which jut out over the trail. You will walk

beneath them (likely marveling at how the rocks in the Shawangunks are so much cooler than rocks elsewhere), before beginning up a winding path at 4.2 miles. The road here will switchback uphill several times before looping you back toward Castle Point. Soon, you will walk by the first of many impressive ledges—these first ledges are the same you passed beneath only minutes ago, and are just as impressive when witnessed from the top as the bottom. The trail continues along these ledges for another quarter mile (passing the blue-blazed Blueberry Run Trail) before reaching the high point of Castle Point. At this expansive vista, you'll discover dramatic views across the Hudson Valley, south to Gertrude's Nose, northwest to Lake Awosting, and due south, where Hamilton Point rises impressively from the surrounding landscape, a rocky prominence craning out above the trees.

When you are ready to go on, head east on the blue-blazed Castle Point Carriageway. For the rest of the way back, you will pass viewpoints on a regular basis—nearly the entire length of this upper ridgeline trail seems to be one unending vista. Just after Castle Point, you will come to the first of these outlooks. All face toward Gertrude's Nose, and thus offer very similar views, but the shift in perspective as you grow ever nearer to this outlying ridgeline is quite interesting to observe. Eventually, you will pass east of the tip of Gertrude's Nose, and enjoy a new perspective on the outcropping as the ravine shrinks back into itself on your right.

At 7.3 miles, you will arrive at Kempton Ledge, an outcropping with views across the ravine to Patterson's Pellet, a large boulder on the far side of the

DRAMATIC CLIFFS TOWER ABOVE THE TRAIL AT CASTLE POINT

ravine. A quarter mile later, you will pass a small side trail to your right—this is the connector trail you passed after starting out on the Hamilton Point Carriageway, connecting you back to the beginning of the loop. You can ignore this trail, as the Castle Point Carriageway will bring you back to Lake Minnewaska at a point closer to the parking area.

The trail slopes gently downhill, but remains wide and easy to follow. Half a mile later, you will pass through an open field with views of the Catskills to the north. Continue for a short distance before the trail intersects with the Lake Minnewaska Carriageway path, marked by the red blazes on which you started out. From here, head to the left, following the trail around the lake and back to the parking area where you began your hike.

# The Trapps Carriageway Loop

| | |
|---|---|
| **TOTAL DISTANCE**: 5.3 miles | |
| **TYPE**: Loop | |
| **HIKING TIME**: 3–4 hours | |
| **TOTAL ELEVATION GAIN**: 375 feet | |
| **MAXIMUM ELEVATION**: 1,000 feet | |
| **DIFFICULTY**: Easy | |

While the many trails of the Shawangunk Ridge are popular among outdoor enthusiasts of all types, this particular hike is actually far better known to climbers than hikers. The easy carriageway trails and relative lack of elevation gain over this 5-mile loop make for an easy walk or mountain bike expedition, but for a long stretch of the dramatic Undercliff Trail, you'll find yourself staring up at looming cliffs to marvel at the humans dangling off of them. Together the Undercliff / Overcliff Carriageway trails form a loop around the famous conglomerate cliffs known as the Trapps, widely considered to be one of the premier rock climbing destinations on the East Coast. On a nice weekend day, the atmosphere on the trail—at least for the first half mile or so—can resemble that of an outdoor music festival more than a backwoods excursion.

Despite the name, the Overcliff Trail merely traverses the other side of the Trapps, but lacks a looming cliff of its own. As a result, this part of the loop is far less busy than the Undercliff route, and boasts endless views north to the Catskill mountains. There are no trails on top of the cliffs, and thus, the only way to enjoy a view from the top is to scramble up the hard way. But even for hikers with a bit of vertigo, this easy hike is highly recommended: the views are great, and you won't even have to work too hard to find them.

## GETTING THERE

From the town of New Paltz, NY, drive west on NY-299 W for about 6 miles. You will reach a T-intersection, with the Mountain Brauhaus restaurant to your left. Turn right onto US-44 E. Follow this road as it climbs the ridge, taking care on the extremely sharp switchback. Drive for 1.8 miles, and the parking area

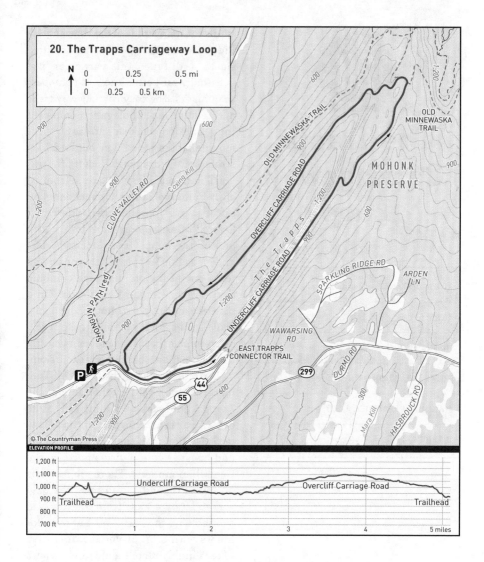

## 20. The Trapps Carriageway Loop

ELEVATION PROFILE

will be to your right. This parking area is managed by the Mohonk Preserve, and there is a $12 fee (as of 2017) per hiker. An annual pass is also available.

## GPS SHORTCUT

Type "West Trapps Trailhead Parking Area" into Google Maps and your GPS will navigate you to the appropriate parking area.

## THE TRAIL

From the parking area, walk to the far end of the long parking lot. You will see an information kiosk situated at the trailhead, and yellow blazes indicating the trail. After about 600 feet, a red-blazed trail marked by a sign—the Shongum Path—intersects on your left. Continue straight on the yellow-blazed trail.

THE OVERCLIFF TRAIL

Soon you will see the bridge crossing NY-55/44, to your right. Here, the trail cuts left through the woods away from the road, ascending briefly before coming to the Carriageway loop. Signs here point out the Undercliff route, to your right, and the Overcliff route, to your left. This loop can be done in either direction. For this guide, turn right to start on the Undercliff Trail.

THE TRAPP CLIFFS ARE ONE OF THE MOST POPULAR CLIMBING DESTINATIONS IN THE EASTERN UNITED STATES

In a short distance, you will see the roadside overlook below you on NY-55/44. The trail begins winding around the edge of the rising cliffs, descending gently downhill. Around 0.4 mile into the hike, you will begin hiking along the stretch of the Trapps cliff that is very popular with climbers. Climbers from all over the world congregate here, and you'll see the biggest crowds along this first section of trail, tackling the routes closest to the parking area. The cliffs continue for another 2 miles, however, and you will see climbers almost anywhere there's a cliff face to tackle. Marvel at the precarious-seeming routes spanning sheer cliffs looming hundreds of feet above the valley—or don't, if you suffer from vertigo. With no hiking trails running over the top of the Trapps, climbing is the only way to access the astonishing views from the top.

Even if the sight of climbers dangling from ropes hundreds of feet above you makes you want to hug the ground, the views of the Hudson Valley are a draw all of their own. With a fairly steep drop-off to your right as well, there is only limited tree cover to block your view of the valley for almost the entire length of the Undercliff Trail.

At 0.85 mile, you will see the East Trapps Connector Trail to your right. This trail connects to the visitor center for the Mohonk Preserve below the cliffs on NY-55/44. The parking area by the visitor center serves as an overflow lot when the West Trapps parking area is full (which is often), and this connector trail offers another access point to the Trapps Carriageway loop.

Continue on the Carriageway trail. After about 2 miles, you will begin hiking away from the east end of the cliff line as the trail makes an S-bend into the woods. At 2.7 miles, you will come to a multi-way intersection. To your left is the Overcliff Carriage Road. Take

this to begin the second half of your loop.

Turn left, following the signs for the Overcliff Trail. The path will begin swerving back west, and around the 3-mile mark, begins to run parallel to your original route along the cliffs. Despite the name of the trail, you will unfortunately not be hiking along the top of the cliffs, merely on the other side of them. The ridge here is sloping and lacks the sheer rock faces of the other side of the Trapps, so you will not see climbers along this part of the route (unless they've decided to enjoy a loop hike themselves).

The route back is similarly unchallenging, with the woods road cutting a mostly straight path back toward the west end of the cliffs. Just as before, practically the entire trail is a viewpoint, with little obstructing the sight of the Catskills to your north.

You will complete the loop around the 5-mile mark, returning to the intersection with the Undercliff Trail and the side-trail leading back to the parking area. Turn right onto this trail, retracing your original path back to the parking lot and your car.

# 21

# High Peters Kill Trail and Awosting Falls

**TOTAL DISTANCE**: 4.7 miles

**TYPE**: Loop

**HIKING TIME**: 3–4 hours

**TOTAL ELEVATION GAIN**: 620 feet

**MAXIMUM ELEVATION**: 1,500 feet

**DIFFICULTY**: Moderate

Heading up to Lake Minnewaska, it's easy to overlook one of the Hudson Valley's best waterfalls if you don't know it's there. And yet Awosting Falls can be reached from the lower (and larger) Minnewaska parking area with only a short walk. This route makes a longer, moderately strenuous loop around the lesser-used Peters Kill Trail, over and then under a scenic ridge, where you'll enjoy a unique perspective over the Shawangunks. You'll finish the hike with a stop at the 60-foot Awosting Falls, the perfect end to a moderate day of hiking. The falls can get quite busy on weekends, as most will simply make the short walk directly from the parking area. Several rocky areas around the falls could be quite dangerous if you were to lose your footing, so practice extra caution, and never approach the edge of a ledge if the stones might be wet.

## GETTING THERE

From the town of New Paltz, NY, drive west on NY-299 W for about 6 miles. You will reach a T-intersection, with the Mountain Brauhaus restaurant to your left. Turn right onto US-44 E. Follow this road as it climbs the ridge, taking care on the extremely sharp switchback. Drive for 4.5 miles, until you reach the Minnewaska State Park Preserve, on your left. Pay the entrance fee at the booth, then continue to park in the Lower Awosting Lot.

## GPS SHORTCUT

Type "Minnewaska State Park Preserve" into Google Maps and your GPS will navigate you to the main Minnewaska Preserve parking entrance. Park in the Lower Awosting Lot.

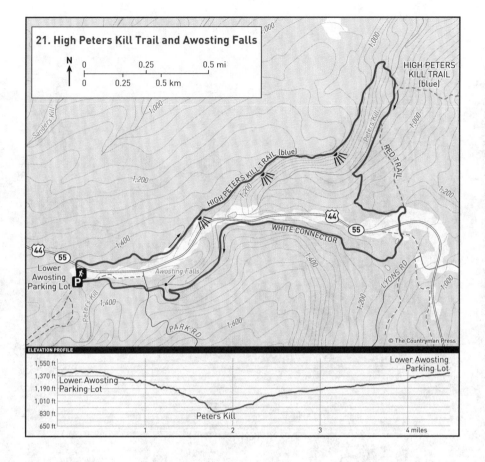

**21. High Peters Kill Trail and Awosting Falls**

N

| 0 | 0.25 | 0.5 mi |
| 0 | 0.25 | 0.5 km |

HIGH PETERS KILL TRAIL (blue)

HIGH PETERS KILL TRAIL (blue)

RED TRAIL

WHITE CONNECTOR

44 55

Lower Awosting Parking Lot

Awosting Falls

Peters Kill

LYONS RD

PARK RD

© The Countryman Press

ELEVATION PROFILE

| 1,550 ft | | | | Lower Awosting |
| 1,370 ft | Lower Awosting | | | Parking Lot |
| 1,190 ft | Parking Lot | | | |
| 1,010 ft | | | | |
| 830 ft | | Peters Kill | | |
| 650 ft | | | | |
|  | 1 | 2 | 3 | 4 miles |

## THE TRAIL

From the large lower parking area, look for a large information sign indicating where the trail crosses NY-55/44. (The crossing is further along the road from where you pulled in to the park, to the northwest of the gatehouse.) This sign clearly indicates where you are, and shows a map of the surrounding area's trails. The High Peters Kill Trail begins on the opposite side of the road. Be very careful crossing here—NY-55/44 is a busy road, even here in the Shawangunks, and traffic approaches quickly.

Cross the road, then begin on the High Peters Kill Trail, following the blue blazes. The trail is a narrow footpath through the unique forestlands of the Shawangunk Ridge, with only a gentle uphill grade at first. This first section of the hike makes for a pleasant, easy stroll through the woods.

Around 0.45 mile, you will begin to encounter a series of ledges facing southeast. The High Peters Kill Trail skirts the edge of this ridgeline, which will grow increasingly prominent the further along you get. You will encounter a viewpoint at 0.75 mile with open views of the ravine below you, as well as the busy roadway running through it. Just under the 1-mile mark, you will arrive at an even larger ledge, with even bigger views. Here, Skytop Tower is vis-

AWOSTING FALLS IN WINTER

ible in the eastern section of the Shawangunk Ridge.

Around 1.1 miles, the trail passes through an interesting split rock—the divide down the center of the stone is so distinct, it looks like it was sculpted by an artist. At 1.3 miles, you will encounter another large rock ledge with similar views, though this ledge is tilted upward at a steep angle, creating another interesting landmark.

Around 1.7 miles, you will begin descending from the ridgeline into the ravine below. The trail switchbacks, and soon you will approach the Peters Kill, which runs below your previous path, parallel to the ridge itself. A short distance later, the creek splits, and two consecutive bridges cross over the water. Just beyond, you will reach a split in the trail, with the blue-blazed trail heading to your left, and a yellow-blazed trail following the creek. Take the yellow path, hiking along the water.

At 2.15 miles, the yellow trail ends at a junction with a red-blazed trail. The red trail itself will split just after this intersection, with the path to your left heading more steeply uphill, and the path to your right keeping close to the creek. Take the trail to the right. You will hike near the water for about another quarter mile, before the trail cuts uphill.

The ascent is moderate, and soon the trail will level as you hear the familiar sounds of traffic from NY-55/44. At 2.75 miles, past a clearing, you will reach the Peters Kill parking area. To your left, you will see a picnic area. Head right, toward the road. With the toll booth behind you, walk toward the road, then carefully cross NY-55/44 once again. On the other side, you will find a white-blazed connector trail heading back into the woods, well-marked by another informational sign.

Follow this trail for a short distance, until it ends at an intersection with the Awosting Falls Carriageway Trail. This broad, mostly flat pathway will bring you back to the parking area where you began—the hike from here on out is easy, though the most interesting feature is yet to come. Turn right onto the Carriageway, heading north, then follow this path for another mile.

Just under the 4-mile mark, you will rejoin the Peters Kill, and at 4.1 miles, you will arrive at Awosting Falls. The views of the waterfall from around the base are magnificent. Being located only a short distance from the parking area, it is an appealing visit all year round, though the trail and surrounding rock ledges can become very icy in winter.

From here, the trail climbs through the woods toward the backside of the falls, and soon passes by a rocky ledge overhang, where you can look down to the cascade below. If you explore this area, be extremely careful—there is nothing to stop you from tumbling over the edge. The trail continues along the creek, toward the roadways that navigate the lower Minnewaska parking area. At 4.5 miles, you will return to the road near the entrance. Walk along the road, following the signs, back to the main parking area.

# 22

# Giant's Workshop and Copes Lookout

| | |
|---|---|
| **TOTAL DISTANCE**: 7.5 miles | |
| **TYPE**: Lollipop | |
| **HIKING TIME**: 4–5 hours | |
| **TOTAL ELEVATION GAIN**: 1,050 feet | |
| **MAXIMUM ELEVATION**: 1,160 feet | |
| **DIFFICULTY**: Difficult | |

As one of the most unique natural places in the eastern United States, the Shawangunks draw considerable attention from outdoor adventurers. Finding solitude on this beautiful ridge can sometimes be difficult. While the Coxing trailhead is itself quite busy, due to a watering hole popular with swimmers just a few hundred feet down the trail, the trails beyond this area remain surprisingly quiet. This route takes hikers along a seldom-used path to a fascinating and secluded area of the ridge, where you'll be shocked to find one of the area's most interesting rock scrambles, and some of the ridge's best views. Copes Lookout arguably rivals the more famous Eagle Cliff, nearby, but is not easily accessible without parking on Mohonk Mountain House property. This is a challenging hike, though the difficult sections are constrained within a short portion of trail—most of the hike simply follows the contour of the ridge as you hike through quiet, peaceful forest.

## GETTING THERE

From the town of New Paltz, NY, drive west on NY-299 W for about 6 miles. You will reach a T-intersection, with the Mountain Brauhaus restaurant to your left. Turn right onto US-44 E. Follow this road as it climbs the ridge, taking care on the extremely sharp switchback. Drive for 2 miles, then turn right onto Clove Road and continue for another mile. This parking area is managed by the Mohonk Preserve, and there is a $12 fee (as of 2017) per hiker. An annual pass is also available.

## GPS SHORTCUT

Type "Coxing Trailhead Parking Lot" into Google Maps and your GPS will

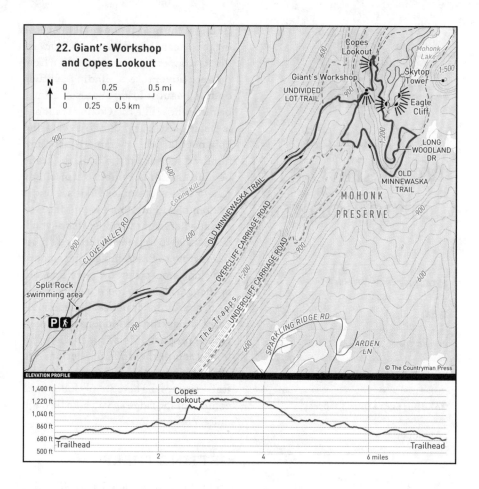

navigate you to the appropriate parking area.

## THE TRAIL

The trailhead begins on the other side of Clove Valley Road, directly across from the entrance to the Coxing parking area. Cross the road carefully.

The trail is a broad, open path to start, marked by blue blazes. You will soon see a number of signs giving information about the area, which was once the site of the Enderly homestead. The foundations of the various buildings that comprised the homestead can be found throughout the woods.

Very soon, you will pass over a creek. To your left is a swimming hole known as Split Rock, through which the Coxing Kill flows. While it may be difficult to find a parking spot in the Coxing parking lot, the trails in this area are not heavily used—most parking at the lot are here simply to swim. Various picnic spots near the watering hole make this an ideal destination on a hot day.

Continue straight, following the blue blazes, to stay on the Old Minnewaska Trail. Just after the swimming hole, you will pass the red-blazed Shongum Path, on your right. The Shongum Path heads south, to the Trapps parking area and its Overcliff / Undercliff Trail loop.

COPES LOOKOUT OFFERS STUNNING VIEWS OF THE TRAPPS CLIFFLINE AND THE CATSKILL MOUNTAINS

The trail past this point is not heavily used, and may be slightly overgrown in spots, though it is still easy to follow. The blue blazes along this stretch are more sporadic. You will make a gentle, but steady ascent up a wide foot trail for a stretch. Shortly after the half mile mark, you will come to a small ravine carved out by a creek. Here, stones embedded on either side of the ravine seem to suggest that there may once have been a bridge crossing here; now, however, hikers must descend toward the creek and back up the other side via stepping stones.

The trail is mostly level over most of the next mile, with occasional mild uphill sections. While the trail is narrow in some spots, this section of the hike is quiet, peaceful, and easy. At 1.5 miles the trees open up to your left, offering limited Catskill views.

Around the 2 mile mark, you will pass an intersection with the Undivided Lot Trail, to your left. Continue straight, and soon the trail will begin to climb. Look carefully as the trees open up above you and you may be able to spot a gazebo perched on the cliff. You'll enter a cool conifer grove, and then you'll arrive at an intersection with a carriage path around 2.2 miles. This is the Laurel Ledge Carriageway. Remember this intersection, as you will eventually return to it later,

A SUMMERHOUSE LOOKING OUT FROM EAGLE CLIFF

after completing the "lollipop" portion of the hike.

At the Carriageway, turn left, then make an immediate right onto a blue-blazed trail. You will see a sign indicating that this is the Giant's Path, and very soon you will enter a section of the trail known as the Giant's Workshop. This intricate climb is even more elaborate than other nearby rock scrambles, like Bonticou Crag, as much of the scramble makes its way through the cave-like interiors of the boulder field. Every segment of the Giant's Workshop seems to involve wedging or contorting your body to slip through some narrow crevasse, or else will find you perched on a narrow rock lip, stretching for your next foothold. Use extreme caution here—while you are not hiking along the edge of a cliff, there are still steep sections where you could easily slip and fall into a crevasse or deep hole. Only attempt this section of trail if you are confident about your climbing abilities.

Just over the 2.5-mile mark, you will reach the top of Giant's Workshop, where a section of flat boulders affords a view over the ridge. The Trapps cliff line and Millbrook Mountain are visible nearby, seen from the back (the slanted rather than sheer side of the cliffs).

From here, the trail begins to climb uphill on a regular footpath. In a short distance, you will intersect with the red-blazed Arching Rocks Path. Turn left, and hike along the underside of the dramatic cliffs. The trail here is rocky, working its way over boulders and stones that have fallen from the cliffs, though as the path is level, this section is not a rock scramble. You will tackle another rock scramble soon, however, as you reach a blue-blazed trail heading up the rocks to your right at the inter-section with the Cathedral Path. Turn right, and begin another, though less intense, rock scramble. After a bit of climbing, the path makes a sharp bend and doubles back the way you came for the final climb. This scramble is much easier than the contortions of Giant's Workshop, though there are a few spots where you must use good judgment and ensure you have a good foothold before making your next move.

Around 2.85 miles, you will reach Copes Lookout. Here, a large "summerhouse," as these pavilions are called, looks out to a classic view of the Trapps and Millbrook Mountain. To the north, the Catskills sprawl across the horizon.

From the Lookout, head into the woods, where you will find wooden stairs making their way to a higher section of the cliff. At the top of the stairs, you will come to a smaller summerhouse and a broad carriage path. Turn right onto the carriage path. The road makes a slight uphill climb, and soon you will pass more summerhouses along the cliff, all with great views of the Trapps.

In a short distance, you will come to a giant boulder field, to the left of the trail, at the underside of Eagle Cliff. At points, you may be able to spot other hikers looking out from a summerhouse on top of this more famous cliff.

At 3.5 miles, you will reach a split with two carriage paths, both heading away from the cliff's edge. To the left, the path heads slightly uphill before reaching the Eagle Cliff ascent path, which will take you to the crest of Eagle Cliff. This optional excursion will add about half a mile to your hike, and an additional two hundred feet of elevation gain. Tackling this scramble is not included in the totals (mileage and elevation) for this hike, but if you have extra energy, it is a fun, strenuous addition to the day.

If sticking to the suggested route, stay straight at the intersection, hiking now on Long Woodland Drive. The path will veer slightly to the right, descend slightly, and make a long curve before intersecting with the Old Minnewaska Drive carriage path at just over 4 miles. There, turn right.

In about a quarter of a mile, you will reach a small opening through the trees with a view to the Trapps, offering a different perspective than your views of the cliffs from before. Around 4.7 miles, you will reach a series of intersections. This is the far end of the loop made by the Undercliff and Overcliff trails, which circle the Trapps (Hike #20). Turn right, and then make another immediate right onto Laurel Ledge Road. Very shortly you will pass the Overcliff Carriage Road, to your left. Stay straight.

Around 5.3 miles, you will return to the intersection with the Old Minnewaska Trail—the long, straight trail you hiked in on. Just past the intersection is the Giant's Path Trail leading to Giant's Workshop. Turn left onto the Old Minnewaska Trail, and retrace your steps from the first leg of the hike to return to the parking area.

# Bonticou Crag Rock Scramble

**TOTAL DISTANCE**: 2.9 miles

**TYPE**: Lollipop

**HIKING TIME**: 2–3 hours

**TOTAL ELEVATION GAIN**: 640 feet

**MAXIMUM ELEVATION**: 1,080 feet

**DIFFICULTY**: Difficult

Want to feel like a climber, without having to actually break out the ropes and harnesses? The Hudson Valley is home to two significant rock scrambles, and Breakneck Ridge, in the Hudson Highlands, is unquestionably the most famous of them. While Bonticou Crag may be shorter and less famous, sections of this scramble are actually more challenging (or intimidating, depending on your perspective) than its rival, and the views from the top are—well, both hikes offer views so exceptional, there's no real sense comparing them. Suffice it to say, if Bonticou Crag had a Metro-North stop at its trailhead, it would probably be world famous too.

Of course, being that this scramble does feature some particularly vertigo-inducing moments, it's not for those with a fear of heights, or anyone uncertain about their balance, or parents with young children. Nor is this a hike to tackle when the rocks may be wet or icy. The Spring Farm trailhead, from which this hike begins, is also an excellent spot for a picnic, with unrivaled views of the Catskills from a large open hill.

## GETTING THERE

From the town of New Paltz, NY, drive west on NY-299 W, crossing the Wallkill River and then immediately turning right onto Springtown Road. After half a mile, turn left onto Mountain Rest Road. Continue for about 4.5 miles. Just before a bend in the road, make a right onto Upper 27 Knolls Road. The parking area is just ahead, to your left, past the toll booth. This parking area is managed by the Mohonk Preserve, and there is a $12 fee (as of 2017) per hiker. An annual pass is also available.

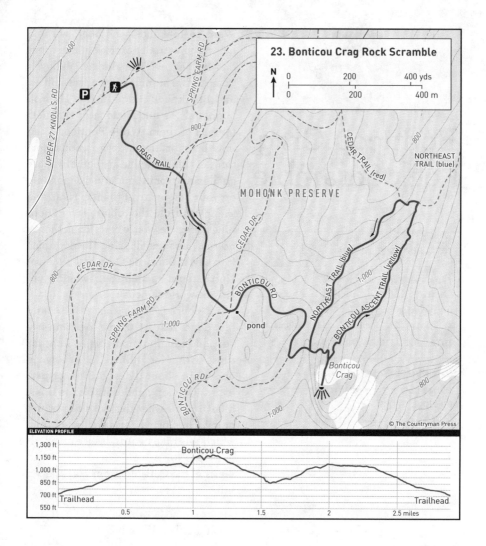

## 23. Bonticou Crag Rock Scramble

ELEVATION PROFILE

## GPS SHORTCUT

Type "Spring Farm Trailhead Parking" into Google Maps and your GPS will navigate you to the appropriate parking area.

## THE TRAIL

Walk to the northern end of the parking area, and cross the road, watching carefully for cars. Look for the blue-blazed Table Rocks Trail, which heads uphill parallel to Spring Farm Road. Soon the trail will come to the top of a hill, with a large open field to your left. Here, you will find one of the best panoramic views of the Catskills in the region.

Shortly past this viewpoint, you will reach an intersection with the Crag Trail. Turn right onto this trail and head uphill. The path continues across a field, near an old stone wall. At 0.35 mile you will come to two parallel carriage roads, one right after the other. The first is Cedar Drive, followed by Spring Farm Road. Keep following the Crag Trail, which continues to gain in elevation.

THE VIEW FROM THE TOP OF BONTICUE CRAG

At about 0.65 mile, you will come to the start of a loop, at a small pond. Turn left, onto Bonticou Road. The trail is now a mostly level carriage road, which will snake through the woods before the Crag itself comes into sight.

At 1 mile, you will reach an intersection with the yellow-blazed Bonticou Ascent Path. Turn left, and the trail heads downhill briefly to reach the rocky base of the Crag. From here, the intimidating-looking jumble of rocks looms above you, and on most days, you will likely see numerous hikers perched at various stages along the climb, and enjoying the views from the ridge above.

The Bonticou Ascent Path is not to be underestimated—while short in mileage, this is a challenging section of trail. Making your way up the Crag, you will climb over giant talus fragments, over ledges, and through crevices. While most of the scramble requires only good balance, several sections may require use of both your arms and legs to find footholds and climb your way up. The yellow blazes painted onto the rocks mark the easiest and safest route of ascent. Pay careful attention, and do not veer off course or you may risk losing the yellow blazes.

Near the top of the climb, the ridge will begin to level out and you will pass pines and laurels. Turn right to reach the crest of Bonticou Crag, where you will find excellent views south toward the Hudson, north to the Catskills, and even across the river toward northern Dutchess County. While pitch pines grow densely in spots, most of the ridge is open, exposed rocks, making for one of the most interesting areas of crumbled and jutting Shawangunk conglomerate anywhere in the ridge. From various ledges along the length of the crest, you can look down at the jumbled mass of rocks that make up the rock scramble you just tackled.

After enjoying the view, follow the yellow-blazed trail as it heads down a rocky, narrow trail along the ridgetop. At 1.5 miles, you will reach an intersection with the blue-blazed Northeast Trail. A sprawling tree with three trunks marks this junction, with a blue-blazed trail to your left descending steeply downhill. Turn left and follow the blue blazes, as they descend steeply for a short distance. At the base of the descent, you'll reach a junction with the red-blazed Cedar Trail.

The Cedar Trail goes straight from this intersection, marked by a large rock covered in small cairns. Turn left, remaining on the blue-blazed Northeast Trail. The path begins to climb slightly uphill, until you return to the intersection with the yellow-blazed Bonticou Crag Ascent Path.

From here, retrace your route from the first leg of the hike to return to the Spring Farm trailhead.

# 24

# Table Rocks

| | |
|---|---|
| **TOTAL DISTANCE**: 4.1 miles | |
| **TYPE**: Out and Back | |
| **HIKING TIME**: 2.5 hours | |
| **TOTAL ELEVATION GAIN**: 600 feet | |
| **MAXIMUM ELEVATION**: 895 feet | |
| **DIFFICULTY**: Easy | |

There are so many staggering sites in the Shawangunks, it would be easy to lose track if they did not also possess so much variety. Fortunately, every route here seems to lead to some unique and unrivaled destination. This is certainly the case with Table Rocks, a unique area of conglomerate cliffs crisscrossed by deep, dramatic fissures. Like nearby Bonticou Crag, this is not the place for hikers with serious vertigo: many of the fissures are wide enough as to be slightly nerve-wracking to cross over, with the sense of height amplified greatly due to the tilted angle of the rocks. The entire slab of stone seems to shift down to a steep drop-off—as if the entire Shawangunk Ridge simply ended here, like the edge of the world. It's a dizzying landmark, and the sense of being slanted toward some great dividing line is further enhanced by the presence of the Catskill Mountains, which loom closer here than anywhere else in the Shawangunks, dominating the horizon beyond the cliffs. There's much to explore here, but you don't really have to hop a single crevasse to take it in: the views open up the moment you approach Table Rocks. Such a dramatic place demands a visit, even if a fear of heights forces you to observe it all from the safety of the uppermost ledge.

## GETTING THERE

From the town of New Paltz, NY, drive west on NY-299 W, crossing the Wallkill River and then immediately turning right onto Springtown Road. After half a mile, turn left onto Mountain Rest Road. Continue for about 4.5 miles. Just before a bend in the road, make a right onto Upper 27 Knolls Road. The parking

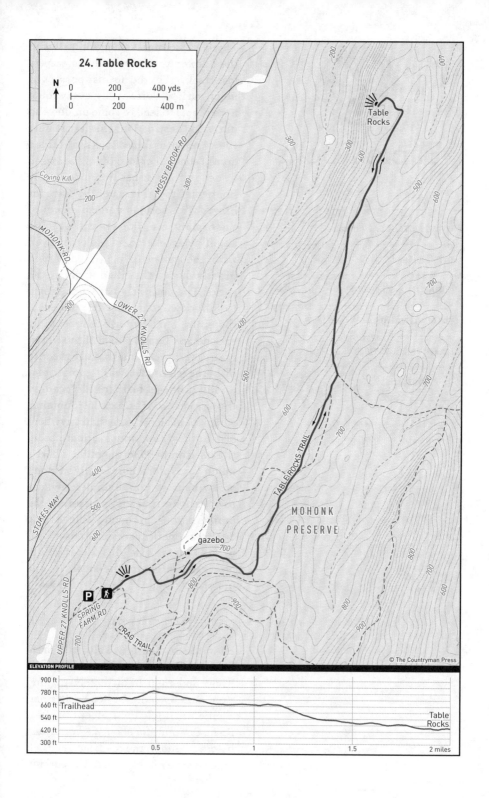

## 24. Table Rocks

N

| 0 | 200 | 400 yds |
| 0 | 200 | 400 m |

Coxing Kill

MOSSY BROOK RD.

MOHONK RD.

LOWER 27 KNOLLS RD.

STOKES WAY

TABLE ROCKS TRAIL

MOHONK
PRESERVE

gazebo

UPPER 27 KNOLLS RD.

SPRING FARM RD.

CRAG TRAIL

P

Table
Rocks

© The Countryman Press

**ELEVATION PROFILE**

| 900 ft |
| 780 ft |
| 660 ft | Trailhead |
| 540 ft |
| 420 ft |
| 300 ft |

Table
Rocks

0.5    1    1.5    2 miles

area is just ahead, to your left, past the toll booth. This parking area is managed by the Mohonk Preserve, and there is a $12 fee (as of 2017) per hiker. An annual pass is also available.

## GPS SHORTCUT

Type "Spring Farm Trailhead Parking" into Google Maps and your GPS will navigate you to the appropriate parking area.

## THE TRAIL

Walk to the far end of the parking area, then walk uphill, toward the path running parallel to the lot on your right. You will see a sign for Spring Farm Road—turn left to follow this road. Just uphill from the parking lot, you will come to an open field. To your left, the hill offers a staggering view of the Catskills. The west-to-east expanse of the mountains is laid out before you with almost no obstructions—this full panorama of the range may be the best of anywhere in the Hudson Valley.

After 0.15 mile, the road turns right, heading into another clearing. Additional roads connect to private property—Spring Farm, the namesake of the parking area—but the intersections here are well-marked by signs. Stay to the right as the path bends into the clearing and begins heading toward the treeline. Look for the sign marking the Table Rocks Trail, then follow this path into the woods.

Just after you enter the woods, you will see another open clearing to your left, and a large wooden gazebo downhill from the trail. Continue as the trail leads you deeper into the forest. Just after the half-mile mark, you will reach an intersection with the Cedar Trail. Turn left, following the blue blazes of the Table Rocks Trail. You will remain on this trail until you reach Table Rocks.

At 0.85 mile, the trail will intersect with a carriage road. Turning left on this road would bring you back to Spring Farm and the parking area. Stay straight, continuing on the Table Rocks footpath. The trail will enter another clearing, with the carriage path making a loop to your right—both trails will intersect again in a short distance. The ground here is often muddy, particularly in spring.

At the far end of the clearing, heading back into the woods, the trails will again intersect. The blue Table Rocks Trail continues straight before reaching one final intersection at the 1-mile mark. Here, a red-blazed trail branches off to your right. This trail can be taken to complete a loop with the Bonticou Crag rock scramble (Hike #23).

Turn left, and the Table Rocks Trail will soon begin to slope downhill. The trail continues mostly straight for the next mile. At 1.5 miles, you will spot a large solitary rock to your left, letting you know that you're getting close. Shortly after, you will begin to see large rocks rising to form a ridge to your left. Soon, the Table Rocks Trail will cut left into the woods through an area of large rocks. In a short distance, you will emerge on the other side of these rock formations to find the sloping expanse of Table Rocks laid out before you.

The rock slabs form a sort of sloping cliff before the ridge drops off entirely. It is possible to navigate over the crevasses to the lowermost slab. However, to dial up the vertigo you'll likely feel

MASSIVE CHASMS CARVE UP TABLE ROCKS, MAKING THIS AN INTIMIDATING DESTINATION FOR ANYONE WITH A SERIOUS FEAR OF HEIGHTS

at this place, the stones are all steeply slanted, making it feel as if you might easily slide and roll down into the next crevasse if you lose your footing. The dangers here are certainly not to be ignored—many of the chasms between rocks do indeed drop down for a significant distance. The deepest of the chasms is more than 60 feet deep, and far too wide to jump across. As with any cliff edge or dangerous perch, always be extra careful of your footing here, and never go exploring here if the rocks may be wet or icy.

When you are ready, retrace your steps to return to your car.

IV.

PUTNAM AND
DUTCHESS
COUNTIES

# 25

# Ninham Mountain Fire Tower

| | |
|---|---|
| **TOTAL DISTANCE**: 1.5 miles | |
| **TYPE**: Out and Back | |
| **HIKING TIME**: 1 Hour | |
| **TOTAL ELEVATION GAIN**: 400 feet | |
| **MAXIMUM ELEVATION**: 1,300 feet | |
| **DIFFICULTY**: Easy | |

Ninham Mountain's steady mountain road up to the top might not be the most exciting trail around, but considering the short distance involved and the views rewarding you at the end, what's not to love? Reach the top of this unassuming summit northeast of the Hudson Highlands and you'll find a tall fire tower with incredible 360-degree views of the countryside, from Connecticut all the way to the Catskills. At more than 80 feet tall, the Ninham Mountain fire tower is one of the tallest in the area. Originally constructed in 1940 by the Civilian Conservation Corps, the tower was eventually restored and opened to the public after being added to the National Historic Lookout Register. Note that various spellings for this site have been used in the past, and you may notice some online descriptions and physical markers—including the historic marker at the site itself—which refer to this area as "Mount Nimham."

## GETTING THERE

From the Taconic Parkway, take the exit for NY-52 toward Fishkill / Carmel. Turn right onto NY-52 E and drive for 5.3 miles. Turn right onto White Pond Road and continue for 2.8 miles, then turn left onto Farmers Mills Road. In less than a mile, turn right onto Gypsy Trail Road. After about 2.5 miles, you'll see the sign on the right for Ninham Mountain Multiple Use Area, next to the historical marker for Mount Nimham. Turn right onto Mount Nimham Ct. and head uphill on the gravel road for about half a mile, until you reach the parking area.

## GPS SHORTCUT

Type "Ninham Mountain State Forest" into Google Maps and your GPS will

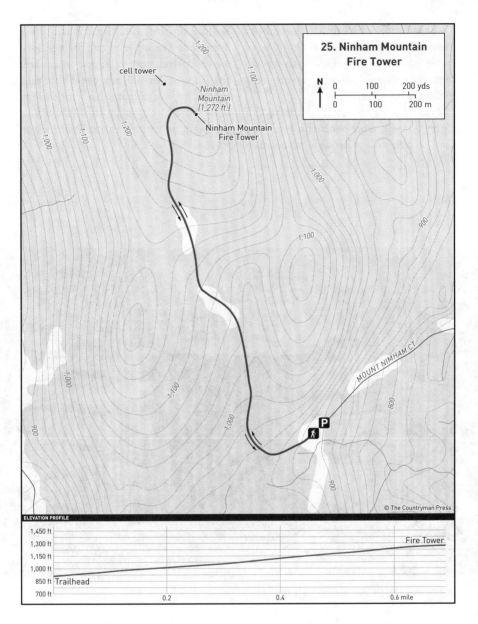

N
0       100       200 yds
0       100       200 m

cell tower

Ninham
Mountain
(1,272 ft.)

Ninham Mountain
Fire Tower

MOUNT NIMHAM CT

© The Countryman Press

**ELEVATION PROFILE**

1,450 ft
1,300 ft                                                        Fire Tower
1,150 ft
1,000 ft
850 ft  Trailhead
700 ft
              0.2              0.4              0.6 mile

navigate you to the appropriate parking area.

## THE TRAIL

From the parking area, the trail begins past a metal gate. The path beyond the gate is a wide gravel road—you will follow this road until reaching the fire tower. The road makes a moderate but steady ascent, and this too will hold true for the duration of the hike. The grade is never severe, but the unrelenting uphill may still start to feel like a chore if you've been deceived into thinking the short trail meant this hike would be without any challenges.

A short distance up the road, you will

pass an old stone building to the right of the trail. There are several abandoned stone buildings throughout the park, including a very similar structure next to the parking area.

Follow the road as it bends to the right. As you approach the top, you may be able to see several structures besides the fire tower through the trees. There are a number of cell towers here as well. After 0.75 mile, you will reach the fire tower. Climb carefully and enjoy the views from the windowless viewing station at the top. When you are ready to return, retrace your steps to your car.

AN OLD STONE CELLAR, JUST OFF THE TRAIL TO NINHAM MOUNTAIN

# Wonder Lake

Wonder Lake may be overcompensating a bit in its name—while this may not be the most memorable or dramatic hike in the Hudson Valley, sometimes a low-key stroll around a pleasant woodland lake is just what a morning calls for. Lacking the serious elevation change of other, more mountainous hikes in the area, Wonder Lake is ideal for an all-ages outing, with just enough up and down to feel like you got some exercise.

**TOTAL DISTANCE**: 3.6 miles

**TYPE**: Lollipop

**HIKING TIME**: 2–3 hours

**TOTAL ELEVATION GAIN**: 550 feet

**MAXIMUM ELEVATION**: 1,065 feet

**DIFFICULTY**: Easy

## GETTING THERE

Heading east on I-84, take exit 17 for Ludingtonville Road, then turn left onto Ludingtonville Road. After 0.7 mile, make a slight right to stay on Ludingtonville Road. Drive for about another mile. The parking area, on your left, is surprisingly large and should hold at least two dozen cars.

## GPS SHORTCUT

Type "Wonder Lake, NY" into Google Maps and your GPS will navigate you a short distance south of the parking area. If arriving via I-84, you will pass the actual parking area before your GPS tells you that you have arrived.

## THE TRAIL

The trail begins from the northeastern end of the parking area. To start, you will be following the double blazes of the yellow trail and the teal-blazed Highlands Trail. The path tackles a moderate incline almost immediately as you make your way up into the hills of the park, with the steady hum of traffic from I-84 at your back. While the trails circumventing Wonder Lake have the look and feel of a tranquil wilderness park, the highway will be providing you

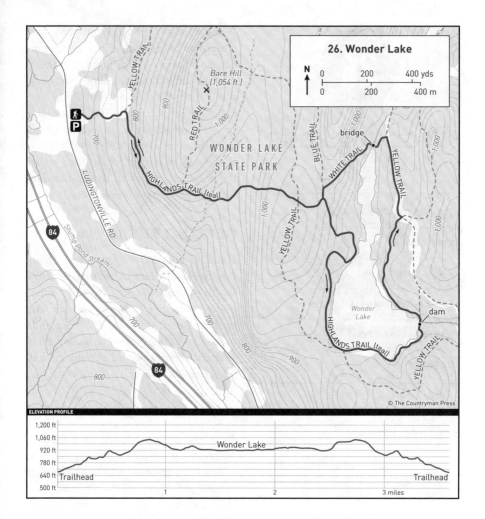

26. Wonder Lake

ELEVATION PROFILE

with white noise most of the time. Fortunately, your brain will soon tune it out!

Cross a stone wall running through the woods. Just beyond, 0.2 mile in, the trail splits. Here, the yellow trail takes a longer arcing route to the north, while the Highlands Trail cuts across the south-side of a hill and heads more directly toward Wonder Lake. Both trails will meet again before you even reach the lake, but for now, stay on the Highland Trail, following the teal blazes.

Following a short, moderate climb, you will arrive at another intersection at 0.5 mile. Here, a red trail running

from north to south connects the Highland Trail with the yellow trail that you just split from, running over Bare Hill in between. Continue straight, following the teal blazes. Soon you will hike over a series of stepping stones placed in the ground, and shortly after cross a small stream gully. Cross the stream and continue until you reach the intersection where the yellow trail reconnects with the Highlands Trail, at about 0.85 mile. Stay straight, still following the teal blazes.

Soon after, you will see a marker indicating the terminus of a white-blazed

WONDER LAKE

trail that heads northeast. You will eventually be returning on this trail. For now, continue still on the Highlands Trail, descending toward Wonder Lake. You will reach the lake just after the 1-mile mark. There are several rocks where you can have a good look out over the water. After briefly arcing away from the water, the teal trail will circle the lake for some time. At about 1.5 miles, the yellow trail once more reunites with the Highlands Trail, before veering off to make a broader circuit of the lake. Stay on the Highlands Trail, which keeps close to the lake shore.

At 1.85 miles, you will reach the southern end of the lake. The trail crosses over a wooden bridge next to a small dam. Just ahead, you will see a white trail which serves as a connector back to the familiar yellow trail. Once again, stay on the teal-blazed trail, still following the edge of the lake as you begin to head north.

At 2.2 miles, you will finally depart the Highlands Trail, turning left onto yellow, which follows a woods road for this section. Your foray onto yellow will be brief, however. At 2.4 miles, turn left onto the white trail. You are now at the narrow northern end of lake, where you will cross a wooden bridge over a small dam, as before. Enjoy the views out over the water before ascending briefly up a moderately steep hill.

At 2.65 miles, you will intersect with a blue-blazed trail that heads north and ends here. Continue on white, and just beyond, you will see the familiar teal blazes of the Highlands Trail. Turn right onto this trail, which is the same you hiked in on. This is the intersection just before you reached Wonder Lake, and now, returning west, you will cross paths will the yellow trail again in a short distance. Continue for another 0.85 mile, following the initial leg of the Highlands Trail again back to your car.

# Mt. Egbert from Depot Hill

**TOTAL DISTANCE**: 3 miles

**TYPE**: Out and Back

**HIKING TIME**: 2 hours

**TOTAL ELEVATION GAIN**: 260 feet

**MAXIMUM ELEVATION**: 1,230 feet

**DIFFICULTY**: Easy

Overall, Dutchess County may largely lack the dramatic landscapes and varied terrain found elsewhere in the area, but the presence of the Appalachian Trail cutting across the southern portion of the county makes for a number of quiet, stately trails. Mt. Egbert offers a nice view from a small rock ledge, but the appeal of this hike may be simply enjoying a scenic, and relatively easy portion of the Appalachian Trail. While there are a few dips up and down small hills, this short route should be accessible to hikers of all skill levels. You may happen to pass a few thru-hikers, but most likely, you'll have the woods to yourself for much of the time you're here.

## GETTING THERE

From the Taconic Parkway, take the NY-52 exit toward Fishkill / Carmel, then turn right onto NY-52 E. Drive for a little over a mile, then turn left onto NY-216 E. Continue for another 4.2 miles, then turn right onto Depot Hill Road. Drive for 2 miles on Depot Hill Road. The parking area will be on the left, under the large communications tower.

## GPS SHORTCUT

Type "Depot Hill MUA" into Google Maps and your GPS will navigate you to the appropriate parking area.

## THE TRAIL

From the parking area, look for blue blazes on a telephone pool marking the start of the hike. An access road continues straight from the road you drove in on; the trail will follow this road for a short distance before meeting with the Appalachian Trail.

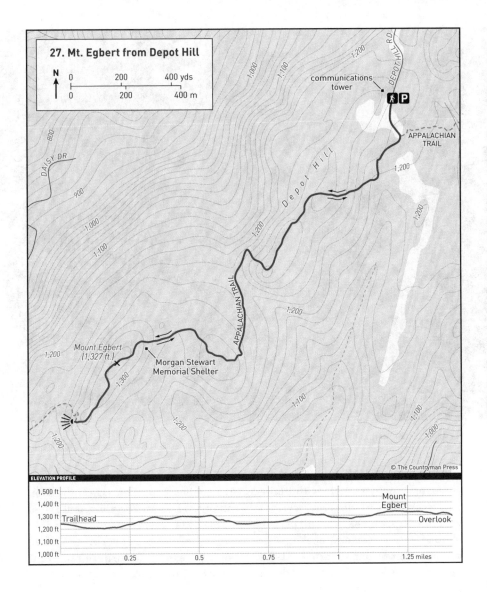

## 27. Mt. Egbert from Depot Hill

N

| 0 | 200 | 400 yds |
| 0 | 200 | 400 m |

communications tower

DEPOT HILL RD

APPALACHIAN TRAIL

DAISY DR

Depot Hill

APPALACHIAN TRAIL

Mount Egbert
(1,327 ft.)

Morgan Stewart
Memorial Shelter

© The Countryman Press

**ELEVATION PROFILE**

| 1,500 ft | | | | Mount |
| 1,400 ft | | | | Egbert |
| 1,300 ft | Trailhead | | | |
| 1,200 ft | | | | Overlook |
| 1,100 ft | | | | |
| 1,000 ft | 0.25 | 0.5 | 0.75 | 1 | 1.25 miles |

Walking down the road, the massive cell tower will loom above you from a hill to your right. After a few hundred feet, you will pass another access road heading uphill, toward the cell tower. Roughly 600 feet from the parking area, you will reach an intersection with the Appalachian Trail. Turn right, now following the white blazes of the AT.

The AT heads west, tackling a slight incline, but the trail is neither challenging nor strenuous. Enjoy the pleasant, meandering stroll through the woods, which remains surprisingly level for most of the hike, with only a few quick dips and climbs here and there.

At 0.6 mile, you will traverse a rocky area and briefly descend. A quarter

THE APPALACHIAN TRAIL AT DEPOT HILL

mile later the trail will once more send you over a rocky stretch, with limited glimpses of the sprawling countryside to your left. At 1.2 miles, you will pass the Morgan Stewart Memorial shelter, where you will often encounter thru-hikers hiking the entire Appalachian Trail during the spring and summer.

Continue on the trail past the shelter. At 1.5 miles, you will arrive at the summit of Mt. Egbert. The viewpoint is just off the peak, where the trail descends to a rocky ledge looking northwest. When you are ready to return, retrace your steps back to the parking area.

# Nuclear Lake

**TOTAL DISTANCE**: 4.3 miles

**TYPE**: Lollipop

**HIKING TIME**: 2.5 hours

**TOTAL ELEVATION GAIN**: 300 feet

**MAXIMUM ELEVATION**: 700 feet

**DIFFICULTY**: Easy

Let's be perfectly up front with this one: unfortunately, Nuclear Lake got its name for the exact reasons you're worried it might have. Yes, there was an accident at a nuclear lab here, several decades ago. But—wait, hey, where are you going? Come back!

Look, it's all fine now. Everything's fine. This is a great hike if you want to walk a peaceful section of the Appalachian Trail, enjoy views over a beautiful lake, spot ducks with a perfectly standard number of heads, or test out your brand new Geiger counter. It's perfectly safe to hike around Nuclear Lake these days, but if the name happens to scare off everyone else, so much the better: you'll just get to experience some solitude on this picturesque loop hike.

Here's the story: in 1959, a private research facility licensed by the government to experiment with bomb-grade uranium and plutonium, United Nuclear Corp., opened its doors next to the lake. UNC operated at this site until 1972, when a chemical explosion unleashed radioactive plutonium dust on the area. The explosion was powerful enough to blow out two windows in the experimental nuclear research lab, but fortunately, the incident went no further than that, and no one in the area was harmed. The National Park Service purchased the land in 1979. Soon after, the site earned a clean bill of health and was opened to the public for hiking. Nowadays, you'd never guess that this was the site of anything so dramatic, if it weren't for the name. Peaceful and scenic, Nuclear Lake is often said to be one of the most picturesque hikes along the Appalachian Trail.

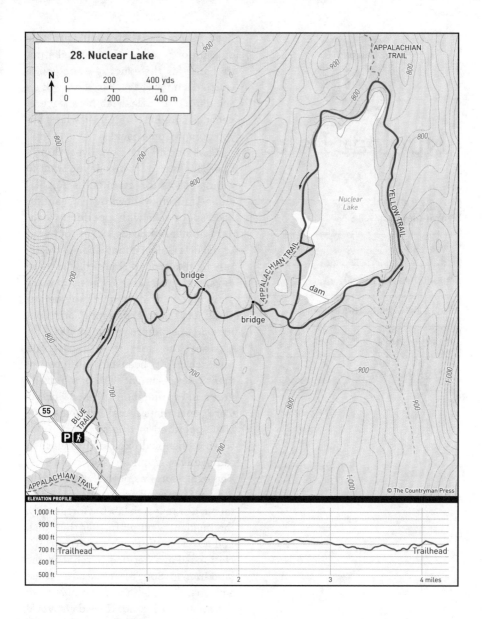

## GETTING THERE

The parking area for the Nuclear Lake trailhead is located on the north side of State Rte. 55 E, about 9.5 miles east of the Taconic State Parkway. The parking area is small, with room for only a handful of cars.

## GPS SHORTCUT

Type "Nuclear Lake Municipal Parking Area" into Google Maps and your GPS will navigate you to the appropriate parking area.

## THE TRAIL

A small foot trail heads into the woods on the right side of the parking area, marked by blue blazes. A short distance down the path, you will pass under power lines, and soon after the blue trail ends at an intersection with the white-blazed Appalachian Trail. The AT heading southwest makes a sharp right turn, while the trail going northeast continues nearly straight-on from your original path.

Continue straight onto the AT. A little under a quarter mile from the trailhead, you will pass the Beekman Uplands Trail to your left, marked by blue blazes. Continue straight, following the white blazes of the Appalachian Trail. In another quarter mile, you will descend past a large rock outcropping, then walk over an area that may be muddy depending on the time of year. At 0.6 mile, you will cross a stream, then hike to the right of it for a short distance.

Just under the 1-mile mark, you will cross the first of two wooden bridges over a stream. The second arrives about a quarter mile further down the trail. Immediately after the second bridge, the trail reaches a split. The Appalachian Trail continues to the left, while a yellow-blazed trail makes its ways up a rocky area to your right. This yellow trail completes a loop of the lake, partly running along the AT.

Take the yellow trail to the right, hiking up the rocks alongside the stream, where a small waterfall is obscured by a large boulder. Soon, at 1.3 miles, you will reach a T-intersection with an access road. Turn right onto the road, then look for the yellow blazes to reappear and make an immediate left, back onto the yellow trail.

About a mile and a half into the hike, you will reach the start of a rocky area that runs along the east side of Nuclear Lake. Soon, as you approach the southern end of the lake, you will spot a rugged side trail that leads down to the shore of the lake. You may choose to take this side trail, to gain a closer vantage of the lake, or continue on the yellow, which runs along the rocky ridge, slightly higher up. The side trail is not blazed, but is relatively easy to follow, and you will see the yellow blazes of the main trail above you on the ridge again after walking along the lake for a short distance.

Back on the main yellow path, the trail veers away from the lake briefly, before crossing another creek around the 2-mile mark. Hike past a stone wall as you near the north end of the lake. Around 2.2 miles, you will encounter the Appalachian Trail once more, and here the yellow trail ends. Turn left, now following the AT south around the west side of the lake.

Around 2.5 miles, you will return to the lakeshore, and a quarter mile later, enter a small clearing. Soon after, look for a broad side trail leading back toward the lake. Take this path for another glimpse over the lake, then follow another broad grassy side path to your left. You will soon hike along the southern end of the lake, and the fenced-off area where the nuclear facility once stood. Don your hazmat suit, test out your Geiger counter, and continue past the lake on the access road that you encountered earlier in the hike.

Soon you will see the yellow-blazed trail that you hiked on previously, at the start of the loop around the lake. Turn right onto the yellow trail. In about a tenth of a mile, you will descend from

NUCLEAR LAKE

the rocks next to the large boulder and rejoin the Appalachian Trail. Ahead of you is the second of the two bridges you crossed earlier.

Continue straight on the Appalachian Trail, now retracing your steps back to the beginning of the hike. Be mindful of the intersection with the first blue-blazed trail that leads back to the parking area—if you miss this intersection and continue on the AT past the power lines, you will find yourself on a whole new hiking adventure. From there, retrace your steps back to your car.

**29**

# Cat Rocks

**TOTAL DISTANCE**: 1.9 miles

**TYPE**: Out and Back

**HIKING TIME**: 1.5 hours

**TOTAL ELEVATION GAIN**: 520 feet

**MAXIMUM ELEVATION**: 1,080 feet

**DIFFICULTY**: Easy

A hike to Cat Rocks (assuming you aren't thru-hiking the Appalachian Trail when you arrive here) is a perfect "Goldilocks" hike: it's not too much or too little of any one thing, and thus it's a perfect little excursion when you're looking for something right in that middle sweet spot. Quiet woods with mossy stones and babbling brooks? Check. An uphill climb to the top of the mountain? Check. But an uphill climb that isn't *too* challenging or strenuous, and short enough that you can reasonably complete it with hikers of any skill level or disposition? Yes, check. Also a check: at under 2 miles round trip, it won't be hard to fit this hike into anyone's weekend schedule. Great vista at the top, more than enough to justify the mile-long climb uphill? Of course.

But wait: there's more! Aside from those agreeable qualities, there's the fact that you'll be following the historic Appalachian Trail. And that one of the most famous trees on the AT is found right by the parking area: the Dover Oak, the largest white oak tree in NY state, and something of a tree-lebrity for AT hikers. Estimated to be around 150 years old, the Dover Oak is thought to be the largest oak tree on the Appalachian Trail.

## GETTING THERE

From the Taconic State Parkway, take the Beekman Road exit toward Hopewell Junction, then turn left onto Beekman Road. Continue for 3.1 miles, then turn right onto Beekman-Poughquag Rd. / Main St. Continue for 2.1 miles.

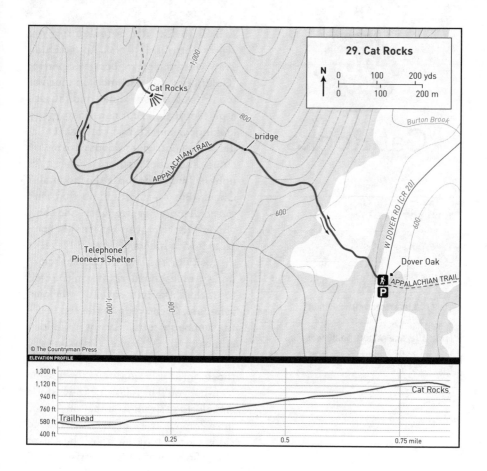

29. Cat Rocks

**ELEVATION PROFILE**

## GPS SHORTCUT

Type "The Dover Oak" into Google Maps and your GPS will navigate you to the appropriate parking area.

## THE TRAIL

From the parking area next to the giant Dover Oak, carefully cross the street. If you take the Appalachian Trail on the same side of the road as the parking lot, you will be heading the wrong direction. Look up after crossing, and you will see Cat Rocks—an area of rocky outcroppings on the ridge—looming above you.

Head down the steps, and cross wooden boards laid into the ground to navigate a wet patch of ground. After this series of boardwalks, you will soon head uphill over a rocky area. After this brief rock scramble, the trail begins a steady, somewhat strenuous incline. At 0.3 mile, cross a bridge over a stream before continuing your ascent. Half a mile in, you will see a blue trail diverging left toward a lean-to. This is the Telephone Pioneers shelter. If you wish to visit this lean-to, take this side trail before returning to the white blazes of the Appalachian Trail and heading to the right, now walking northeast.

Continue uphill again. The trail marches up an incline fairly steadily for most of the way. At 0.9 mile, the trail begins to level as you near the

THE DOVER OAK

peak of West Mountain. Just before the 1-mile mark, you will spot side paths to your right, leading to the Cat Rocks viewpoint. A mix of farmland and suburbs sprawls out before you, looking east and south, toward Pawling, Wingdale, and Connecticut beyond. The rocks themselves provide plenty of perches for relaxing with a picnic or just basking in the sun (like a cat, you might even say).

When you are ready, return to the Appalachian Trail and retrace your steps back to your car.

# 30

# Red Wing Recreation Area

**TOTAL DISTANCE**: 2 miles

**TYPE**: Out and Back

**HIKING TIME**: 1.5 hours

**TOTAL ELEVATION GAIN**: 620 feet

**MAXIMUM ELEVATION**: 730 feet

**DIFFICULTY**: Easy

If nearby Cat Rocks (Hike #29) is right in the middle of the Goldilocks scale of ambition and reward, then Red Wing Recreation Area offers similar qualities, but dialed down a few notches on the "easy" side of things. At 2 miles round trip, an excursion here won't eat up too much of your afternoon, nor will you have to work all that hard to reach the park's 700-foot-high summit. With a number of benches and tables stationed around Red Wing's overlook, this is a great place for a picnic. With the presence of various communications towers looming behind you at the top, there's no mistaking this for a serious backwoods excursion, but the humble ambitions of this hike doesn't demand such trappings. This is simply a nice stroll in the woods with a surprisingly good view to reward you at the end. Sometimes, that's all one really needs.

## GETTING THERE

The parking area is located approximately 2 miles east of the Taconic State Parkway, off of NY-55. Driving east on NY-55, turn left onto NY-82 N. Continue for 0.2 mile, and the parking area will be on your left, at what looks like an access road closed off by a large metal gate. Across the street, you will see a sign for Red Wing Sand & Gravel.

## GPS SHORTCUT

Type "Red Wing Recreation Area - Hudson Valley Admirals, Lagrangeville, NY" into Google Maps and your GPS will navigate you to the appropriate parking area. Of note, the Red Wing Recreation Area should not be confused with nearby Red Wing Park, which is located in East Fishkill.

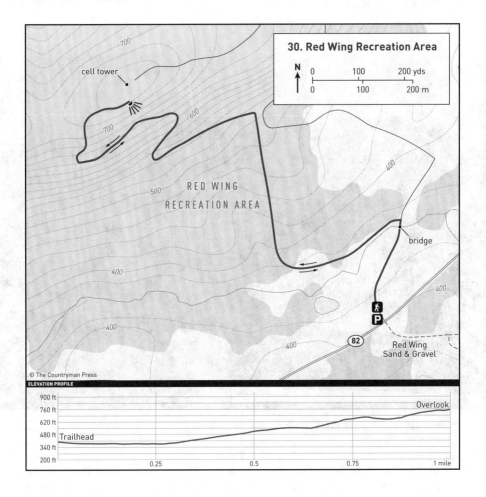

**ELEVATION PROFILE**

Overlook

Trailhead

900 ft
760 ft
620 ft
480 ft
340 ft
200 ft

0.25    0.5    0.75    1 mile

## THE TRAIL

From the parking area, cross around the gate and walk down the road. A giant stone sign marks the entrance just inside the gate. Soon you will cross a bridge over a stream. Just beyond the bridge, look for the blazes indicating the footpath where the trail cuts into the woods, to your left.

The trail is marked by red blazes, and for the much of the hike, extensive signs posted on trees will serve to steer you as well. At this intersection, however, the signs are actually more confusing

than helpful (at least as of the time of this writing). Several signs suggest to continue to the right through the woods, along a path that will shortly bring you back out onto the road that you just left. Here, the signs seem to indicate that you should cross the road, and guide you down a trail on the other side. Ignore these signs, as the trail you want to follow actually heads left immediately upon entering the woods. Upon first leaving the road to take this footpath, you will see a broad, straight trail running for some distance before ending at what looks like a wooden barrier. While

THE VIEW FROM THE TOP AT RED WING RECREATION AREA

it is unclear based on the signage, this is in fact the path you want to take.

Walk down this straight trail toward the wooden roadblock. You should be walking parallel to a stream at this point, and just before the roadblock, a path will diverge to the right. Take this trail, heading uphill. At 0.3 mile, the trail begins a moderate ascent. Soon you will reach a 4-way intersection. Stay straight. In another quarter mile, you will arrive at an intersection adjacent to a gravel road. Ignore the road and continue on the footpath; just ahead, the trail Ts, and you will head to the left.

Around 0.6 mile, the trail begins a steeper ascent of the hill. Through the trees above, you will soon spot a cell tower on top of the ridgeline. At 0.8 mile, switchback around, heading toward the crest of the ridge, before arriving at an intersection shortly after. Here, directional signs have been placed on a tree to steer you: to the left, the path heads toward Velie Road, while to the right, you will reach the overlook. Head right. At 1 mile, you will arrive at the overlook. Benches have been set up before the vista, while the cell tower looms behind you.

When you are ready to return, retrace your steps back to the parking area.

# Dover Stone Church

**TOTAL DISTANCE**: 2.6 miles

**TYPE**: Out and Back

**HIKING TIME**: 1.5 hours

**TOTAL ELEVATION GAIN**: 550 feet

**MAXIMUM ELEVATION**: 775 feet

**DIFFICULTY**: Easy

Many visitors to Dover Stone Church explore only the most notable feature of this park: the dramatic, cathedral cavern housing a waterfall for which the site is named. Such an abbreviated out-and-back version of this hike would be one of the shortest hikes covered by this guide, and yet there's no questioning the incredible payoff. Any way you look at it, the Dover Stone Church is one of the region's most unique places. But recent expansions to the property have added over 5 miles of new trails looping around the ridge behind the cavern, allowing hikers to extend their visit and take a pleasant, quiet woods walk to a scenic overlook.

The "Church" itself may seem utterly out of a place in this area of New York, a geological anomaly even beyond its unique shape. Leading up to the dramatically framed waterfall and cavern, a vibrant, mossy gorge seems as if it must have been stolen from somewhere in the Pacific Northwest. The cavern itself is like no other waterfall around, though more famous (and much taller) waterfalls like Bash Bish and Kaaterskill receive considerably more tourism. For now, the Dover Stone Church is a bit of a local secret, and you'll be delighted to have discovered it. The trail leading up to the cavern becomes quite intimate with the brook next to it at times, and visitors should exercise extra caution at all times. During winter or early spring, the trail may be unsafe without the use of traction devices.

## GETTING THERE

Dover Stone Church is located in the town of Dover Plains, on NY-22. While there is, unfortunately, no parking area for Dover Stone Church itself, several

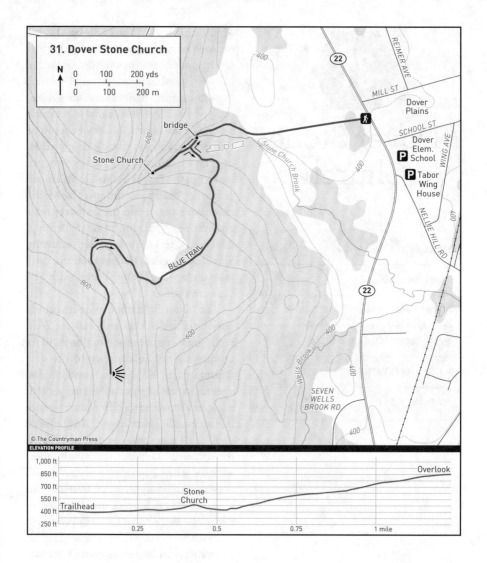

31. Dover Stone Church

N

0    100    200 yds
0    100    200 m

bridge

Stone Church

BLUE TRAIL

Stone Church Brook

Wells Brook

REIMER AVE

22

MILL ST

Dover
Plains

SCHOOL ST

Dover
Elem.
School

Tabor
Wing
House

WING AVE

NELLIE HILL RD

22

SEVEN
WELLS
BROOK RD

600

800

600

400

400

400

400

400

400

© The Countryman Press

**ELEVATION PROFILE**

1,000 ft
850 ft
700 ft
550 ft
400 ft
250 ft

Overlook

Stone
Church

Trailhead

0.25      0.5      0.75      1 mile

businesses in Dover Plains close to the trailhead allow hikers to park in their lots during their visit.

The following locations allow parking for Dover Stone Church: Dover Elementary School (when school is not in session—after 3 pm during the week, on weekends, and holidays); The Tabor Wing House; Silver Screen Deli; Four Brothers Restaurant; and La Famiglia Restaurant. The trailhead begins up a hill off a private driveway, near the traffic light; while there may appear to be parking spots next to the trailhead, visitors are not allowed to park here.

## GPS SHORTCUT

Type the name of any of the businesses listed above into Google Maps and your GPS will navigate you to the appropriate parking area.

## THE TRAIL

From NY-22, the trailhead is located at the first right after the traffic light going south, up a gravel driveway. The right-of-way road crosses private property, so please respect the landowners. Follow the driveway uphill toward the oddly shaped sign for Dover Stone Church (while the sign may look as if it's cut in the shape of a leaf, it's actually the shape of the Stone Church cave opening). At the top of the hill is a small parking area, though parking is not permitted here for hikers.

Beyond the sign, a set of stairs leads back downhill, to a scenic pathway between fields. Rows of trees parallel to the path make the trail here resemble something you'd encounter while exploring a city park rather than a backwoods adventure. Cross to the other side, where the path climbs up another set of steps. You will begin walking on a more traditional hiking trail, and pass a stream to your left. Cross through a wire fence, and a quarter mile from the road, arrive at a large information sign. Here, you can find more information on the history of the site, as well as a trail map.

Turn left and follow the path. Very soon you will approach a shady clearing where the Stone Church Brook emerges from its gorge. A bridge crosses over the water, and you will arrive at a trail sign pointing out the three trails that head to your left, into the woods. To your right, the path continues into the gorge, toward the Stone Church.

Follow the brook as the trail heads into the gorge. In places, the trail is only a narrow series of stepping stones to the left of the water. While you should be extra careful with your footing, especially during times when the trail may be wet or icy, the path is not especially difficult.

Continue deeper into the gorge, enjoying your mossy, cool surroundings, and soon you will see the Stone Church ahead. Just under half a mile from the trailhead, you will arrive at the opening of the cave. At the entrance, massive metamorphic rocks converge in a unique diagonal, shaping the cave entrance with the rough appearance of a church's cathedral window. Inside the cavern is a rock ledge known as the "Pulpit," and a 30-foot waterfall cascading into a pool of water in the Church and out into the gorge. Due to the pool inside the cavern, it may be difficult to enter the Stone Church itself without getting—your feet, at the least—very wet.

When you are done attending the Church, return to the intersection about a tenth of a mile down the trail. Here the directional trail sign points out the red, yellow, and blue trails awaiting you, now to your right. Follow these trails up the hill. After crossing through a fence, you will come to another intersection. The yellow- and blue-blazed trails make a steady climb up the hill to your right.

Turn right, and begin to climb. The ascent is moderately strenuous, but not difficult. In a few hundred feet the trail will begin to level out once more. Pass through an old stone wall as the trail bends to the right. Just under a mile into the hike—including your out-and-back to the Stone Church—you will come to another intersection, where the yellow Upper Loop Trail splits left. Take the blue trail to the right.

At one mile, the trail bends left up a small incline. Continue through the woods for another quarter mile, reach-

THE TRAIL TO THE DOVER STONE CHURCH

ing the overlook at 1.3 miles. Here, you can enjoy somewhat obstructed views over Dover Plains and east, toward Connecticut.

When you are ready to return, retrace your steps back to the intersection in the clearing, then continue over the bridge, away from the Stone Church. At the information sign, turn right, then follow the path out to the driveway and NY-22.

# 32

# Mills Norrie State Park

| | |
|---|---|
| **TOTAL DISTANCE**: 4.5 miles | |
| **TYPE**: Loop | |
| **HIKING TIME**: 3–4 hours | |
| **TOTAL ELEVATION GAIN**: 270 feet | |
| **MAXIMUM ELEVATION**: 145 feet | |
| **DIFFICULTY**: Easy | |

A hike at Mills Norrie is really a two-for-one deal: Margaret Lewis Norrie State Park is situated just next to Ogden Mills and Ruth Livingston Mills Memorial State Park, and the 1,000 acres of the two parks together are as nice of a hiking destination as they are overly verbose. Hereafter, we'll simply refer to the two parks together as Mills Norrie State Park, as it is commonly called. Situated on the banks of the Hudson River, the trails here are mostly level, and make for an easy day of hiking, but the views are stunning despite the lack of a summit. A large field sloping downhill toward the water opens up views of the Esopus Meadows lighthouse and the Catskills almost at once, and the vistas only continue from there. With a unique footpath hugging a cliff line right above the Hudson, a trek around numerous historic buildings, a scenic campground, and an optional extension to visit the Norrie Point Environmental Center, Mills Norrie is one of the finest parks along the Hudson River.

At the center of the Ogden and Ruth Livingston Mills State Park is the Staatsburgh State Historic Site, or Mills Mansion, the Beaux-Arts style country home of Ogden Mills and his wife, Ruth Livingston Mills. The Gilded Age mansion, completed in 1896, features more than 60 rooms, with 14 bathrooms and 23 fireplaces. The house and nearly 200 acres of land were donated to New York state in 1938. The mansion is open for tours, programs, and special events, with a small entrance fee.

## GETTING THERE

The parking area for Mills Norrie is located at the northern end of the park, by Mills Mansion. The entrance is located off of US-9N, about 10 miles

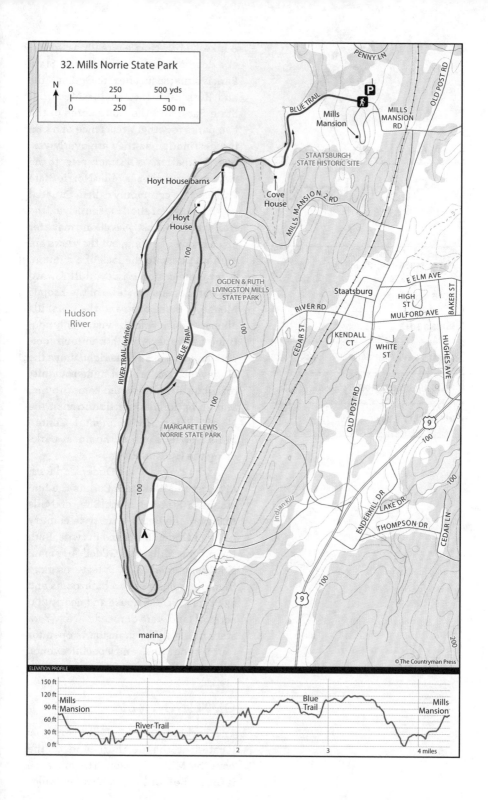

32. Mills Norrie State Park

N

| 0 | 250 | 500 yds |
| 0 | 250 | 500 m |

PENNY LN

OLD POST RD

P

BLUE TRAIL

Mills Mansion

MILLS MANSION RD

STAATSBURGH STATE HISTORIC SITE

Hoyt House barns

Cove House

MILLS MANSION 2 RD

Hoyt House

100

OGDEN & RUTH LIVINGSTON MILLS STATE PARK

Staatsburg

E ELM AVE

HIGH ST

BAKER ST

MULFORD AVE

Hudson River

RIVER RD

RIVER TRAIL (white)

BLUE TRAIL

100

CEDAR ST

KENDALL CT

WHITE ST

HUGHES AVE

100

OLD POST RD

MARGARET LEWIS NORRIE STATE PARK

100

9

100

Indian Kill

ENDERKILL DR

LAKE DR

THOMPSON DR

CEDAR LN

100

100

100

9

marina

200

© The Countryman Press

ELEVATION PROFILE

150 ft
120 ft
90 ft
60 ft
30 ft
0 ft

Mills Mansion

River Trail

Blue Trail

Mills Mansion

1
2
3
4 miles

north of Poughkeepsie. From 9N, turn left onto Old Post Rd., then drive for another 1.2 miles. Turn left onto Mills Mansion Rd., then turn right into the parking area.

## GPS SHORTCUT

Type "Mills Mansion, Staatsburg, NY" into Google Maps and your GPS will navigate you to the appropriate trailhead.

## THE TRAIL

From the parking area, walk toward the hill, with the mansion above you. Just before the intersection where the road leads up the hill, the path begins to your right, following the paved roadway that heads downhill. Two Greek columns mark the entrance to the road, as well as blue trail blazes.

Follow this road as it heads toward the Hudson River. In a short distance, it will veer to the south, along the lawn below the mansion, before running parallel to the river itself. Here, you will catch your first views out over the Hudson, with the Esopus Meadows Lighthouse and the Catskill Mountains visible in the distance. At about 0.25 mile, you will see a small stone building down the hill to your right, right on the water's edge. This is an old power house, accessible by descending a flight of stone steps.

At 0.4 mile, you will see an old house before you, with an open lawn to your right. This is the Cove House, and the road splits in several directions here. The footpath trail that you will want to follow leaves the roadway and crosses the lawn, as indicated by the blue blazes. Follow the trail as it heads across the lawn and then downhill, toward the river. At the riverbank, the trail passes only a few feet from the water, and here

you will have an excellent view out over the Hudson, perfectly framing both the distant mountains and the picturesque lighthouse on its diminutive island.

The trail heads back uphill slightly, as more structures become visible through the trees. This is the Hoyt House barn complex. Here, at 0.6 mile, the trail splits. Take the white-blazed trail to your right, which sticks close to the river's edge. The blue-blazed trail heads deeper into the woods, away from the river—you will return on this trail later, at the end of the loop.

Follow the white trail as it banks left to run parallel to the river, now following a ridge with a steep drop off to the water below. The trail here is quite dramatic and unique for the area, following the ridge above the water for some distance. Be very careful of your footing and enjoy this unique trek alongside the Hudson.

At 1 mile, the trail heads back into the woods briefly, before returning to the ridge-edge a quarter mile later. At 1.3 miles, you will see an abandoned shack covered in graffiti to your right. Soon after, you will come to an open clearing, with large stone walls to your left indicating the presence of another abandoned structure. A portion of the clearing by the water is fenced in, and there are picnic tables here for you to break.

Down a hill from here is another, even larger picnic area. Here, you will find a sizeable wooden pavilion, with more picnic tables and grills.

At 1.85 miles, the trail ascends briefly uphill, and just past 2 miles, you will reach the campground area. The campground is open from May to October, so for much of the year, you will want to be courteous and quiet through this part of the hike. The trail first passes a series of

MILLS NORRIE OFFERS AN EXCELLENT VIEW OF THE HUDSON RIVER, WITH THE ESOPUS MEADOWS LIGHTHOUSE BACKED BY THE CATSKILL MOUNTAINS

cabins perched on the hill, overlooking the Hudson. Hike along a steep bank before the trail cuts to the left, looping back around and heading north once more. You will be able to see the Norrie Point Marina through the trees.

Follow the white blazes as the trail heads back into the woods, passing an information center at 2.4 miles. Here, take the paved road to the right, away from the campground. The road forks, with the left fork heading toward a series of camping sites. Keep to the right, and soon the roadways merge once again as you leave the campground behind. You will see blue blazes marking the way.

At 2.7 miles, turn left at the intersection in the road, keeping an eye out for the blue blazes that mark the trail. Just down the road, a foot trail enters the woods. Take this path, following the blue markers. At 3.15 miles, you will cross another road, and soon after meet an intersection with a green-blazed trail heading to the right. Stay on the blue trail, to the left. Soon after, at 3.5 miles, the same intersection setup is repeated: ignore the green trail to your right, and stay left on the blue trail.

At 3.7 miles, you will reach the Hoyt House. This property is fenced in and off-limits to hikers. Continuing on, you will soon see another abandoned property through the woods. This is the old Hoyt House barn complex, which you passed earlier as the trail originally split into its loop, along the ridge. Here, you will return to the edge of the Hudson. Turn right, and follow the path uphill, returning to the paved road, with Mills Mansion visible in the distance. Follow the paved path back uphill to the parking area and your car.

# Ferncliff Forest

**TOTAL DISTANCE**: 1.25 miles

**TYPE**: Out and Back

**HIKING TIME**: 1 hour

**TOTAL ELEVATION GAIN**: 250 feet

**MAXIMUM ELEVATION**: 180 feet

**DIFFICULTY**: Easy

It would be odd to complain that a park contains too many trails, though Ferncliff Forest may push the boundary. Dozens of short paths weave and bend around this small park, often completing parallel trajectories to their immediate neighbors for no discernible reason. This short hike to the fire tower and back can easily be extended into a full loop of the park, or something more intricate and meandering, though you should obviously be very careful when wandering the woods here. Even with a map, it can be quite easy to get lost. (Some of the trails are present on Google Maps, but many others are missing.) For most, a short and simple trip up to the fire tower will be the most appealing approach; the views from the tower toward the Catskills are exceptional. On the way back, stop by the scenic pond to relax or enjoy a picnic.

## GETTING THERE

Ferncliff Forest is located about 2 miles north of the town of Rhinebeck, NY. From Rhinebeck, turn onto Montgomery St. where it splits with US Rte. 9, heading north. Drive for half a mile, then veer left onto Mt. Rutsen Rd. where the road forks. Continue for another 1.2 miles, then you will arrive at the Ferncliff Forest parking lot, on the left.

## GPS SHORTCUT

Type "Ferncliff Forest" into Google Maps and your GPS will navigate you to the appropriate parking area.

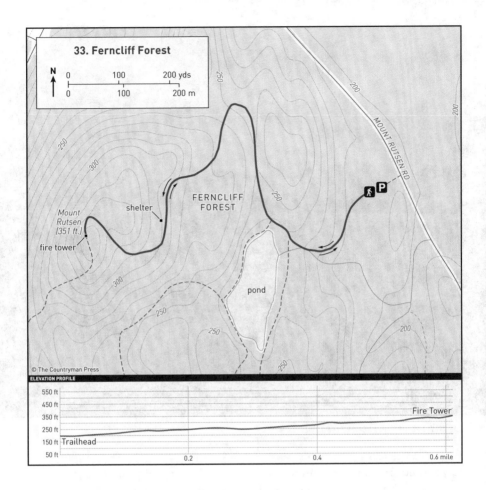

33. Ferncliff Forest

N

| 0 | 100 | 200 yds |
| 0 | 100 | 200 m |

250

200

MOUNT RUTSEN RD

200

FERNCLIFF
FOREST

250

shelter

300

250

Mount
Rutsen
(351 ft.)

fire tower

300

pond

250

250

250

250

200

© The Countryman Press

ELEVATION PROFILE

| 550 ft | | | |
| 450 ft | | | |
| 350 ft | | | Fire Tower |
| 250 ft | | | |
| 150 ft | Trailhead | | |
| 50 ft | 0.2 | 0.4 | 0.6 mile |

## THE TRAIL

From the parking area, cross around the gate and start down the trail next to the information kiosk. The trail begins on a wide gravel road, with a mild uphill grade. Soon you will pass a large, hilly field to your left, before reaching a pond and a camping area with a pavilion and several shelters.

Several trails will branch off from the one you are on as you continue, but the first several intersections are well marked. The first shelter points you toward the fire tower itself, and

another sign beyond indicates where the trail that you should follow enters the woods. At 0.3 mile you will pass a trail marked by red and white blazes to your right, but keep left to stay on the yellow trail. Immediately after, a green trail will head into the woods to your right. Again stay left, as yellow makes a hard turn.

A few more trails will branch off to your right as you continue, but stay on the main yellow path. Soon you will pass a lean-to next to the trail. At 0.6 mile, you will come to a trail that heads steeply up a short hill to the fire tower,

THE VIEW FROM THE FERNCLIFF FIRE TOWER

to your left. Head up the hill to reach the tower. The viewing platform is open all year round and offers an excellent view out over the Hudson River, the Kingston-Rhinecliff Bridge, and the Catskill Mountains.

When you are ready, retrace your steps to return to your car.

# 34

# Stissing Mountain

| | |
|---|---|
| **TOTAL DISTANCE**: 2.2 miles | |
| **TYPE**: Loop | |
| **HIKING TIME**: 2 hours | |
| **TOTAL ELEVATION GAIN**: 920 feet | |
| **MAXIMUM ELEVATION**: 1400 feet | |
| **DIFFICULTY**: Moderate | |

The Hudson Valley contains a surprising number of fire towers—six are covered by this guidebook, with five more featured in *50 Hikes in the Catskills*—together offering commanding views of nearly the entire region. Stissing Mountain, located just to the south of the town of Pine Plains, looks out over the northern tip of Dutchess County and southern Columbia County. Surrounded by (mostly) flat land, Stissing Mountain's long profile dominates the landscape around it. The hike to the tower can be done as a moderately strenuous loop, with a short stretch of scrambling up a rocky ridgeline. Hikers wishing to make a full day of this adventure can also explore the Thompson Pond Preserve, located at the foot of the mountain. The swamp around the pond is home to a diverse collection of wildlife, and the pond itself forms the headwaters of a major tributary of the Hudson River.

## GETTING THERE

From the Taconic State Parkway, take the NY-199 exit toward Pine Plains / Red Hook, then turn right onto NY-199 E. Continue for about 6 miles, then turn right onto Lake Rd. Drive for another 1.4 miles. The parking area will be on the left.

## GPS SHORTCUT

Type "Stissing Mountain Parking Area" into Google Maps and your GPS will navigate you to the appropriate parking area. Note that typing just "Stissing Mountain" into Google Maps will not lead you to the correct parking area for this hike.

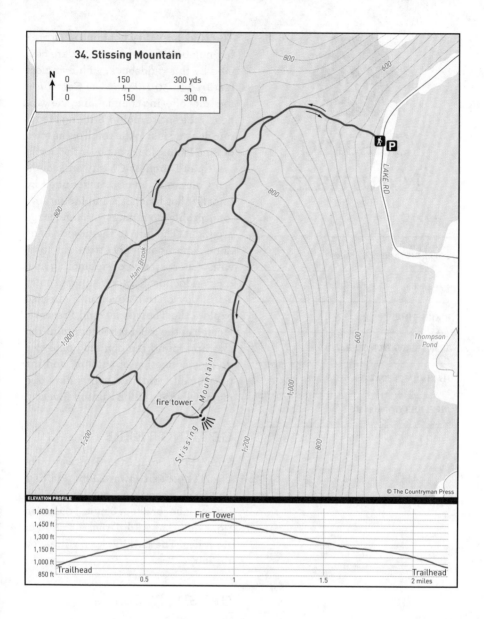

**34. Stissing Mountain**

0      150      300 yds
0      150      300 m

N

LAKE RD

Thompson Pond

fire tower

Stissing Mountain

© The Countryman Press

**ELEVATION PROFILE**

| | | | |
|---|---|---|---|
| 1,600 ft | | Fire Tower | |
| 1,450 ft | | | |
| 1,300 ft | | | |
| 1,150 ft | | | |
| 1,000 ft | | | |
| 850 ft | Trailhead | | Trailhead |

0.5          1          1.5          2 miles

## THE TRAIL

From the parking area, carefully cross
the road to the gated trailhead. Cross
through the opening in the wire fence
gate, and you will begin uphill almost
immediately. The climb is moderate and
steady—a good indication that you'll get

a solid workout, in spite of this hike's
short length!

This initial ascent will have you slog-
ging up through a gully, and soon, you'll
pass an area with several small waterfalls as a stream runs along the trail. The
trail in this initial section is often quite
wet, so be mindful of your footing. At

THE STISSING MOUNTAIN FIRE TOWER RISES TO 90 FEET, UNCOMMONLY HIGH FOR A FIRE TOWER IN THE REGION

about 0.2 mile, you will cross over the stream and continue uphill.

At 0.3 mile, the trail forks. Both paths will bring you to the fire tower, though the difficulty you will face on the way up will be determined by the route you take, and your preference for a steep up or downhill. The path to the left is shorter and steeper, while the path to the right is slightly longer, but tackles the hill at a more moderate grade. It's generally safer to climb steep sections than it is to descend them, so for the purposes of this guide, go left at the fork.

Over the next half mile, you will climb the ridge to the tower, with the forest opening up around you and occasional glimpses of the valley through the trees. The trail is rocky and fairly steep in sections, but not to the point of a full-fledged scramble. Take your time on this challenging section and you'll be at the top fairly quickly.

You will reach the fire tower around the 1-mile point, just past an area with a number of side trails weaving around the ridgeline and summit. This fire tower is exceptionally tall—90 feet, much higher than the 60 feet that most fire towers reach—and thus often extremely windy. Of course, due to the tower's height, you will begin to enjoy views out over the treeline from only halfway up, and a wide-open panorama of the northern Hudson Valley will sprawl out before you from the cabin of the tower. To the northeast, Pine Plains is visible in the near distance, with the Taconic Ridge beyond. Immediately below you, Thompson Pond stretches out before the land turns into farms. And to the west, in the distance, the Catskills can be glimpsed on the clearest days. Enjoy this spectacular view before continuing back on the second leg of the loop.

To the west of the tower, you will see a trail heading downhill and back into the woods. (This trail will be to your right, if facing the tower from the direction by which you originally approached.) Climb downhill. Shortly after you will come to a T-intersection. Head to the right. Climb down a rocky area, then cross a series of logs placed into the ground to form a bridge over a wet area. Continue downhill, and about a quarter mile from the tower, you will reach an overlook to your left with views out to the Catskills.

Shortly beyond, a fork in the trail doubles back to your left; ignore this side path and continue straight. Cross a stream, then begin a steady downhill through another gully. Soon after you will come to the original fork of the main loop. Here, continue straight, heading downhill. After making the stream crossing once more, you will notice another side trail heading left, away from the parking area. Stay to the right, and continue along your original route to the trailhead. Cross the road and return to the parking area.

# Poets' Walk

| | |
|---|---|
| **TOTAL DISTANCE**: 2.4 miles | |
| **TYPE**: Loop | |
| **HIKING TIME**: 1.5–2 hours | |
| **TOTAL ELEVATION GAIN**: 160 feet | |
| **MAXIMUM ELEVATION**: 205 feet | |
| **DIFFICULTY**: Easy | |

Well known and very popular among locals, don't expect to have Poets' Walk to yourself, especially if venturing here on a weekend. This gorgeous park—with its short, easy hiking trails and memorable wooden structures—draws the crowds even on winter days, but it only takes a few minutes to see why. With a grand pavilion of the same intricate, woven-wood design common across parks in the northeastern Hudson Valley, and a perfect view across the river to the Catskills from a sloping bucolic field, a stroll around Poets' Walk truly feels like you've stepped into a painting (or perhaps a . . . poem?). This spot has been inspiring Hudson Valley residents for many, many years: it's thought that Washington Irving conceived of "Rip Van Winkle" and his long slumber in the Catskill Mountains while gazing at those dramatic peaks from Poets' Walk.

The perfection of this site is no coincidence: all aspects of the park were carefully considered by landscape architect Hans Jacob Ehlers. Hired in 1849 by the Astor and Delano families, who lived on bordering estates, Ehlers was tasked with sculpting the land into a series of "outdoor rooms." This intention can be easily felt today, as everywhere you go at Poets' Walk, it seems as if some master painter has unfurled a new masterpiece in front of you.

## GETTING THERE

Poets' Walk is located just northeast of the Kingston-Rhinecliff Bridge. At the intersection of NY-199 and NY-103 / River Rd., drive north on NY-103 / River Rd. for half a mile. Turn left onto the entrance road for Poets' Walk.

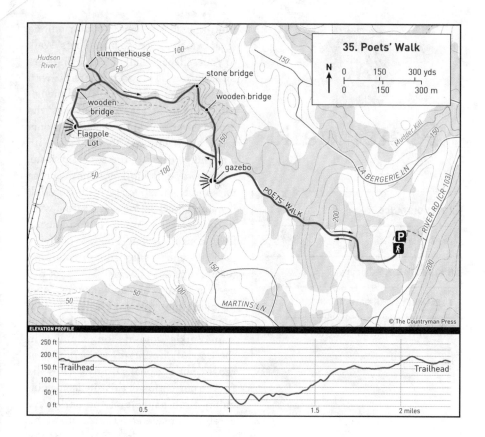

ELEVATION PROFILE

## GPS SHORTCUT

Type "Poets' Walk" into Google Maps and your GPS will navigate you to the appropriate parking area.

## THE TRAIL

From the parking area, walk toward the sign by the start of the trail, which offers a map of the property and information about Poets' Walk. The trail begins by making its way through a large hilly clearing. The trail here is broad, and while it is not marked by blazes, it is very easy to follow.

After a quarter of a mile, you will crest a small hill and pass by a wooden bench, fashioned in a signature style that you will see repeated with the benches and structures throughout the park. At 0.4 mile, the path passes through a wooded area briefly, before entering a large clearing. The main site of Poets' Walk awaits you just ahead: the large gazebo on the hill in this clearing is the primary destination for most visitors to the park.

Follow the path toward the gazebo, which you will reach at 0.6 mile. From this structure, perched on a hill, the Catskills are visible across the Hudson, and the Kingston-Rhinecliff Bridge spans the river to the south. This is an incredibly charming spot, and accordingly, it can be difficult to enjoy it without a crowd surrounding you. On a quiet weekday, this would be a lovely spot for a picnic.

From the gazebo, walk through the structure and turn right. The path follows the top of the hill for a short distance, passing several more wooden benches, which face out over the fields to the river. Soon, you will reach a trail intersection marked by signs. Turn left, following the sign for the Flagpole Lot. At 0.7 mile, the trail crosses an interesting hill, which runs like a ridge toward the Hudson. The trail continues along the crest of this hill ridge, and at 1 mile, after descending slightly, you will reach an overlook with wooden benches. The views here, looking out toward the Catskill Mountains, are particularly dramatic around sunset. As with the pavilion earlier in the hike, it may be difficult to have this place all to yourself on a weekend, but during the week, this can be an ideal destination for a romantic, late-afternoon picnic.

The hill drops off quickly after the viewpoint, and the trail continues to the right. Descend the hill and cross a wooden bridge over a stream. The path now will become a standard footpath marked by red blazes as it enters a wooded area. At 1.2 miles, a side trail to your left heads a short distance to a pavilion lookout by the river. Continue on the main path, following the red markers, as it heads through the woods parallel to the stream below you. At 1.45 miles you will cross a stone bridge, then shortly after a wooden bridge.

At 1.6 miles, the trail heads back uphill toward the open clearing. Soon after, you will reach the intersection marked by wooden signs below the gazebo. Continue straight, following the trail back through the gazebo. From here, retrace your steps to your car.

THE PAVILION AT POETS' WALK

# V.
# NORTHEASTERN HUDSON VALLEY

# 36

# Bash Bish Falls

| | |
|---|---|
| **TOTAL DISTANCE**: 1.5 miles | |
| **TYPE**: Out and Back | |
| **HIKING TIME**: 1–2 hours | |
| **TOTAL ELEVATION GAIN**: 195 feet | |
| **MAXIMUM ELEVATION**: 1,110 feet | |
| **DIFFICULTY**: Easy | |

Bash Bish Falls, located almost precisely on the border of New York state and Massachusetts, draws crowds of visitors from across the region. Located in a particularly beautiful stretch of the Taconic Mountains, Bash Bish claims the distinction of being the highest waterfall in Massachusetts. While several other falls in New York may overshadow it, there's no denying the specialness of this place, no matter where you're from. This short hike follows an easy trail alongside a loud wide brook, through a shady, steep gorge: a surprisingly severe landscape compared to the rolling hills of New England. The falls loom almost 200 feet high, and are composed of a series of cascades, with the final cascade split into twin falls by a jutting rock. Opposite the falls is a sheer rock wall, almost equal in height, and just as dramatic in its own way, a reminder of the many varied landscapes pressed violently into being during the last ice age.

The falls are accessible from parking areas located in both states, though this hike will, of course, start from the NY-side parking lot. The hike to Alander Mountain (Hike #37) begins from the same parking area, and can be followed to access another view of the waterfall from near its top. While this is a short hike, there is a small picnic area just before the base of the falls where you can enjoy the view and the cool mist coming off the water. As you sit and enjoy the beauty of this spot, consider perhaps the most important quality of this hike: Is Bash Bish Falls the most fun name to say of any waterfall out there?

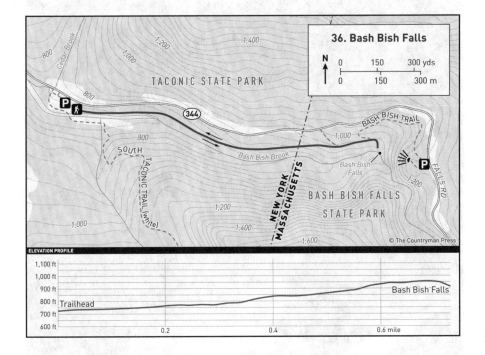

## GETTING THERE

From the town of Copake, NY, drive north on NY-22 N for 1 mile, then turn right onto NY-344 E. Continue for 0.3 mile, then turn right to stay on NY-344 E, and continue for another 0.3 mile. Make a slight left to stay on NY-344 E, and drive for another 0.7 mile. The parking area will be on the right. Note that there is a second parking area for the Massachusetts side of the trail, located on the other side of the valley.

## GPS SHORTCUT

Type "Bash Bish Falls (NY Parking Area)" into Google Maps and your GPS will navigate you to the appropriate parking area.

## THE TRAIL

From the parking area, walk to the far end of the lot, where an information kiosk stands next to the trailhead. The trail begins between the road, to your left up the bank, and the creek, downhill to your right.

Follow this wide, easy trail as it climbs gently uphill, overlooking the creek. Situated deep in the ravine, and well shaded by tall conifers, this pathway is strikingly beautiful. Various benches along the way provide opportunities to relax and reflect by the water.

After about half a mile, you will see a sign indicating your arrival at the New York–Massachusetts border. Around 0.6 mile, you will pass a steep access road to your left.

Soon you will see the viewing area for the falls just ahead. A set of steep stairs work their way uphill to your left, leading

BASH BISH FALLS

to the Massachusetts-side parking area. Tables around the viewing area give you the opportunity to prolong your stay here with a picnic.

Closer to the falls, a set of stairs descends down the rocky hill to bring you closer to the waterfall itself. Use extra care here, as the waterfall casts off a significant amount of mist, and the rocks can be very slippery as a result.

When you are ready to return, retrace your steps back to the parking area.

# 37

# Alander Mountain

**TOTAL DISTANCE**: 6.8 miles

**TYPE**: Out and Back

**HIKING TIME**: 4.5 hours

**TOTAL ELEVATION GAIN**: 1,360 feet

**MAXIMUM ELEVATION**: 2,200 feet

**DIFFICULTY**: Strenuous

Plenty of mountains feature a fire tower at the top, but how many offer a rustic cabin where you can bunk for a night, free of charge? Sure, the cabin just off the summit of Alander Mountain may, possibly, give off the vibe of the setting for a horror film, but that's just part of the charm of the place. And if you're too intimidated by rickety remote wooden structures to pay the cabin a visit, the mountain itself is more than enough to justify the trip. Alander's summit is basically a long stretch of incredible vistas, with mesmerizing views over rural Columbia County and the Catskills beyond.

Of course, it should be mentioned that nothing good comes easy, and reaching the top of Alander Mountain requires one of the most strenuous ascents of any hike in this guide. While not technically challenging, the 1,200 feet you'll ascend in little over a mile is going to leave even seasoned hikers winded and sweaty. There are three trailheads from which one can reach the top of Alander, but this route gets the elevation gain out of the way early, rewarding you with a pleasant ridgetop stroll over 2 miles of easy trail before arriving at the mountain itself. The hike begins at the parking area for Bash Bish Falls (Hike #36), itself an extremely popular destination. If the challenge of Alander hasn't completely worn you out, the short stroll to the waterfall would be an excellent addition at the end of the day.

## GETTING THERE

From the town of Copake, NY, drive north on NY-22 N for 1 mile, then turn right onto NY-344 E. Continue for 0.3 mile, then turn right to stay on NY-344 E, and continue for another 0.3 mile. Make a slight left to stay on NY-344 E,

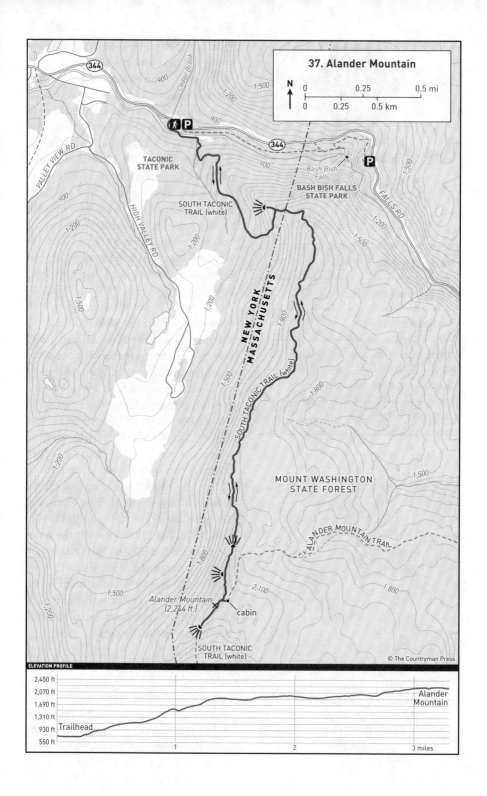

## 37. Alander Mountain

N

| 0 | | 0.25 | | 0.5 mi |
| 0 | 0.25 | | 0.5 km | |

344

TACONIC
STATE PARK

SOUTH TACONIC
TRAIL (white)

Cedar Brook

VALLEY VIEW RD

HIGH VALLEY RD

344

Bash Bish
Falls

BASH BISH FALLS
STATE PARK

FALLS RD

NEW YORK
MASSACHUSETTS

SOUTH TACONIC TRAIL (white)

MOUNT WASHINGTON
STATE FOREST

ALANDER MOUNTAIN TRAIL

Alander Mountain
(2,244 ft.)

cabin

SOUTH TACONIC
TRAIL (white)

© The Countryman Press

**ELEVATION PROFILE**

| 2,450 ft |
| 2,070 ft |
| 1,690 ft |
| 1,310 ft |
| 930 ft |
| 550 ft |

Trailhead

Alander
Mountain

1          2          3 miles

and drive for another 0.7 mile. The parking area will be on the right. This parking lot is also used to access Bash Bish Falls (Hike #36).

## GPS SHORTCUT

Type "Bash Bish Falls (NY Parking Area)" into Google Maps and your GPS will navigate you to the appropriate parking area. Both hikes begin from this shared parking area.

## THE TRAIL

From the parking area, walk west (the direction from which you entered the lot). At the end of the lot, by the road, you will see a sign indicating the direction of the South Taconic Trail. At the start, this trail follows another gravel road, branching off from the main road right before the parking lot. Follow this road as it slopes downhill, toward the broad Bash Bish Brook, then turn left. Cross over the bridge to the other side of the brook, then turn left again, walking parallel to the water.

Soon you will pass a small shack. Continue walking on the gravel path through a clearing, toward a campground. A sign ahead of you reads: STOP! THIS AREA FOR CABIN PATRONS ONLY. While the sign may appear alarming from a distance, you won't have to worry about accidentally trespassing: the trail cuts right just before entering the "cabin patron" area, heading steeply uphill past another shack containing bathroom facilities.

Follow the trail alongside a stream cascading down this steep bank, and soon you will arrive at an intersection. To the left, you will see one of the cabins belonging to the campground—turn right. Soon the trail will switchback up a steep hill. The elevation gain to access Alander Mountain is heavily stacked against you all at the beginning of this hike: you will climb about 1,200 feet in the first mile, so get ready for a challenge. The trail will level for short sections, before swooping sharply uphill again just after. Pace yourself in this section, as there's likely yet another big ascent to tackle just around the corner. But remember: at the end of this hike is a cabin in the woods, offering a well-stocked bar, and a masseuse on weekends to ease your pain, all for free! (Though it should be noted that the cabin is rather rustic, the bottles at the bar are all empty, and the masseuse may have just been a very large spider present during the author's most recent visit).

Ascend through a tranquil mixed forest. About three-quarters of a mile into the hike, you will come to a rocky area where the trail makes a very steep ascent. At the 1-mile mark, you will spot a short side trail to your left leading to a viewpoint, marked by blue blazes. Follow the blue blazes over rocks, descending slightly, to a rocky outcrop looking over the farmland of Columbia County, with dramatic views of the distant Catskills.

After enjoying the pastoral scene from this vista, return to the main trail and continue uphill, again following the white blazes. The trail briefly levels, making a sharp right turn at 1.25 miles, before ascending uphill yet again. At 1.3 miles, you will pass a sign indicating the distances to various trail-side destinations. Climb for a short distance more and the trail will finally begin to level. Congratulations, you have just gained over 1,000 feet of elevation from the parking area. While the high point of the hike is still a few hundred feet higher than where you stand now,

A SMALL CABIN SITS JUST BELOW THE SUMMIT OF ALANDER MOUNTAIN, WHERE OVERNIGHT HIKERS CAN CAMP FOR FREE

you will ascend these last few hundred feet much more gradually, over the next 2 miles.

Continue following the white blazes as the trail heads south along the ridge. There are a few dips and climbs, and of course twists and turns, but for the most part, the trail here is easy. After the challenging climb at the start of the hike, this section makes for a pleasantly relaxed anti-climax, a peaceful mountain stroll to reward you for your earlier effort. At 2.7 miles, you will pass through a small area of dwarf pitch pine trees, before tackling another brief uphill section just after.

At 2.85 miles, you will arrive at the first of many viewpoints from Alander Mountain's shoulder, looking north. At 3 miles, from a rocky outcrop, you'll find more views to the west and east. Continue on this rocky ridgeline until you come to an intersection with a blue-blazed trail to your left. Take this trail as it drops downhill, and you will arrive at Alander Mountain's cabin. This cabin is open to hikers, free of charge, and is the only place where overnight camping is permitted on Alander Mountain. Indeed, it is very rare to find such a structure near the summit of a mountain in this area, and past hikers have left behind quite a collection of empty bottles (remember that well-stocked bar mentioned before?), trinkets, tools, and notes. Embodying both a quirky rustic vibe and the atmosphere of someplace where a horror movie might be filmed, this cabin certainly adds appeal to an already intriguing hike. If you decide to linger at this spot, or camp here, as always, pack out any trash and leave the cabin in better condition than when you got there.

When you are ready, climb back up the hill and return to the intersection with the white-blazed trail. Turn left, to continue heading in the direction you were originally hiking. Just past the intersection you will emerge onto the open, rocky top of Alander Mountain, which is unusually free of tree cover, and provides excellent views to the southwest. Gaze out over the farmland of rural Columbia County. In the distance, you may be able to see the hazy outline of the Shawangunk Ridge, as well as the Catskill Mountains.

When you are ready to return, retrace your steps back to the parking area.

# 38

# Olana

| | |
|---|---|
| **TOTAL DISTANCE**: 2.4 miles | |
| **TYPE**: Loop | |
| **HIKING TIME**: 1.5–2.5 hours | |
| **TOTAL ELEVATION GAIN**: 230 feet | |
| **MAXIMUM ELEVATION**: 480 feet | |
| **DIFFICULTY**: Easy | |

Masterminded by successful Hudson River School painter Frederic Edwin Church, a student of Thomas Cole, Olana is a picturesque estate featuring a farm, meadows, a man-made pond, carriage trails winding leisurely through the woods, and dramatic Catskill overlooks. Even sticking to the hiking trails alone, Olana would be a remarkable place for a walk. But like many of the other beautiful parks in the area, it is a site as rich with history as views. At the heart of the Olana estate is a one-of-a-kind mansion: a villa designed with a blend of Victorian, Persian, and Moorish architectural styles, and named after a fortress house in Persia. From the hill on which the house is perched, and from various other points around the property, one can enjoy views not only over the Hudson Valley and its mountains, but across four states. It is hard to imagine a more perfect setting for a country house than this.

Indeed, Church searched for years to find the ideal property on which to oversee his dream house, considering locations all across New England, but eventually settling on the Hudson Valley, where he'd studied with Cole during his youth. After selling his famous Niagara painting in 1859, Church began to shape his vision of the perfect country estate, sculpting the rolling hills and forests of the property into a "living landscape." Church wrote of his work on the grounds at Olana, "I can make more and better landscapes in this way than by tampering with canvas and paint in the studio."

Olana was designated a National Historic Landmark in 1965 and today is owned and operated by the New York State Office of Parks, Recreation and Historic Preservation, and supported by the Olana Partnership. The interior

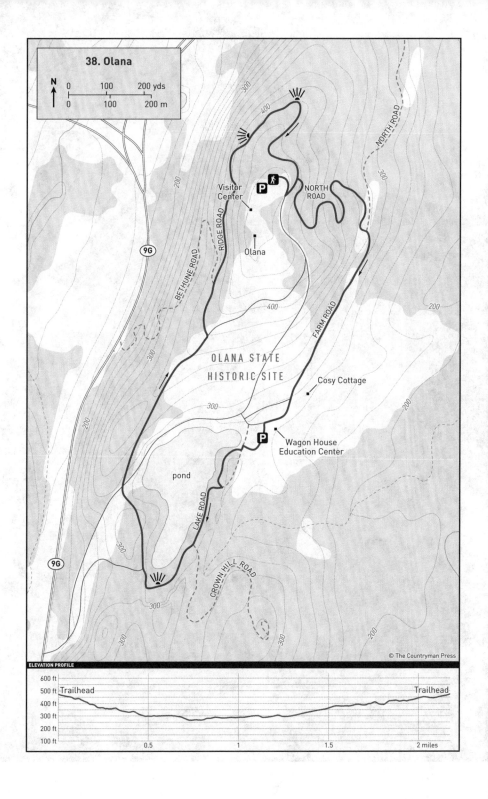

## 38. Olana

N

| 0 | 100 | 200 yds |
| 0 | 100 | 200 m |

9G

BETHUNE ROAD

RIDGE ROAD

NORTH ROAD

Visitor Center

P

NORTH ROAD

Olana

FARM ROAD

OLANA STATE HISTORIC SITE

Cosy Cottage

P

Wagon House Education Center

pond

LAKE ROAD

CROWN HILL ROAD

9G

300

400

200

© The Countryman Press

**ELEVATION PROFILE**

| 600 ft |
| 500 ft | Trailhead | Trailhead |
| 400 ft |
| 300 ft |
| 200 ft |
| 100 ft |

0.5   1   1.5   2 miles

THE OLANA HOUSE

has been maintained to resemble its appearance during Church's lifetime, and contains prizes and furnishings from his worldwide travels, as well as several dozen paintings by Church and his peers.

## GETTING THERE

Olana is located just south of the Rip Van Winkle Bridge, off of NY-9G. The entrance for Olana is 0.7 mile south of the intersection of NY-9G S and NY-23 E. The entrance road winds up the hill, toward the mansion. Park in the lot next to the mansion. An alternate lot is located lower down the hill, near the pond.

## GPS SHORTCUT

Type "Olana State Historic Site" into Google Maps and your GPS will navigate you to the appropriate parking area.

## THE TRAIL

From the parking area, walk back to the road as it begins to curve downhill. Cross, watching carefully for cars making their way up the hill, and walk alongside the road. A short distance downhill, you will encounter a trail on your left. Most of the trails at Olana are wide gravel paths and thus are easily traversed.

Cross the wooden barrier to take this trail. A short distance beyond you will reach an intersection with the Ridge Road path, which heads to your left. Turn right onto the North Road path, which snakes downhill through the woods. At 0.5 mile, you will come to a T-intersection. The North Road heads left, while the Farm Road path heads right.

Turn right, and walk for another quarter mile until you cross a wooden barrier. You will see a number of buildings just ahead. Here, you can further explore the history of the property at the Cosy Cottage, barnyard, and Wagon House Education Center. Past the buildings is a secondary parking lot. You may complete this loop hike starting from this parking area as well.

Walk along the road, past the parking area, then turn left. Follow the path around the edge of the pond. Just ahead you will see a small wooden dock, and past it, a mossy hill with a narrow footpath overlooking the water. Turn right to take this footpath and head uphill. From here, continue down the other side of the hill toward a picnic bench, then follow a rough trail back out to the main path.

Soon you will come to an intersection with the Crown Hill Road path. At 1.25 miles, you will reach the southern end of the lake, where you can enjoy a beautiful view toward the open grassy hill on which the Olana house is perched.

When you are done enjoying this scene, continue on the path until you reach the paved road. Cross this road and walk uphill, watching carefully for traffic. (If you do not wish to walk alongside the road, you may also choose to turn around and retrace your steps back to your car at this point. Whether as a loop or an out-and-back, from this point the total mileage will be roughly the same). The road here offers a wide shoulder to walk along. Pass the entry kiosk that you drove by on your way in, and cross to the second road on the other side. Walk past the WRONG WAY GO BACK sign—which is directed at cars, not you—and carefully cross once again to the far side of the road. Walk along the left shoulder of the road, heading uphill.

OLANA OFFERS AN EXCELLENT VIEW OF THE HUDSON RIVER AND CATSKILL MOUNTAINS

At 1.65 miles, you will reach the Ridge Road Trail on your left, heading back into the woods. The Bethune Road heads downhill at 1.75 miles—stay right to keep on the Ridge Road path. As you walk along this beautiful ridgeline, you will see the Olana house looming above you to your right. The trail winds moderately uphill through the woods, though even here, the hiking is never difficult.

At 2 miles, you will come to a stunning scenic overlook: a small clearing with wooden benches, overlooking the Hudson River, Rip Van Winkle Bridge, and Catskill Mountains. This is one of the best viewpoints in the northeastern Hudson Valley, and you will want to take the time to savor it. With furniture here built for relaxing, this makes the perfect spot to plan a picnic around.

After you're done taking in the views, continue on the path toward the northern end of the property. Soon you will reach a second overlook, this time facing north, toward the town of Hudson. At 2.3 miles you will return to the original intersection, completing your loop. Turn right and head uphill, toward the road. At the paved road, follow the bend back uphill to the parking area and your car.

# 39

# High Falls

**TOTAL DISTANCE**: 1 mile

**TYPE**: Loop

**HIKING TIME**: 1 Hour

**TOTAL ELEVATION GAIN**: 150 feet

**MAXIMUM ELEVATION**: 525 feet

**DIFFICULTY**: Easy

With 47 total acres and several miles of trails, the High Falls Conservation Area, managed by the Columbia Land Conservancy, is perfect for a more relaxed stroll to a scenic waterfall view. Some 50 feet shorter than nearby Bash Bish Falls, the High Falls waterfall is nonetheless a dramatic sight. And due to its relative obscurity, the crowds that flock to the area's other famous waterfalls seldom find their way here. The falls and their creek were once looked upon for industrial use rather than beauty, as a hydropower dam built above High Falls provided power to more than a dozen mills in the area. From the falls, the Agawamuck Creek continues northwest before joining the Claverack Creek on its way to the Hudson River.

## GETTING THERE

From the Taconic State Parkway, take the exit for NY-23 toward Claverack / Hillsdale. Drive east on NY-23 E, and a short distance down the road, make a left onto County Road 11. Continue for 2.2 miles, then turn left onto Stevers Crossing Road. Continue for another mile, then turn left to stay on Stevers Crossing Road, and continue for another mile. Turn right onto Roxbury Road, and after half a mile, the entrance to the High Falls Conservation Area will be on your right.

## GPS SHORTCUT

Type "High Falls Conservation Area" into Google Maps and your GPS will navigate you to the appropriate parking area.

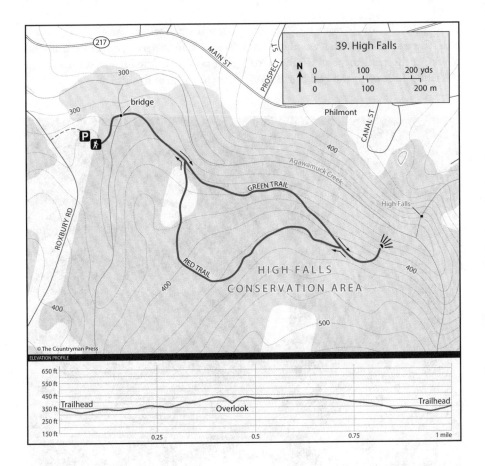

## THE TRAIL

Pass through the wooden entrance gate to find an information kiosk just inside, by the trailhead. Begin your hike following the green blazes.

A small stream meanders through the woods, briefly running alongside the trail. Cross a wooden bridge over the stream, heading deeper into the woods. Soon the trail will fork, with a blue-blazed trail running left, parallel to another stream. Stay to the right, following the green blazes.

At 0.15 mile, a red-blazed trail splits off from your path to the right. Continue straight. You will soon see a much larger creek downhill to your left.

At 0.35 mile, the blue-blazed trail will rejoin your route from the left, as the path begins to make its way more steeply uphill. Shortly after, you will pass another branch off from the red trail to your right, which you will take on your way back.

Just ahead, the green trail splits to form a short loop. You may take either route around the loop, as both meet at the viewing area above the waterfall. At the viewing area, there are several places to sit and relax. There is no path down to the base of the waterfall, but the elevated view from this vista is quite impressive as it is.

When you are ready to start back, return along the loop to the red trail branching off, now to your left. At 0.75 mile, the trail forks, with a wooden gate blocking the trail to your left. Stay to the right, following the red blazes. At 0.9 mile, you will rejoin the green trail. Turn left and retrace your steps from the first section of the hike to return to the parking area and your car.

THE HIGH FALLS WATERFALL

# Greenport Conservation Area

**TOTAL DISTANCE**: 2.5 miles

**TYPE**: Loop

**HIKING TIME**: 2 Hours

**TOTAL ELEVATION GAIN**: 85 feet

**MAXIMUM ELEVATION**: 170 feet

**DIFFICULTY**: Easy

Just north of the town of Hudson, neighboring Greenport Conservation Area and Harrier Hill Park offer a similar setting as the far more popular Poets' Walk. With ornate gazebos looking out to the eastern Catskill escarpment, and large, open, scenic fields, all three parks are ideal for a meditative walk or romantic picnic. But at Greenport (and Harrier Hill), you'll have a much better chance of finding solitude, especially if you arrive on a weekday. Here, a short walk through a field to a pavilion is only the first section of a scenic loop hike, but the views are stunning every step of the way. Proximity to the town of Hudson, with ample shopping and dining options, makes this a worthy destination for a weekend outing, even if the hike itself won't take you more than a few hours to complete.

## GETTING THERE

The Greenport Conservation Area is located about 2 miles north of the town of Hudson, NY. Drive north on Harry Howard Ave. for about 1 mile, then make a left onto Joslen Blvd. Continue for half a mile. When you pass Daisy Hill Rd., a restricted access road on the left, you are almost there. The parking area is on the west side of the road, a short distance past Daisy Hill Rd.

## GPS SHORTCUT

As of the time of this writing, the parking area for the Greenport Conservation Area does not appear on Google Maps. Inputting the park itself into your GPS will bring you to Daisy Hill Road, which accesses private property, and should not be taken by hikers. However, instruct your GPS to navigate you to this

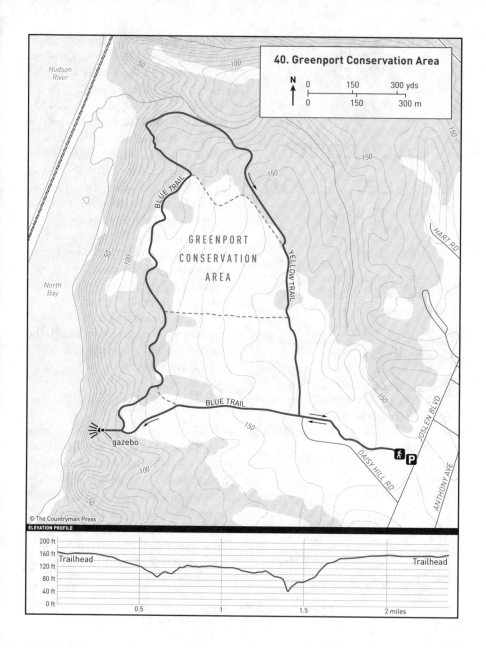

point, and you will find the parking area just a short distance north of Daisy Hill Road, marked by a sign.

## THE TRAIL

As with most of the parks managed by the Columbia Land Conservancy, the trailhead is accessed through a wooden gate, next to an information kiosk. The Greenport Conservation Area offers many more miles of trails than the loop described in this guide, and also connects to Harrier Hill (Hike #41) Park, to the north. A map of the park's trails is displayed at this kiosk, though many of

THE GREENPORT CONSERVATION AREA FEATURES EASY TRAILS WITH STUNNING VIEWS

these trails are infrequently used compared to the route you will be taking, and not as clearly marked.

The "all-access trail" is a gravel path next to private land, fenced in, broad, and flat. This easy section of trail will bring you quickly to the ruins of an old farm, with two silos lurking in an overgrown patch of woods. Beyond is an expansive field sloping down toward the Hudson River. There is another large gravel lot here, fenced in so that you cannot wander beyond onto private property, as you will see private homes next to the field to your left. Beyond the lot is another info kiosk and gate.

At the gate, yellow blazes indicate a trail heading to your right, to the north. You will return along this route later, but for now, continue straight on the main path, heading toward the river with the

Catskill Mountains looming in the distance. This expansive open area is quite beautiful, and one of the best places in all of the Hudson Valley to take in the sight of the Catskills.

At 0.3 mile, a sign indicates another trail cutting left through the field, away from the main path. Stay straight on the all-access trail and soon you will be able to see a gazebo in the distance. At 0.5 mile the trail will split; go left, toward the gazebo. The view here is even better than before, with the mountains rising up over the wooden structure, framing a swath of swampland that runs along the Hudson.

Walking back from the gazebo, take the trail left, heading north along the river. Very soon you will split left once again, on a side trail leading to an overlook bench with similar views as the

A LARGE PAVILION LOOKS OUT OVER THE HUDSON RIVER

gazebo. This is an excellent backup spot to take in the scene, should the gazebo happen to be overcrowded—or a lovely primary destination too, should you happen to prefer a more intimate, wooded atmosphere.

Continuing on from the bench, at 0.85 mile you will reach another fork. Once again, stay to the left. Just after the 1-mile mark, the trail splits at a picnic shelter. Here, another beautiful wooded structure looks out to the river from a shaded forest perch, though the

view is more limited than those previous. Beyond the structure, a green trail heads downhill on the left, while the blue trail goes right. Keep right to stay on blue.

At 1.25 miles, the trail cuts through an area of dense briers, though the path itself is well-maintained and free from intrusion. You will reach a wooden boardwalk that navigates a marshy patch of ground. At 1.3 miles, you will reach an intersection with the green-blazed trail, which previously diverged from your route by the picnic shelter. Continue following blue over another wooden boardwalk.

Soon, you will reach a split, where a yellow side trail to the right cuts across the field, offering a shortcut for those wishing to reduce the length of their hike. Taking this shortcut would shave about half a mile from the total distance. Continuing on the slightly longer route, following the blue blazes, you will walk in the direction of the river before crossing a third boardwalk. Soon you will reach another bench overlook tucked into the woods.

At 1.55 miles, you will arrive at an intersection marked by two bridges. Here, the blue path continues to your left over one bridge, meandering north through the upper sections of the Green-port Conservation Area before eventually connecting to Harrier Hill Park. To the right, a yellow-blazed trail crosses the second trail to loop you back around toward the start of your hike.

Head to the right, following the yellow blazes. Soon the trail will run alongside the large open field once again, rejoining the shortcut trail you passed previously at 1.8 miles. Continue straight, and shortly the path will leave the woods and begin crossing the field, with the silos of the abandoned farm visible in the distance. At 2.2 miles, you will reach the patch of forest where the yellow trail reconnects to the all-access trail by the large gravel lot. Retrace your steps from the beginning of the hike back toward the parking area and your car.

# Harrier Hill Park

**TOTAL DISTANCE**: 3.6 miles

**TYPE**: Out and Back

**HIKING TIME**: 2 hours

**TOTAL ELEVATION GAIN**: 80 feet

**MAXIMUM ELEVATION**: 180 feet

**DIFFICULTY**: Easy

From Harrier Hill Park's impressive pavilion, shaped like a corncrib in homage to the land's previous incarnation as a dairy farm, you can escape the sun, but keep your binoculars handy. The surrounding fields, also protected by Scenic Hudson, support a wide variety of birds—including the northern harrier, the hawk for which the park is named. Grasslands in the valley and elsewhere are vanishing at an alarming rate, reducing essential bird habitat, and making protected sites like Harrier Hill all the more important.

From the parking area, hikers can access several miles of trail, though there are essentially two separate and very distinct hikes starting from this trailhead. Immediately up the hill from the parking area is the aforementioned pavilion, overlooking the river and the Catskills—another grand viewpoint similar to those found at Poets' Walk (Hike #35) and the Greenport Conservation Area (Hike #40). The walk to the pavilion is easy, and (aside from the time you spend there) will take only a few minutes. The bulk of the hike, however, begins across the street, meandering through fields, woods, and ravines. Enjoy this quiet woods walk, then return to the pavilion afterward to relax and soak in the view.

## GETTING THERE

Harrier Hill Park is located about 3 miles north of the town of Hudson, NY. Drive north on US-9 N, then, at the intersection next to the shopping center, make a sharp left onto W. Atlantic Ave. Immediately after, turn right onto Rod and Gun Rd. Continue on Rod and Gun Rd. for 0.8 mile. The parking area will be on the left.

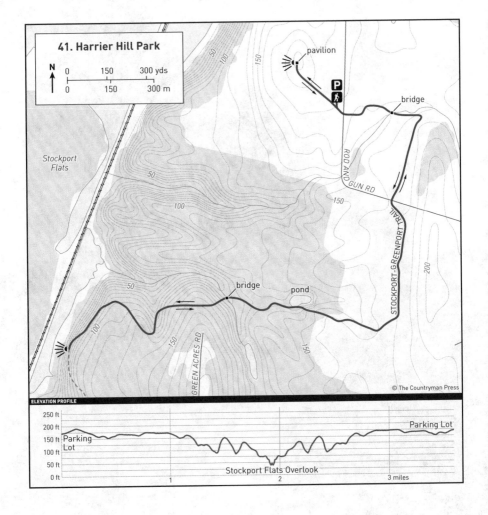

## 41. Harrier Hill Park

N

| 0 | 150 | 300 yds |
| 0 | 150 | 300 m |

pavilion

P

bridge

Stockport
Flats

ROD AND GUN RD

STOCKPORT-GREENPORT TRAIL

bridge

pond

GREEN ACRES RD

© The Countryman Press

**ELEVATION PROFILE**

250 ft
200 ft
150 ft — Parking
100 ft — Lot
50 ft
0 ft

Parking Lot

Stockport Flats Overlook

1          2          3 miles

## GPS SHORTCUT

Type "Harrier Hill Park" into Google Maps and your GPS will navigate you to the appropriate parking area.

## THE TRAIL

From the parking lot, you have two options. The pavilion overlook—undoubtedly the highlight of the hike, for most—heads in the opposite direction from the main trail right from the parking area. However, the trail to the

pavilion overlook is only 0.1 mile long, so this side trip can be tackled on either end of the main hike with very little extra effort.

The trail to the pavilion is self-evident, and is not marked with blazes. You will pass a small pond about halfway to the pavilion, with a bench overlooking the water. Several more benches are situated around the pavilion to take in the incredible views of the Hudson River and Catskills. An old silo from an abandoned farm property nearby adds to the grandeur of the scene. The pavilion is

THE BEST VIEWS AT HARRIER HILL ARE FOUND ONLY A SHORT WALK FROM THE PARKING AREA

not huge but offers enough space for several parties to enjoy a picnic here. And given that this park is not quite as well-known as some others, you have a good chance of experiencing solitude at this wonderful place.

When you are ready to continue, return on the trail to the parking lot. The rest of the trail continues across the road. Carefully cross the street, then start on the trail as it passes through a wooden arch and descends a short flight of wooden steps. Immediately the trail heads over a boardwalk, to the right side of the large open meadow. There are no blazes on this section of the trail, but the path is wide and easy to follow.

About a quarter mile from the parking area, watch for a smaller trail that cuts into the woods on the right. The wide meadow path which you have been on continues straight, and this turn is not marked or blazed, unfortunately making this section an easy place for confusion. The only indication that the trail veers here is the consistency of the trail itself: watch for the path of the gravel stones heading into the woods. If the trail is obscured (or you've merely spaced out, lost deep in thought about what to make for dinner later), it is very easy to miss this turn. If you do miss the trail and continue straight on the previous path, it will continue through meadows and fields for another half mile before dead-ending at private property on a farm (as the author discovered himself on his first hike in this park, when the gravel path was obscured by snow).

Following the correct path, you will cross a stream on a wooden bridge through a shady strip of woods, before returning to another wide path, which heads southeast through another field. The path here will cut to the right after a short distance, then continue straight for a while, before crossing over Rod and Gun Rd., the paved road on which you drove in. On the other side of the road, look for the path to pick up again through the meadow.

At 0.85 mile, the trail forks, with a maintenance road heading to the left, grooved by tire ruts. Turn right. The trail is still not blazed, but gravel on the path indicates the way. At 1 mile, the trail enters a scraggly woods, then soon skirts a small pond. Leaving the pond, the trail turns left then descends stairs built into the ground. Cross a bridge over a small stream and arrive at the first trail blaze on this hike.

Following the blue blazes, you will now hike through an attractive, shady forest. Here, the trail descends into a ravine, where various streams cross during high season. In spring, the intersection of murky, fast-flowing water at the bottom of this deep, shady ravine makes for a dramatic backwoods site.

Look for the blue blazes to continue on the other side of the stream crossing, then continue up the other side of the ravine. At 1.5 miles, you will reach a long stretch of boardwalk winding through the woods. Soon after, cross another wooden bridge. The trail will begin to run parallel to the river, with limited views out over the water below, and glimpses of the Catskills in the distance. Below you are the Stockport Flats, a mosaic of landforms on the east bank of the Hudson River dominated by marshes and swamplands.

Here, the trail continues south, soon joining the Greenport Conservation Area (Hike #40) trail system. Your hike can be extended to include many more miles of hiking thanks to these trails.

When you are ready, retrace your steps to return to your car.

# Beebe Hill Fire Tower

| | |
|---|---|
| **TOTAL DISTANCE**: 1.8 miles | |
| **TYPE**: Out and Back | |
| **HIKING TIME**: 2–2.5 hours | |
| **TOTAL ELEVATION GAIN**: 500 feet | |
| **MAXIMUM ELEVATION**: 1,820 feet | |
| **DIFFICULTY**: Easy | |

The northernmost fire tower covered in this guide, Beebe Hill offers another excellent option for a not-too-strenuous hike to far-ranging views. From the tower, the city of Albany is visible on a clear day, nestled beyond the hills and forests of Columbia and Rensselaer County. The fire tower was originally constructed on nearby Alander Mountain in 1928, but was moved to Washburn Mountain in Columbia County five years later. Finally, in 1964, the tower was moved to Beebe Hill. The cab of the 60-foot-tall tower is open year round. Beebe Hill, miles from any highway or town of significant size, is far more remote than most of the Hudson Valley's fire towers, and while the Catskill Mountains are still visible in the distance, the endless rolling hills and vibrant forests that surround you are perhaps the most captivating sight. Nearby, a lean-to just off the trail next to a pond gives the option to turn this into an overnight stay, with unbeatable sunrise and sunset views.

## GETTING THERE

Beebe Hill State Forest is located about 4 miles southeast of the town of Chatham, NY. From the Taconic State Parkway, take the exit for Rigor Hill Rd. Drive for 1.3 miles, then turn left onto Crow Hill Rd. and drive for another 1.7 miles. Here, Crow Hill Rd. becomes South St. Continue for an additional mile, then turn right onto NY-203 S. Drive for 4 miles, then turn left onto NY-22 N. After 0.3 mile, make a slight left onto Osmer Rd. Drive for 1.8 miles, and then make a sharp left onto Beebe Forest Rd. Drive down this forest road for a short distance and you will arrive at the parking area.

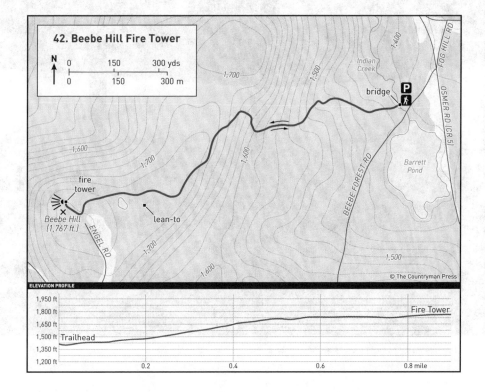

## 42. Beebe Hill Fire Tower

N

| 0 | 150 | 300 yds |
| 0 | 150 | 300 m |

Indian Creek

bridge

fire tower

Beebe Hill (1,767 ft.)

lean-to

Barrett Pond

BEEBE FOREST RD.

ENGEL RD.

OSMER RD. (CR 5)

FOG HILL RD.

© The Countryman Press

**ELEVATION PROFILE**

1,950 ft
1,800 ft
1,650 ft
1,500 ft Trailhead
1,350 ft
1,200 ft

Fire Tower

0.2    0.4    0.6    0.8 mile

## GPS SHORTCUT

Type "Beebe Hill State Forest" into Google Maps and your GPS will navigate you to the appropriate parking area.

## THE TRAIL

The trail begins at the far end of the parking loop. Cross a wooden bridge over a stream, then stay straight when an overgrown woods road cuts across the trail. Barrett Pond will be to your left. This first section of trail is marked by blue blazes

At 0.1 mile, you will encounter the trail register. Stop and take the time to log your hike. Here, the blue blazes end, and continuing straight from the register, you will now follow red blazes for the rest of the hike.

Soon, you will cross another wooden bridge. A little over a quarter mile into the hike, the grade picks up significantly, and you will tackle a short climb up to the top of the hill. Continue on the path, and at 0.7 mile you will pass a small pond with a lean-to on the far side, which can be reached by taking a short side trail. This lean-to is open to the public, should you wish to turn this short hike into an overnight camping trip.

Past the pond and lean-to, you will spot a wooden outhouse lurking (somewhat creepily) deeper into the woods. Shortly after, the trail will bring you to a large open clearing, with a boarded up cabin on a hill and several other old structures lurking nearby. Turn to the right, where the fire tower awaits. The cabin is open and offers fantastic

STUNNING VIEWS FROM THE BEEBE HILL FIRE TOWER

views over Columbia County, the capital region, western Massachusetts, and northwestern Connecticut.

When you are ready to return, retrace your steps back to the parking area.

# Schor Conservation Area

**TOTAL DISTANCE**: 3.6 miles

**TYPE**: Out and Back

**HIKING TIME**: 2 hours

**TOTAL ELEVATION GAIN**: 320 feet

**MAXIMUM ELEVATION**: 1,420 feet

**DIFFICULTY**: Easy

In this quiet northeastern corner of Columbia County, the Schor Conservation Area is home to one of the most remote and little-known hikes covered in this guide. On a gorgeous spring evening, a stroll through this park is as quiet and beautiful as one could ever hope of a nature walk, and yet you'll possibly not see a single other person. Beebe Hill is only a short drive away, but likely due to its fire tower, that park is much better known. Schor is tucked away behind several miles of backroads, but the trip here is well worth it—and easily paired with a hike to the Beebe Hill fire tower, as both are fairly short and easy hikes. Schor does offer a hilltop vista, with Albany visible on a good day, though the more subtle aspects of the park may actually be the highlight. Hiking up to the vista, you'll wander through a shady and grand pine forest that feels as if you've suddenly been teleported out of the Hudson Valley altogether. And near the start of the hike, you'll encounter a pond with a picnic area, a grill, and a bench swing, making this an ideal spot to relax before or after your hike.

## GETTING THERE

The Schor Conservation Area is located about 8 miles east of the town of Chatham, NY, just south of I-90. From the Taconic State Parkway, take the exit for NY-203 S and drive east for about half a mile. Turn left onto Red Rock Rd., then drive for 2.5 miles.

## GPS SHORTCUT

Type "Schor Conservation Area" into Google Maps and your GPS will navigate you to the appropriate parking area.

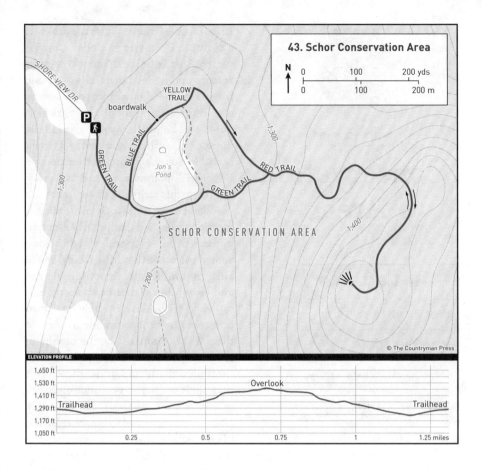

## THE TRAIL

Two trails branch off from the parking area, both marked by green blazes. While not covered by this guide, the green trail makes a circle around the edge of the Schor Conservation Area, giving the option for an easy loop hike. The green trail loop begins from the parking area, and you will begin by starting on the portion of the trail that heads southeast, toward the pond. Look for the green-blazed trail at the far end of the lot. This path will run alongside a woods road, and as you walk down the trail, you will spot Jon's Pond through the trees almost immediately.

At the pond, you will find a pavilion, grills, and a nice bench swing positioned to overlook the water. This tranquil, quiet spot is perfect for a picnic or an evening of reflection and rest.

Facing the pond, turn left past the bench swing and follow the trail around the edge of the water. Cross a wooden boardwalk over a muddy area as you approach the far end of the pond. Soon you will come to an intersection with a yellow-blazed trail. Turn right at the intersection, following the yellow trail for a short time. Soon you will arrive at another intersection, where you will veer left and then immediately turn right, onto the red-blazed trail. Look for wooden signs pointing you toward the summit.

At 0.4 mile, the trail begins to climb uphill, and soon passes an intersection with a green-blazed trail, which you will return to later. Cross another bridge, and soon you will pass a bench overlooking a quiet part of the woods. Enter a dark, majestic forest of pine and hemlock that is especially peaceful on a warm spring or fall day. The trail will begin to climb moderately uphill as you approach the high point of the park.

About 0.65 mile from the trailhead, you will reach the top of the ridge, and the trail levels out. Follow the path as it hooks right, and you will reach the summit and its vista at 0.8 mile. Enjoy the view looking west over this quiet corner of the Hudson Valley.

From the summit, retrace your steps down the red trail, through the shady pine forest along the ridge, until you have reached the intersection with the green trail. Turn left onto green, and soon you will return to the edge of the pond, on the opposite side from where you started earlier. The trail forks here, with the blue trail to the right tracing the edge of the pond heading north. Turn left, and walk along the dam past a bench, back toward the pavilion and picnic area. From here, simply retrace your original steps up the green trail to return to your car.

THE POND AT THE SCHOR CONSERVATION AREA IS A QUIET, BEAUTIFUL PLACE TO RELAX, OR ENJOY A PICNIC

# VI.
# NORTHWESTERN HUDSON VALLEY

# 44

# Illinois Mountain

**TOTAL DISTANCE**: 4.2 miles

**TYPE**: Loop

**HIKING TIME**: 2–3 hours

**TOTAL ELEVATION GAIN**: 500 feet

**MAXIMUM ELEVATION**: 910 feet

**DIFFICULTY**: Moderate

Illinois Mountain rises subtly over one of the most developed portions of the Hudson Valley, and the trails here offer a relatively new and little-known option for hikers seeking an outing without steep trails and strenuous climbs. The paths around this park form a series of staggered partial loops, all connected by an access road running toward private property (a broadcast tower) at the mountain's high point. Several different routes could be composed here, ranging from short and easy, to a thorough loop requiring several hours. However, the trails at Illinois Mountain are not particularly challenging, and hikers will enjoy the serenity and variety found in this park. The small pond by a picnic area near the start of the hike sees the most traffic, while wetlands and several water reservoirs along the service road create a scenic contrast to the rocky, wooded first section of trail. The land here is owned by the Town of Lloyd Water Department, so please do not wander off of the marked trails, and respect the opportunity to escape to this quiet corner of the Hudson Valley.

## GETTING THERE

Illinois Mountain is located on the western fringes of the town of Highland, NY. From the Mid-Hudson Bridge, drive west on US-44 W, then keep right at the fork. Follow signs for US-9W N / US-44 / NY-55 / Highland / Kingston and merge onto NY-55 W / US-44 W / US-9W N. After 0.3 mile, turn left onto Haviland Rd. Just after, turn right onto Tillson Ave. Continue for half a mile, then turn left onto Vineyard Ave., then right onto Reservoir Rd. Continue to the end of Reservoir Rd. and you will enter Berean Park. Park in the lot to

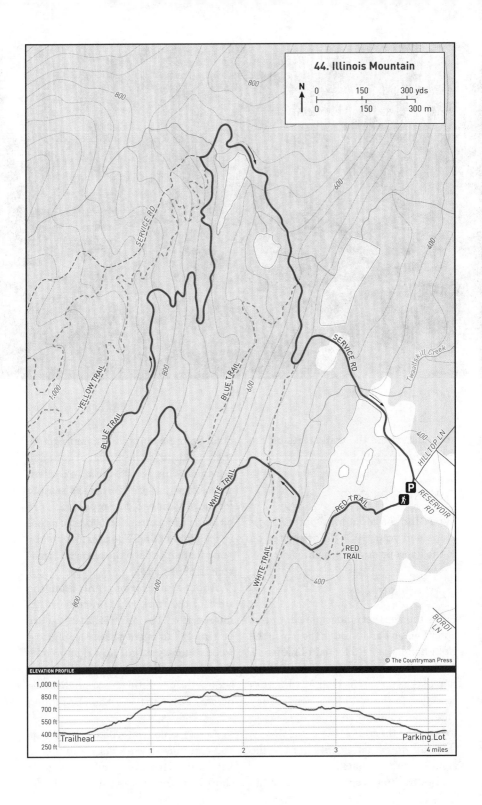

44. Illinois Mountain

N

| 0 | 150 | 300 yds |
| 0 | 150 | 300 m |

SERVICE RD

YELLOW TRAIL

BLUE TRAIL

BLUE TRAIL

WHITE TRAIL

SERVICE RD

Twaalfskill Creek

HILLTOP LN

RED TRAIL

RED TRAIL

WHITE TRAIL

RESERVOIR RD

BORDI LN

© The Countryman Press

**ELEVATION PROFILE**

| 1,000 ft | | | | |
| 850 ft | | | | |
| 700 ft | | | | |
| 550 ft | | | | |
| 400 ft | Trailhead | | | Parking Lot |
| 250 ft | | | | |
| | 1 | 2 | 3 | 4 miles |

A LARGE PICNIC AREA AT BEREAN PARK

your left, where the trail starts on the hill above the pond.

## GPS SHORTCUT

Type "Illinois Mountain" into Google Maps and your GPS will navigate you to the appropriate parking area.

## THE TRAIL

From the southernmost parking area, enter Berean Park through the gap in the right-hand side of the chain-link fence. A wooden sign points you in the direction of the start of the trail. Walk across the lawn to the red blazes where they enter the woods, then cross the barrier to begin on the trail. Once in the woods, the trail immediately cuts hard to the right, toward the water.

The trail makes its way around the pond before coming to a camping area with a large semi-circle of wooden benches. This would be an excellent place for a gathering—there is seating for more than two dozen people, a fire pit, and the construction of the furniture is itself interesting. The proximity of the pond further adds to the pleasant atmosphere of this site.

About a quarter of a mile from the start of the trail, you will come to an intersection. The red trail that you are on cuts left to make a short loop in the woods. Here, you will turn right to take the white trail. This trail follows the edge of the pond still for a short distance before cutting to the left and beginning a moderate ascent.

At 0.75 mile, you will switchback as you continue to work your way uphill. Afterwards, the trail levels again for a short distance. At the 1-mile mark, the white blazes will suddenly transition to blue blazes. Continue onward, following the blue blazes.

At 1.25 miles, you will follow a nice ridgeline trail through a conifer forest up a series of switchbacks. Now on the semi-loop of the blue trail, you will meander through the woods for some time, with occasional, mild uphill and downhill tangents. The climb is never severe, and overall this section makes for a very pleasant walk through the woods.

At around 2.4 miles, you will wind down from the ridge on another series of switchbacks. At 2.8 miles, you will come to the end of the blue trail. The yellow trail cuts to the left, and skirts the northwestern ridgeline in a very similar manner as the blue trail. This trail can also be taken if you wish to add an additional 2 miles onto your hike.

Walk over a small wooden bridge to the service road beyond. Turn right onto the service road. This road heads back to the pond and parking area where you began the hike. Along the way, you will pass several reservoirs, which are the property of the Town of Lloyd Water Department. Stay on the trail, and respect private property. Near the third reservoir, you will see a blue trail intersecting with the service road to your right. This is another end of the blue trail which you had been hiking on before, completing a partial loop at two spots along the service road. Soon after this, you will also pass the terminus of the white trail along the road.

Continue along the road until the pond is in sight, then walk along the path, through a secondary parking lot, to return to the parking area where you began the hike.

AUTUMN ARRIVES AT ILLINOIS MOUNTAIN

# 45

# Joppenbergh Mountain

**TOTAL DISTANCE**: 1.3 miles

**TYPE**: Loop

**HIKING TIME**: 1 hour

**TOTAL ELEVATION GAIN**: 360 feet

**MAXIMUM ELEVATION**: 450 feet

**DIFFICULTY**: Moderate

Despite sitting at less than 500 feet, Joppenbergh Mountain's profile is so distinct that it seems to bear the drama—and offer the views—of a mountain many times its size. It helps that its rocky western face, with jagged cliffs dropping steeply down toward the town of Rosendale, looks out to one of the best vistas in the Hudson Valley, with a picture-perfect view to the Rosendale Trestle, the Rondout Creek, and the northernmost end of the Shawangunk Ridge. This viewpoint can be reached with only a few minutes of moderately strenuous uphill hiking, or as part of a loop hike—both versions quite short and shockingly rewarding, all-in-all. Joppenbergh may be one of the best reward-to-effort ratio hikes in the Hudson Valley.

Even more surprising, Joppenbergh has only been a park for a handful of years. The Open Space Institute bought the land in 2011. Earlier in the mountain's life, the area was mined through the nineteenth century for materials used in the manufacture of cement, until 1899 when over-mining resulted in a massive cave-in. Joppenbergh still undergoes periodic tremors to this day as a result of rockfalls resulting from the mining. Decades later, the mountain became a center for long-distance ski-jumping competitions. You'll encounter few signs of these activities today while hiking along this loop, but given that this property was not open to the public until very recently, you will come to appreciate how lucky we are to have organizations working for the preservation of such memorable sites.

## GETTING THERE

The trailhead for Joppenbergh Mountain is found in the center of the town of

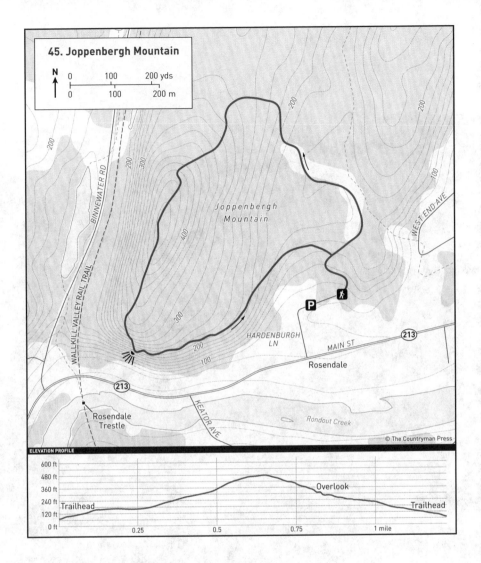

## 45. Joppenbergh Mountain

N

| 0 | 100 | 200 yds |
| 0 | 100 | 200 m |

*Joppenbergh Mountain*

BINNEWATER RD

WALL KILL VALLEY RAIL TRAIL

WEST END AVE

HARDENBURGH LN

MAIN ST

213

Rosendale

213

KEATOR AVE

Rosendale Trestle

Rondout Creek

© The Countryman Press

**ELEVATION PROFILE**

600 ft
480 ft
360 ft
240 ft — Trailhead
120 ft
0 ft

Overlook

Trailhead

0.25    0.5    0.75    1 mile

Rosendale, NY, just off of Main Street. Take NY-213 into Rosendale, then turn onto Hardenburgh Lane. Here you will find the large town parking lot. The trail begins by Willow Kiln Park, on the northeast side of the lot.

## GPS SHORTCUT

Type "Willow Kiln Park" into Google Maps and your GPS will navigate you to the appropriate parking area. The directions to "Joppenbergh Mountain"

will not take you to the trailhead for this hike.

## THE TRAIL

From the large municipal lot, a number of signs point you toward the start of the trail. The hike begins at the far end of the parking area, where a slope cuts up next to the rocky ridgeline. Walk up this slope to a large open area above the stone cave structures that faced the lot. From here, the trail continues to

THE VIEW FROM JOPPENBERGH MOUNTAIN LOOKS OUT OVER THE TOWN OF ROSENDALE AND THE ROSENDALE TRESTLE

the right and is extensively marked by signs. Continue up a moderate slope.

At 0.2 mile, the trail splits at a four-way intersection. Stay straight. The trail here is still very broad and well-marked by large, obvious signs. Soon you will pass a wide, open clearing. At 0.35 mile, the trail narrows to the width of a traditional foot trail, and crosses under power lines. You will begin to climb uphill more steeply. There are multiple signs here designating the area off-trail as private property; be sure to stay on the trail at all times.

Soon the trail hooks back left, and at 0.5 mile, you will cross back under the power lines. Immediately after, you will tackle the most serious uphill section of this hike. The ascent here is not challenging on a technical level, but the trail is quite steep. This segment is short, however, and soon the trail will level again as you approach the summit of Joppenbergh. The high point of the mountain is reached at 0.7 mile, though there are no views from the peak. A wooden bench marks the spot. The sensation of standing on top of a narrow island above the earth is quite noticeable here, given the small area of the summit, despite the fact that this moun-tain is minuscule in stature compared to others in the area. However, the best is still ahead.

There are no blazes marking the trail here, but the path is easy to follow none-theless. Descend from the summit down a moderate slope. At 0.85 mile, you will reach the lookout—there's no mistaking this one. A rocky outcropping juts out from the mountainside over the town of Rosendale, with a direct view down to the trestle below. The whole valley stretches before you, and for only 500-foot elevation, the view here is quite remarkable, among the best in the area. The unique staging of the rocky ledge, overlooking a river, running through a valley, with a rail trestle spanning the space below, all work together to create a truly memorable place.

When you are done enjoying this excellent view, descend again down a steady, moderate slope. Very soon the descent becomes even more gradual. At 1.15 miles, the trail splits, with a brick shack lurking just off the trail. Signs point to the way out; follow them down until you have returned to the flat open area above the parking lot. From here, take the broad path down to the lot to return to your car.

# Shaupeneak Ridge

| | |
|---|---|
| **TOTAL DISTANCE**: 3.5 miles | |
| **TYPE**: Loop | |
| **HIKING TIME**: 2.5 hours | |
| **TOTAL ELEVATION GAIN**: 250 feet | |
| **MAXIMUM ELEVATION**: 875 feet | |
| **DIFFICULTY**: Easy | |

This 936-acre park occupies a ridge just south of the city of Kingston, cradling the beautiful Louisa Pond at its center. There are enough trails around the ridge to enjoy a variety of hikes, but this guide makes use of several of the trails to complete a broad loop. You'll encounter the full variety of terrain and habitats that the Shaupeneak Ridge has to offer, and you can easily choose to extend your hike, should you wish to explore further. There is little elevation change on this route, though some of the trails do tackle rocky areas and small hills.

Note that there are actually two parking areas for Shaupeneak Ridge: the second, east of the ridge and lower in elevation, can be used for a more strenuous hike up the ridge itself. Both approaches will bring you to the park's main viewpoint, looking out over the Hudson Valley, though the tranquil pond and its wetlands may be the park's true payoff. In spring and fall, Shaupeneak is an especially peaceful setting for a woodland walk.

## GETTING THERE

From US-9W N, in the town of Esopus, turn onto Old Post Rd. heading west. A few hundred feet down the road, you will pass the secondary parking area for Shaupeneak Ridge, which requires hikers to climb the ridge to reach the main section of the park. This route is not covered by this guide; continue driving past this parking area. Drive for about 1.7 miles, then make a slight right onto Popletown Rd. Continue for another mile and the main parking area will be on your left.

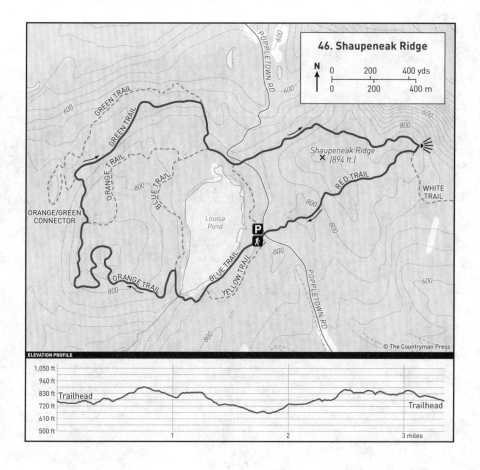

ELEVATION PROFILE

## GPS SHORTCUT

Type "Shaupeneak Ridge" into Google Maps and your GPS will navigate you to the appropriate parking area.

## THE TRAIL

A number of trails branch off right from the parking area: to the south, the yellow trail climbs up a small ridge; the red trail crosses back over the road before heading east; to the west, the blue-blazed trail follows the edges of Louisa Pond. Follow the blue blazes along the bank of the pond, where benches are perched to offer a waterfront view. You will pass several signs indicating kayak launch points. After 0.25 mile, the yellow trail branches back and rejoins the blue trail. Continue straight.

Just beyond, you will reach the southern end of the pond. Enjoy the view before continuing as the trail hooks north. At 0.45 mile, turn left onto the orange-blazed trail and begin a modest ascent up a ridgeline. Around 0.75 mile, the trail levels. The path winds through the forest, making broad switchbacks before ultimately heading north. At 1.35 miles, look for the orange-green blazed trail continuing north down the ridge just as the orange trail begins looping back to the east. After descending briefly, the trail will level.

LOUISA POND

At 1.5 miles, turn right onto the green trail. The green trail makes a narrow loop along the ridgeline connected to the blue trail that circles the pond—heading east, you will reach the intersection where the green loop closes, and a single green trail heads to the right, south, toward the pond. Make a brief uphill, before the green trail ends completely at 2.14 miles. Turn left onto the blue trail, then shortly after, left onto red. A short distance beyond, the red trail crosses over a service road.

Around 2.6 miles, you will be able to see large antennas through the trees to your right. This area is private property, so stay on the trail at all times. To the left, you may be able to catch limited views of the Catskills in the distance when there are no leaves on the trees. On older trail maps for this park, Scenic Hudson had even designated a Catskill Mountain overlook near this spot on the map. Sadly, whatever view there was in the past is now overgrown. What can be glimpsed through the trees of the mountains looming in the distance suggests that it would have been quite impressive.

At 3 miles, just before the red trail makes a complete reversal and bends back toward the pond, you will come to a still-existing overlook with views out to the Hudson River.

Immediately after the bend, now heading back west, you will pass a white trail to your left. This trail leads to the secondary parking lot below the ridge, 1.6 miles to the southeast, and passes a waterfall about halfway down. As this hike is much more strenuous than others included in this route, and cannot be hiked as part of a loop, it is skipped for the purposes of this route. Remain on the red trail. At 3.2 miles, you will cross a wooden bridge over a wet area. Continuing threading through the woods, until you come to Poppletown Road at 3.5 miles. Checking for cars, cross the road, and arrive back at the parking area on the other side.

# Esopus Meadows Preserve

**TOTAL DISTANCE**: 1.7 miles

**TYPE**: Loop

**HIKING TIME**: 1 hour

**TOTAL ELEVATION GAIN**: 200 feet

**MAXIMUM ELEVATION**: 160 feet

**DIFFICULTY**: Easy

This family-friendly park on the river's edge, only a few miles south of the city of Kingston, is a perfect spot for a quiet, easy stroll through the woods, or simply a picnic with Hudson River views. Several trails make short loops throughout the park, though this route takes you on a greater loop covering each of the different areas of the preserve. In less than 2 miles, you will enjoy a wide variety of terrain, and perhaps even spot a bald eagle. But the memorable scenery starts right in the parking lot, where you'll enjoy a great view of the Esopus Meadows Lighthouse. Save the picnic for your return, and reward yourself after your hike with some quiet time by the water.

## GETTING THERE

Esopus Meadows Preserve is located about 1.5 miles east of the town of Esopus, NY. From US-9W, turn onto River Rd. heading east. Drive for about 1.5 miles, and the parking area will be on your right.

## GPS SHORTCUT

Type "Lighthouse Park" into Google Maps and your GPS will navigate you to the appropriate parking area.

## THE TRAIL

Begin on the path next to the information kiosk, heading alongside the water. Soon you will reach a fork in the trail, with both paths marked by blue blazes. Stay to the left, continuing to hike along the river's edge, though the trail meanders briefly into the woods. After a short distance, you will come to another fork, with the continuation of your loop head-

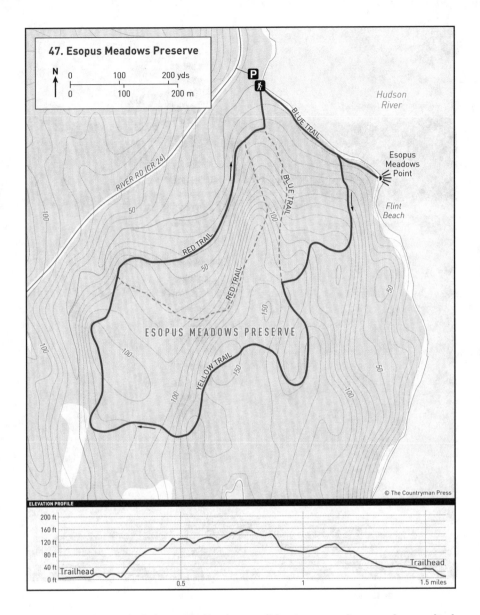

## 47. Esopus Meadows Preserve

N

| 0 | 100 | 200 yds |
| 0 | 100 | 200 m |

RIVER RD (CR 24)

BLUE TRAIL

Hudson
River

Esopus
Meadows
Point

Flint
Beach

RED TRAIL

BLUE TRAIL

RED TRAIL

ESOPUS MEADOWS PRESERVE

YELLOW TRAIL

© The Countryman Press

**ELEVATION PROFILE**

200 ft
160 ft
120 ft
80 ft
40 ft
0 ft

Trailhead

Trailhead

0.5          1          1.5 miles

ing to the right. To the left is a small side trail leading to Esopus Meadows Point. Take this side trail, which goes for a short distance before reaching an excellent view over the Hudson River.

After taking in the viewpoint, return to the intersection and continue on the trail that heads deeper into the woods, which is now to your left. The blue trail begins to make a moderate climb uphill but levels off after a few hundred feet. At about 0.5 mile, you will reach a T-intersection with a yellow-blazed trail. Turn left onto this trail to continue your loop of the preserve. Soon you will cross an overgrown woods road that rambles through this part of the park—you will cross this road again several times.

ONLY 87 MILES FROM MANHATTAN

Just before the 1-mile mark, the trail will switchback downhill, past a stone wall. A short distance beyond you will pass an old access road and a collapsed bridge. At 1.25 miles, the trail reaches a scenic ravine, with a steep drop-off below the path. Continue as the trail makes its way downhill to your right.

At 1.3 miles, you will reach an intersection with a red-blazed trail. Turn left onto red, then continue on the red trail as it bends right and crosses over a stone wall. You will now hike alongside the creek, heading back in the direction of the Hudson. At 1.6 miles, the red trail completes its loop. Continue straight onto the blue trail, turning left at the river's edge to return to the parking area.

# 48

# Falling Waters Preserve

**TOTAL DISTANCE**: 1.7 miles (additional 0.6 mile optional)

**TYPE**: Loop

**HIKING TIME**: 1.5–2 hours

**TOTAL ELEVATION GAIN**: 160 feet

**MAXIMUM ELEVATION**: 50 feet

**DIFFICULTY**: Easy

Tucked behind a suburban development, off a secluded side road south of the town of Saugerties, you would never find Falling Waters Preserve if you weren't looking for it. Even then, with your GPS guiding you, this park feels almost intentionally hidden. Its seclusion and quiet trails only add to its many appealing qualities, however, and there's a good reason why the site appears so obscure. Only opened in 2011, the Falling Waters Preserve is a collaboration between Scenic Hudson and the Esopus Creek Conservancy. The property is owned by the Dominican Sisters, and the park was created through a generous arrangement to allow public access over a portion of the land, creating the Preserve. Existing trails were updated by Scenic Hudson and the ECC, enabling the beautiful riverside loop hike covered by this guide. With benches perched at waterfall overlooks, spots to enjoy Catskill views, and several stone beaches with a unique perspective of the Hudson River, this quiet gem is an excellent addition to the parks of the Hudson Valley. As the Dominican Sisters property is situated adjacent to the park's trails, please respect their privacy and stick to the designated, well-marked pathways.

## GETTING THERE

Falling Waters Preserve is located about 3 miles south of the town of Saugerties, NY. From Saugerties, drive south on US-9W for about 1.5 miles, then turn left onto Josephs Drive. Continue for 0.8 mile, then turn right at the T-intersection onto York Street. A few hundred feet down the road, make a sharp left onto Dominican Lane. The parking area is 0.3 mile down the lane.

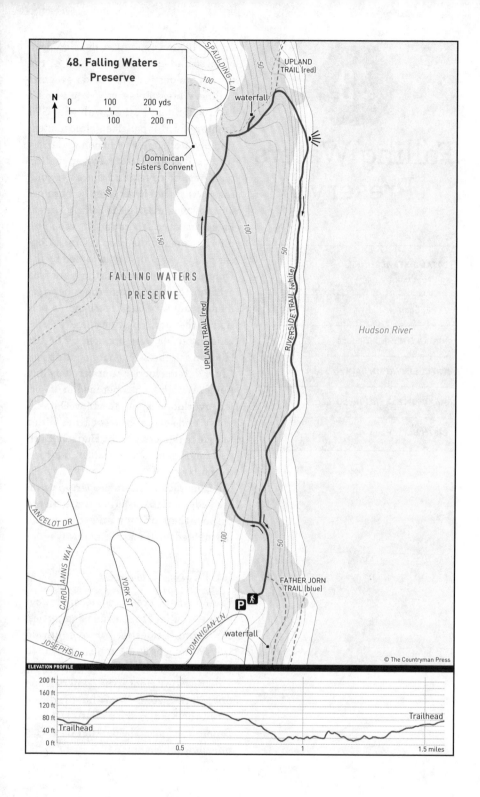

**48. Falling Waters Preserve**

N

| 0 | 100 | 200 yds |
| 0 | 100 | 200 m |

SPAULDING LN

UPLAND TRAIL (red)

waterfall

Dominican Sisters Convent

FALLING WATERS PRESERVE

UPLAND TRAIL (red)

RIVERSIDE TRAIL (white)

Hudson River

LANCELOT DR

CAROL ANNS WAY

YORK ST

DOMINICAN LN

JOSEPHS DR

P

FATHER JORN TRAIL (blue)

waterfall

© The Countryman Press

**ELEVATION PROFILE**

200 ft
160 ft
120 ft
80 ft
40 ft
0 ft

Trailhead

Trailhead

0.5     1     1.5 miles

SUNSET AT FALLING WATERS PRESERVE, WITH THE CATSKILLS RISING IN THE BACKGROUND

## GPS SHORTCUT

Type "Falling Waters Preserve" into Google Maps and your GPS will navigate you to the appropriate parking area.

## THE TRAIL

From the parking area, walk to the information kiosk. The trail begins here, past a wooden gate. The first section of the trail is an easy gravel path. To your left, across a field and up a hill, you will see a barn and silo. After walking for only a few hundred feet, you will cross a blue trail which slopes downhill to your right, toward the river. This optional trail can be taken to one of the preserve's two waterfalls and an additional Hudson River "beach" spot, adding only approximately 0.6 mile to your

hike, and a small amount of elevation gain while working your way back up from the river.

From this side trail, continue straight on the main red-blazed gravel path. Very soon after, you will pass another trail intersecting to your right. You will later complete your loop on this white-blazed Riverside Trail. For now, stay to the left, sticking to the red-blazed Upland Trail.

Soon you will be able to spot glimpses of the Catskills looming over the field to your left. Several benches here provide the perfect place to enjoy an afternoon picnic or watch the setting sun over the mountains.

Continue on the trail past the meadow. At 0.75 mile, the path ends at a gate to private property. The trail continues to the right, descending slightly. Follow the trail along the creek, then stay to the left where it splits. The main trail veers to the right, while a side trail goes left to the falls. Take the left branch and continue downhill to the benches overlooking the waterfall. This cool, shady spot, with the water babbling nearby, is another wonderful place to spend a few relaxing minutes.

Continue past the falls on the path until it intersects back with the main trail in a short distance. Turn left onto the main trail. Just under a mile from the trailhead, you will arrive at the northern terminus of the white-blazed Riverside Trail. Turn right to begin the second half of your loop. Very soon you will arrive at the banks of the Hudson River, where you can explore a small stone beach and enjoy views up and down the river. On the far bank is Tivoli Bays.

From the beach, return to the trail as it ascends a narrow footpath along the ridge above the river. After a short distance, you will encounter another wooden bench, overlooking more views.

At 1.4 miles from the trailhead, the trail heads down to another stone beach via a short side trail to your left. Continue on the main path, and shortly cross a board over a section of muddy trail. About a quarter mile later, you will return to the red-blazed trail and the end of the loop portion of the hike.

Turn left, and retrace your steps along the gravel path back to the parking area.

BENCHES BY THE WATERFALL OFFER A PLACE TO RELAX AND REFLECT

**49**

# Vroman's Nose

**TOTAL DISTANCE**: 2.4 miles

**TYPE**: Lollipop

**HIKING TIME**: 1.5–2 hours

**TOTAL ELEVATION GAIN**: 475 feet

**MAXIMUM ELEVATION**: 1,100 feet

**DIFFICULTY**: Easy

The Hudson Valley is home to several excellent vistas which can be reached with a minimum of effort. Little Stony Point (Hike #3), Bear Hill Preserve (Hike #14), Table Rocks (Hike #24), and Joppenbergh Mountain (Hike #45) all offer stunning vistas available with just modest effort, though Vroman's Nose may rival all of them for views. This uniquely shaped hilltop rises like a cresting wave over the farmland of the Schoharie Creek Valley near Middleburgh. The south-facing side of Vroman's Nose drops off dramatically, making this landmark immediately recognizable for miles in every direction, and the flat, open rocks on top of the cliff allow for expansive 180 degree views. Vroman's Nose was formed by the Wisconsin glacier moving across the hills of the region thousands of years ago, plucking huge chunks of rock away as it moved, and forming these distinctly shaped cliffs. With such incredible views, accessed by generally easy trails, Vroman's Nose inevitably became one of the most popular hiking destinations in the Upper Hudson Valley. Expect to encounter many other hikers on this distinct route.

## GETTING THERE

Vroman's Nose is located 1.5 miles west of the town of Middleburgh, NY. From Middleburgh, cross over the Schoharie Creek on NY-145, heading west. Just past the creek, turn left onto NY-30 S. Drive for 0.6 mile, then turn right onto W Middleburgh Rd. / Mill Valley Rd. Continue for another 0.6 mile and the parking area will be on the left.

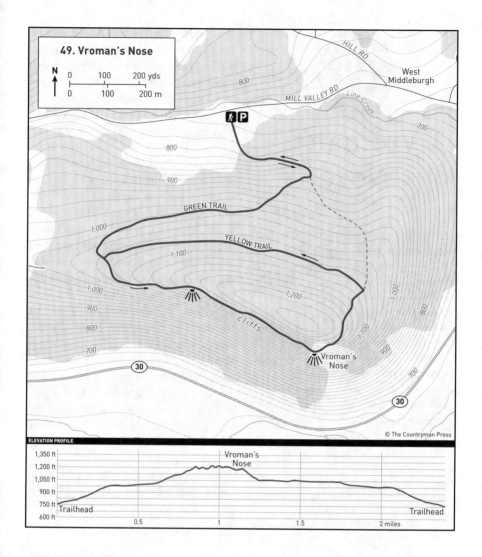

## 49. Vroman's Nose

N
| 0 | 100 | 200 yds |
| 0 | 100 | 200 m |

West Middleburgh

HILL RD

MILL VALLEY RD

Line Creek

800

700

GREEN TRAIL

800

900

1,000

YELLOW TRAIL

1,100

1,000

900

800

700

1,200

cliffs

1,100

1,000

800

900

700

Vroman's Nose

30

30

© The Countryman Press

**ELEVATION PROFILE**

| 1,350 ft | | | Vroman's Nose | | |
| 1,200 ft | | | | | |
| 1,050 ft | | | | | |
| 900 ft | | | | | |
| 750 ft | Trailhead | | | | Trailhead |
| 600 ft | | 0.5 | 1 | 1.5 | 2 miles |

## GPS SHORTCUT

Type "Vroman's Nose Hiking Trail" into Google Maps and your GPS will navigate you to the appropriate parking area.

## THE TRAIL

From the parking area, head uphill through the grassy field. Turn left after the information sign at the top of the hill, and walk until you come to the trail register, just into the woods.

The trail makes a moderate ascent, following green blazes. About 1,000 feet from the trailhead, you will reach an intersection with a yellow-blazed trail. Turn right and stay on the green trail. Here, the trail is a broad dirt path, still climbing fairly steadily uphill. Soon, however, the grade levels, and heads straight through a stately pine forest. Portions of the trail here are frequently muddy throughout the year.

Shortly after the half-mile mark, you will pass a side trail to your left—the trail you will return on, after completing a loop around the "Nose." To your right, through the trees, you will spot a residence. Continue straight, though the trail begins to veer left, soon making its way up to the ridge.

At 0.75 mile, you will reach the ridge and enjoy your first glimpse of Vroman's incredible views. From here, the trail follows the cliff's edge. Use caution, particularly if the rocks are wet or icy. The setting is particularly epic due to

A HIKER CLIMBS TO THE VIEWPOINT AT VROMAN'S NOSE

THE VIEW FROM VROMAN'S NOSE

the sheer drop from this ridgeline, which makes any accident here a potentially fatal one. Below you, farmland fills the valley, giving this vista a pastoral vibe—there's no mistaking this for the remote wilderness, but the scene is no less stunning for it.

Continue along the cliffs, enjoying the shifting views and rocky outcroppings. At 0.95 mile, after descending slightly along a narrow path, you will come to the last set of rock ledges, which loom dramatically over the fields below.

From here, the trail cuts away from the ridge and begins to descend steeply downhill.

At 1.2 miles, you will reach another intersection. The Long Path continues straight; turn left to follow the yellow trail. After about half a mile, you will return to your original route, intersecting the trail just before it ascends to the ridge top. Turn right, heading back through the muddy section of pine forest. Continue downhill, retracing your steps to return to the parking area.

# Indian Ladder Trail

**OTAL DISTANCE**: 2.4 miles

**TYPE**: Lollipop

**HIKING TIME**: 1.5–2 hours

**TOTAL ELEVATION GAIN**: 475 feet

**MAXIMUM ELEVATION**: 1,100 feet

**DIFFICULTY**: Easy

Like the Shawangunk Ridge and the eastern edge of the Catskills, the Helderberg Escarpment is a dramatic run of cliffs rising steeply up from the Hudson Valley, with incredible views out over the countryside. The most dramatic section of the escarpment cliffs is found within John Boyd Thacher State Park, which is home to numerous trails, campgrounds, and picnic areas. With the numerous amenities and attractions here and the park's proximity to the city of Albany, it's no wonder that these trails are extremely busy. Indeed, the Indian Ladder Trail, which descends partway down the escarpment to view a series of dramatic waterfalls from behind cave-like rock overhangs, is one of the busiest trails in all of New York, and on some afternoons hiking here can feel more like waiting in line at an amusement park than an outdoor excursion. Still, the crowds shouldn't keep you away from visiting, though it may be worth planning your trip around a less busy time if you value your solitude. The Indian Ladder Trail is popular for good reason: its sights are unique and breathtaking. And while you likely won't encounter any fossils on your hike, the area is significant for scientific reasons, as well: the Helderberg Escarpment is one of the richest fossil-bearing formations in the world.

## GETTING THERE

If arriving from the south, take I-87 N. Drive north on I-87 until you reach exit 21B for US-9W toward Coxsackie / Ravena / NY-81. Turn right onto US-9W N. Continue for 4 miles, then turn left onto Aquetuck Rd., and continue for 1.5 miles. Turn left onto NY-143 W and drive for 7.5 miles, then turn right onto NY-32 N.

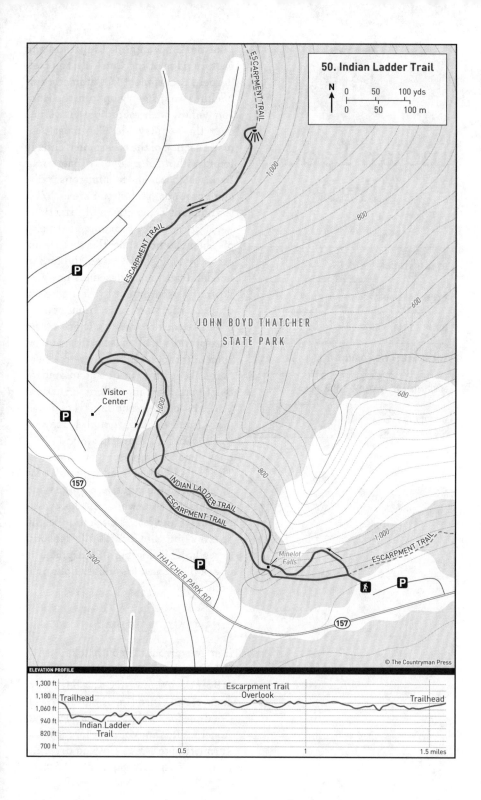

## 50. Indian Ladder Trail

N
| 0 | 50 | 100 yds |
| 0 | 50 | 100 m |

ESCARPMENT TRAIL

JOHN BOYD THATCHER
STATE PARK

P

Visitor
Center

P

INDIAN LADDER TRAIL

ESCARPMENT TRAIL

157

THATCHER PARK RD

1,200

P

Minelot
Falls

ESCARPMENT TRAIL

P

157

© The Countryman Press

**ELEVATION PROFILE**

| | | | | Escarpment Trail | | |
| 1,300 ft | | | | Overlook | | |
| 1,180 ft | Trailhead | | | | | Trailhead |
| 1,060 ft | | | | | | |
| 940 ft | | Indian Ladder | | | | |
| 820 ft | | Trail | | | | |
| 700 ft | | | | | | |
| | | 0.5 | | 1 | | 1.5 miles |

THE VIEW FROM ALONG THE ESCARPMENT TRAIL

Continue for 3.4 miles. Turn left onto Tarrytown Rd. and drive another 2.5 miles. Turn left onto NY-443 W and drive for 0.4 mile, then turn right onto Stove Pipe Rd. After 2.7 miles, make a slight right onto NY-85 E, and after another 0.3 mile, make a slight left onto NY-157 E. The road will now begin to ascend the escarpment of John Boyd Thacher State Park. Continue for about 2 miles. The parking area will be the second parking area you come to, on the right.

## GPS SHORTCUT

The Google tag for the Indian Ladder Trail is set to the north end of the trail—this route begins from the south, to make a loop hike easier. Type "Thacher Park Visitor Center" into Google Maps and continue past this parking area. The correct parking area is two lots south, just past Mine Lot Falls.

## THE TRAIL

The trail begins at the end of the parking lot—look for wooden stairs and a sign pointing you in the appropriate direction. Teal blazes mark the start of the trail, which splits to continue along the edge of the escarpment, and also heads down cement stairs to begin the Indian Ladder Trail. Head down the stairs, which cut steeply down the escarpment. At the bottom of the stairs, the trail continues northwest, following the escarpment once again.

MINELOT FALLS ALONG THE INDIAN LADDER TRAIL

A rock shelf protruding out from the escarpment, over the trail, requires ducking to pass beneath. Emerging from the other side, you will continue along a mostly level path. A few hundred feet from the stairs, you will arrive at Minelot Falls. This majestic waterfall cascades in front of a broad cave, with the hiking trail following the cave behind the falls for a unique perspective. The name originated from the site's original use as a mine for iron pyrite or Fool's Gold.

Past the falls, the trail remains relatively flat around the steep, sheer rock cliffs. Soon you will reach a second waterfall, with a similar cave-like opening bringing you behind the falls, under the escarpment.

At 0.6 mile, you will climb up another set of stairs, nearing the end of the Indian Ladder Trail. Before the trail heads back to the top of the escarpment, however, there is a short boardwalk to a viewing platform, to the right. From this T-intersection, turning left brings you up another set of stone steps, returning to the top of the cliffs.

Back up top, you will reach an intersection, with the Escarpment Trail heading both right and left. Ahead of you is the large visitor center. Turn right. A dirt path heads uphill through the woods, and a broader trail follows the escarpment cliffs. Make a hard right to stay on the Escarpment Trail, and follow the path along the cliff edge. A wooden fence separates you from the steep drop-off only feet away.

Continue along the Escarpment Trail, enjoying occasional glimpses of the far side of the escarpment cliffs. At the 1-mile mark, you will reach a fantastic vista, with dramatic views of the Indian Ladder Trail and the meandering cliff line.

From here, the Escarpment Trail continues for some distance. If you wish to extend your adventure and enjoy a longer hike, you can follow the trail to its terminus, past several more picnic areas and viewpoints. However, from this spot, you have already covered most of the notable features of the park, making this a good point to turn around. Retrace your steps back along the Escarpment Trail, to the intersection with the Indian Ladder Trail at the visitor center. Here, continue straight, with the fence along the escarpment now to your left. The path will follow the route of the Indian Ladder Trail that you hiked earlier, this time from the top of the cliffs. Continue until you reach the original trailhead and the parking area.

# Index

# S